OUR HOME

OR

NATIVE LAND?

WHAT GOVERNMENTS' ABORIGINAL POLICY IS DOING TO CANADA

MELVIN H. SMITH, Q.C.

FOREWORD BY RAFE MAIR

Stoddart

Published in 1996 by
Stoddart Publishing Co. Limited
34 Lesmill Road
Toronto, Canada
M3B 2T6
Tel. (416) 445-3333
Fax (416) 445-5967

First published in 1995 by Crown Western

Stoddart Books are available for bulk purchase for sales promotions,
premiums, fundraising, and seminars. For details, contact the
Special Sales Department at the above address.

Canadian Cataloguing in Publication Data

Smith, Melvin H. (Melvin Henry), 1934 –
Our home or native land?

Includes bibliographical references.
ISBN 0-7737-5821-6

1. Native peoples – Canada – Government relations.*
2. Native peoples – Canada – Claims.*
3. Native peoples – Canada – Land tenure.*
4. Native peoples – Canada – Land transfers.*
5. Native peoples – Canada – Legal status, laws, etc.*
I. Title.

E92.S64 1996   323.1'197071   C96-930471-4

Cover Design: Bill Douglas at the Bang

Printed and bound in Canada

*Stoddart Publishing gratefully acknowledges the support
of the Canada Council and the Ontario Arts Council
in the development of writing and publishing in Canada.*

Contents

Figures

Figure 1
Rafe Mair (right) and the author before
the Senate Commons Committee on the Constitution,
Ottawa, September 1978.

Foreword

Mel Smith has been a friend of mine for 20 years. It is a friendship which was forged in the fire of constitutional changes in this country which, in some ways, contributed to the necessity of this book.

I was a Cabinet Minister in the Bill Bennett government when I met Mel in the mid 70s. I had been made Chairman of the Cabinet Committee on Confederation as well as Chairman of the Western Premiers' Task Force on Constitutional Trends, and Mel was the Deputy Minister responsible for Constitutional Affairs. Though never officially designated as such, I became responsible for constitutional affairs in the run up to the Patriation of the Constitution and this placed Mel and me in the closest contact.

Under my formal chairmanship, but actually under the watchful guidance of Mel Smith, British Columbia developed, in 1978, a set of constitutional proposals which were as far reaching and thoroughly researched as they were under-read. This product of countless hours of work by some of the best brains in British Columbia—brains trained in law, government, political science, and business—was seen by keen observers of these matters, like Gordon Gibson, as the best set of constitutional proposals of any government in Canada very much including the Government of Canada.

To get ideas, Mel and I went to Europe in early 1978 where we conferred with high officials and politicians in Switzerland and West Germany about how their federal systems worked and also met British officials in London working on proposals for "devolution" of parliamentary power to Scotland and Wales.

Over the years, we travelled the length and breadth of Canada as we tried to convince other Premiers, Cabinet Ministers and decision-makers that B.C.'s proposals were worth careful consideration. We met in private with people who were involved in these issues like Claude Ryan, Ken Dryden, and Jean Luc Pepin; we gave speeches in places like Toronto, Montreal and even Harvard; we appeared before the Pepin-Robarts Commission, both publicly and privately; we attended ad hoc conferences on constitutional matters; we met constitutional

vii

experts at breakfasts, lunches and dinners all across the country; we appeared before Parliamentary Committees; we attended every meeting of Ministers, Premiers and First Ministers from 1976 until I left government at the end of 1980. These proposals were, alas, utterly ignored by those set in authority over us. That B.C. wasn't listened to is sad indeed since in these days, post-Meech and Charlottetown, these proposals make even more sense than they did in 1978.

While B.C. was ignored, Mel Smith could not be. He developed into one of the major constitutional experts in the country. I claim no credit for that. All I contributed, perhaps, was a degree of hawkishness on behalf of what was right for all of Canada rather than that which was traditionally convenient in the interests of the central Canadian establishment.

In more recent times, Mel and I were kindred spirits in our opposition to the Charlottetown Accord. His writings, and particularly his paper "Why I Must Vote 'No' in the Referendum," which was distributed or reproduced in the scores of thousands throughout western Canada, provided analytical support to the 'No' forces.

Through it all, Mel and I argued together, swapped opinions on all subjects, laughed a lot, and shared disappointments. I saw Mel Smith the lawyer, the constitutional expert, and the man. It was, then, with the highest hopes that I read this book. I was not disappointed.

The native agenda has taken us on a frightening journey through the looking glass where everything is backwards. Whatever the courts say, governments do the opposite. Victories in court are treated as losses. Winning lawyers are fired and new lawyers hired with instructions to lose on appeal. We are indeed "through the looking glass" where the Queen demands that the sentence be carried out before the case is even heard and Tweedledum and Tweedledee are pushed at us as knowing what they are talking about.

Tiny communities are given enormous tracts of land while the majority of Canadians is not only ignored but kept in the dark. Incredible sums of money are spent—worse, even larger amounts are committed to be paid by future generations. The Constitution of the country is ignored. The Referendum of 1992, wherein the people rejected the very notions now propounded by our leaders, is arrogantly cast aside.

We have committed ourselves to a land full of native homelands, the very notion which revolted the civilized world when they were created in South Africa. How ironic it is that Mel Smith, in pointing out the folly of states within the state, where rights are determined by the colour of one's skin, must fight off the claim that *he* is a racist.

We have developed a huge industry around "native land claims" and the rewards for the participants are enormous. Staggering sums are spent on "research," lawyers, bureaucrats, and sundry hangers-on.

This is not a happy book at all. It is a catalogue of continuing Canadian catastrophes. But it is a book which every thinking Canadian has an obligation to read. Not to read this book and then demand a full accounting from government, especially the government of B.C., is to silently collude in a massive fraud on future generations.

This is not a book about the left or the right—it is about fools. Well-meaning fools, no doubt, but nonetheless fools. It is easy to read—though thoroughly researched and footnoted, it can be understood by any person who recognizes humbug, stupidity (if not cupidity) and deliberate deception of the public.

British Columbians especially will want to read this book for it is they who have the most to lose and it is they who are being deliberately kept in the dark. It is also they who, after agreements have been reached, will witness the charade of legislation forced upon us by party whips exercising party discipline.

This book is not without its optimistic moments for Mel Smith tells us how we can get out of the unholy mess we are in—at least we can do so in B.C. where the final hammer has yet to sound.

But time is short—very short. The government of B.C. is determined to change us from a peace-loving democratic province, under the rule of law being equally applied to all, to a state where in large areas race counts for everything. If the government has its way, sad as this is to say, it is hard to believe that we will be a peaceful people for very long.

If this book doesn't wake up a sleeping public, God help us all, including the generations to come.

Rafe Mair
Vancouver, B.C.

Acknowledgements

This book could not have been written in the relatively brief period of ten months that the author has been engaged in its writing without the assistance of others. Steve Vanagas, a Victoria-based journalist, collaborated on Chapters 4 and 10. I am most grateful for his effort.

Others have also contributed much time and effort. No one knows the federal aboriginal fisheries strategy issue better than Phil Eidsvik, the Executive Director of the B.C. Fisheries Survival Coalition, and I am grateful for his contribution in Chapter 9. Norman Mullins, QC, an authority on Indian taxation, was of much assistance on that subject. Bent Sivertz, former Commissioner of the Northwest Territories, was most helpful on the High Arctic Relocation issue, while John Watson of Victoria and my daughter, Sandra, did valuable research on the same subject. The Canadian Taxpayers' Federation provided research material on the Prairie treaties. Don Scott, a management consultant who lived in Yellowknife for six years, provided valuable insights on political developments in the NWT.

To Hilary Watson, who inputted the manuscript on the word processor through what must have seemed an endless number of alterations, drafts and adjustments with such expertise, patience and good cheer, I extend my very grateful thanks.

And finally, to my wife Beverley, who endured long hours of my seclusion and my more than usual irritability, while foregoing leisurely and pleasant mutual activities, I extend my gratitude and my love.

I alone am responsible for any errors that are contained in the text. These are bound to occur in dealing in such a relatively short time with a subject of such complexity. Nonetheless, I believe such errors, if any, will not be of an egregious nature or detract from this book's essential message.

Melvin H. Smith
Victoria, B.C.

Preface

This book is written for all Canadians, regardless of their race or ethnicity, who are concerned about their country's future. It deals with governments' actions of alarming proportions that have been quietly yet inextricably unfolding over the past decade in particular, under the broad label of aboriginal or native policy. The greatest concern of all is this: although major concessions are being made on the aboriginal front almost daily, most Canadians are blissfully unaware of the effect these developments will have on them and on future generations.

Consider just a few of them:

- a new "province" is being created in the North having dubious constitutional validity;
- vast areas of the public lands of Canada are being conveyed forever to a relatively few aboriginal people;
- governments ignore the decisions of our courts by settling land claims far beyond constitutional entitlement;
- the federal Aboriginal Fisheries Strategy establishes a racially segregated commercial fishery without judicial support;
- billions of dollars are spent each year on seemingly ineffective government native programs;
- governments are entering into formal accords with the native leadership that concede the inherent right to native self-government when the courts have found no such right exists;
- existing treaties are "topped up" to the tune of hundreds of millions of dollars and millions of acres of land;
- new and more "governments" are springing up like mushrooms; and,
- close to $60 million is being spent by a Royal Commission that seems more interested in settling old scores than in prescribing practical solutions to today's problems.

Most of all, this book is a wake-up call to all Canadians. I can state categorically that, if the Canadian public knew what was going on, most of them would be appalled. The whole process is driven by the unrelenting efforts of what has been called the "Indian Industry": the national native leadership, the many lawyers, consultants, advisers and academics—all government-funded—who would keep it going in perpetuity. Over-zealous bureaucrats and compliant politicians complete the loop. But the Canadian public is out in the cold. One would have thought that cutting off the common people went the way of the Charlottetown Accord. But no, paternalism, for so long the bane of native policy, is now being visited on all Canadians.

Most politicians in power have taken it upon themselves to act as Canada's conscience on these matters. One editorial writer has questioned whether recent pronouncements from the Royal Commission represent "a retroactive morality, satisfying a need to assert the contemporary cant of 'political correctness'." (*Globe and Mail*, July 15, 1994).

This book will anger some readers. Those with a vested interest in the Indian Industry will condemn it. Well-meaning past, and some present, politicians who have had a hand in these matters will take umbrage. The national native leadership—but not many native Canadians who live under the inadequacies of the present system—will reject it and incorrectly brand the author as racist. (An ironical condemnation from those who perpetuate and advocate a system premised solely on race and ethnicity.)

Those who respond in this way will have missed the point, for this book is not anti-native. Quite the reverse. In calling for an end to more than 125 years of a flawed and failed government policy, it holds out the prospect of removing the shackles of government dependency caused by discriminating against people because of their race, replacing it with individual opportunity, self reliance and success—and national unity in place of fragmentation.

Note: Certain terms and definitions are used throughout this book. The reader is invited to consider these at the outset by referring to the Appendix.

A Vision Short-Lived

"We can go on treating the Indians as having a special status . . . adding bricks of discrimination around the ghetto in which they live. . . . Or we can say you're at a crossroads—the time is now to decide whether the Indians will be a race apart in Canada or whether [they] will be Canadians of full status." Prime Minister Trudeau, 1969.

The 1969 White Paper

In a bold government initiative that was designed to "lead to the full, free and non-discriminatory participation of the Indian people in Canadian society,"[1] the Minister of Indian Affairs and Northern Development, Jean Chrétien, stood in the House of Commons on June 25, 1969, to unveil the Trudeau government's White Paper on Indian Policy. The policy proposed the most significant change in government-native relations in a hundred years.

Seated in the Speaker's Gallery were Indian leaders brought to Ottawa by the government to witness what had been billed as an "historic occasion." Although over the previous year there had been a substantial measure of consultation with native peoples on the inadequacies of the *Indian Act*, most of the native leaders present had little knowledge of what the White Paper contained.

The White Paper clearly presented a fork in the road for native people in Canada and their place in, and relationship with, the rest of Canadian society. It put the issue squarely and eloquently:

"Canadians, Indians and non-Indians alike stand at the crossroads. For Canadian society the issue is whether a growing element of its population will become full participants contributing in a positive way to the general well-being or whether, conversely, the present social and economic gap will lead to their increasing frustration and isolation, a threat to the general well-being of society. For many Indian people, one road does exist, the only road that has existed since

*Confederation and before, the road of different status, a road
which has led to a blind alley of deprivation and frustration.
This road, because it is a separate road, cannot lead to full
participation, to equality in practice as well as in theory. . . . the
Government has outlined a number of measures and a policy
which it is convinced will offer another road for Indians, a road
that would lead gradually away from different status to full
social, economic and political participation in Canadian life.
This is the choice."*[2]

Specifically, the White Paper's six major points were:

1. **The legislative and constitutional bases which set Indians
   apart from other Canadians must be removed.**

A word of explanation on the enormous significance of this
proposal. Under S.91(24) of the Canadian Constitution, the federal
Parliament is given the power to legislate specifically for "Indians and
Lands reserved for Indians." The consequence is two-fold: Parliament
can legislate over Indians in ways in which it cannot over other
Canadians; and secondly, the provincial legislatures are precluded
from legislating specifically for Indians. Thus many provincial programs
and benefits, which bind citizens to the province and to the local
community of which they form an integral part, are not available to
Indians. They are displaced by federal programs that treat Indians
differently from other Canadians.

The classic example of such discriminatory legislation is the *Indian
Act,* which deprives Indians of benefits enjoyed by other Canadians
but, conversely, extends other benefits to Indians not enjoyed by
others. The White Paper summed up the point this way:

*". . . the separate legal status of Indians . . . [has] kept the
Indian people apart from and behind other Canadians. The
Indian people have not been full citizens of the communities
and provinces in which they live and have not enjoyed the
equality and benefits that such participation offers. The
treatment resulting from their different status has been often
worse, sometimes equal and occasionally better than that
accorded to their fellow citizens. What matters is that it has
been different."*[3]

The White Paper would have seen the 95-year-old *Indian Act* repealed and specific programs for Indians replaced by the full range of provincial and federal programs available to all other Canadians. No constitutional amendment would have been necessary. The federal government would have simply "vacated the field," i.e. ceased to have specific legislation for Indians.

2. **There must be a positive recognition by everyone of the unique contribution of Indian culture to Canadian life.**

    The White Paper stressed that the new policy need not result in the destruction of the native peoples' cultural identity but, in fact, it could flourish and be enriched in a broader Canadian society.

3. **Government services must come through the same channels and from the same government agencies for all Canadians.**

    This would be a natural consequence of implementing point 1 and would see the Department of Indian Affairs dismantled within five years.

4. **The title to Indian reserves (now held by the federal government) would be transferred to the Indian people of each reserve.**

5. **Lawful obligations must be recognized.**

    Any outstanding commitments the federal government might have had in setting aside reserves under a few existing treaties in northern parts of the Prairie provinces and in a small part of the Northwest Territories (NWT) would be fulfilled. Pointing out that modern-day government services provided to the Indians benefits that went far beyond what could have been foreseen by those who signed treaties, the White Paper suggested that the annual treaty requirement on government to provide twine, agricultural implements, ammunition and minuscule payments to each treaty Indian should be reviewed and phased out.

    On the question of land claims, so eagerly embraced subsequently by federal and provincial governments alike, the White Paper said this:

    "These are so general and undefined that it is not realistic to think of them as specific claims capable of remedy except through a policy and program that will end injustice to Indians

as members of the Canadian community. This is the policy that the Government is proposing for discussion."[4]

In other words, dealing with nebulous land claims would not be entertained. On another occasion Prime Minister Trudeau said:

"It's inconceivable . . . for one section of the society to have a treaty with the other section of the society. We must be all equal under the law and we must not sign treaties amongst ourselves . . . I don't think that we should encourage Indians to feel these treaties should last forever within Canada. . . . They should become Canadians as all other Canadians."[5]

6.   **Those who are furthest behind must be helped the most.**

As an interim measure, the White Paper proposed that the Government would make substantial additional funds available to ensure a greater equality in social and economic conditions to those Indians that needed it most. Also, all programs and advisory services at both the federal and provincial level available to other Canadians would be available to native Canadians.

———

Claiming that the new policy had been the result of "a year's intensive discussions with Indian people throughout Canada,"[6] Mr. Chrétien concluded his speech by promising early meetings with the provincial premiers or their representatives and proposed a close working relationship with the Indian community to implement the policy. The White Paper recognized the heavy burden that would be placed on Indian leaders to implement the policy and agreed to pay $50 million to them and their advisers to assist in doing so.

How did it come to be that such a revolutionary approach to dealing with Indian policy was developed in 1969? DIAND was not noted for developing new perspectives, as evidenced by the fact that the 95-year-old *Indian Act*, which that Department administered, had not been significantly up-dated over many years. The initiative came from Prime Minister Trudeau. The election of the Trudeau government resulted in a dramatic shift in the way public policy was developed in government. Up until then, each department of government had the primary responsibility to develop policy in its particular sphere of activity. Under Mr. Trudeau, a greatly increased role for the Privy

Council Office, the policy arm of the Prime Minister's Office, was brought about. The old assumptions on which native policy had been based by DIAND were now open to question. It is no accident therefore that this fresh approach of government policy towards the native people represented a dramatic shift from the status quo of the previous hundred years. Such a proposal was entirely in keeping with the liberal democratic principles of equality which Mr. Trudeau espoused.

Reaction to the White Paper

Copies of the White Paper had been made available to the Opposition in advance. The official spokesman for the Conservative Party, Mr. G. W. Baldwin, MP (Peace River), responded in the House that day and pledged his party's support "for the general goals which are outlined."[7] Mr. Frank Howard, NDP MP (Skeena), responded for the New Democratic Party. He rode the fence. At one point in his speech, he claimed that what Mr. Chrétien and the government proposed "was a reiteration of what many of us in this House have been saying for the last five or ten years."[8] Later on he stated that some solution to the land question in Quebec, the Territories and British Columbia would need to be found.

However, it wasn't long before opposition to the proposed policy began to emerge from several quarters. Foremost among them was the native leadership itself. Representatives of the National Indian Brotherhood and provincial Indian organizations signed a statement expressing the view that the end result would be "the destruction of a nation of people by legislation and cultural genocide."[9] They made it very plain that they did not want to give up the special status which the Constitution and government policy over the past hundred years had given them.

Opposition also arose among provincial governments who did not wish to assume the fiscal responsibility for delivering programs to native people, which up to that time had been delivered by the federal government. This, in spite of the fact that Ottawa was agreeable to funding each province with an amount equivalent to what the federal government was spending on Indian services in that province. This federal funding to the provinces would be phased out over a 30-year period.

Likewise, there was a decided change of heart on the part of certain elements in the opposition parties in the House of Commons.

A special debate took place in the House on July 11, 1969. The NDP was now deathly opposed to the White Paper even though three months before its release, on March 6, 1969, Mr. Howard had said this in the House:

> *"The Indian Act gave birth in 1867 to a system of paternalism which has been like a fungus growth that unfortunately is still with us today and still growing. As long as we have an Indian Act, a special law relating to people with a different cultural inheritance from everybody else, and as long as we have a separate department, we will have discrimination and denials of fundamental human rights."* [10]

Some Conservatives in the opposition ranks also began attacking the policy laid out in the White Paper. For his part, Indian Affairs Minister Chrétien, facing mounting opposition, began to back down, assuring critics that the policy was not cast in stone and that there was still ample time for consultation.

Prime Minister Trudeau entered the fray in support of the White Paper and made a major speech on the subject in Vancouver, on August 8, 1969. In it he said:

> *"We have set the Indians apart as a race. We've set them apart in our laws. We've set them apart in the ways the governments will deal with them. They're not citizens of the province as the rest of us are. They are wards of the federal government. They get their services from the federal government rather than from the provincial or municipal governments. They have been set apart in law. They have been set apart in the relations with government and they've been set apart socially too. . . .*
> *"We can go on treating the Indians as having a special status. We can go on adding bricks of discrimination around the ghetto in which they live and at the same time perhaps helping them preserve certain cultural traits and certain ancestral rights. Or we can say you're at a crossroads—the time is now to decide whether the Indians will be a race apart in Canada or whether [they] will be Canadians of full status."* [11]

At first it was thought that the White Paper would survive the criticism; that it was misunderstood and misconstrued, and that there was simply an over-reaction to it. However, the protests ran much deeper. As one author notes:

"Federal policy-makers were caught off guard by the aboriginal reaction to the White Paper. Deeply committed to liberal values, and resentful of special status as discriminatory and regressive, many of those policy-makers were convinced that conferral of formal equality and protection of individual, civil and human rights represented a step forward for aboriginal peoples, accelerating their movement into the 20th century. To their surprise, aboriginal groups condemned the White Paper as racist in its intent and potentially genocidal in its consequences. Obviously Ottawa had miscalculated aboriginal grievances and aspirations. Aboriginal peoples did not want Ottawa to get out of the aboriginal business."[12]

It was all too much for Minister Chrétien, and the Government ignominiously withdrew the White Paper in the Spring of 1970. Ironically though, the White Paper's funding initiative to Indian organizations nonetheless went forward. The $50 million, which was intended to be used to assist the native leadership in implementing the White Paper's proposals, "helped these native groups take their battle for rights to other forums."[13] It financed lawyers, consultants, advisers, academics, and others. Thus the Indian Industry was born.

But the $50 million was only the beginning. By 1985 federal funding to 57 native political organizations had increased to $100 million annually.[14] What it is now we can only guess, but we do know that total program funding for natives, discussed at greater length in Chapter 10, has gone up over 260% since 1985.

The policy vacuum that developed at the federal level after the defeat of the White Paper was met by an increase in sophistication on the part of the native leadership, first to advocate for the negotiation of land claims, then self-determination, and ultimately the concept of the inherent right to self-government. The $50 million paved the way.

Looking back, instead of embarking upon the White Paper's new approach, requiring thirty years to fully phase-in, the record of government expenditure in furtherance of the status quo or the special status option has shown that in the last twenty years at least $40 billion has been spent on what one native author admits was "an attempt to help Indians out of their social-economic gutter—with virtually no success."[15] More about this in Chapter 10.

The 1973 Land Claims Policy

Not only did the Trudeau government with Mr. Chrétien as Minister withdraw the White Paper of 1969, but it did a complete about face from its earlier expressed intention not to entertain comprehensive land claims as being "vague, general and undefined."

On August 8, 1973, the Minister announced the federal government's land claims policy, which is with us today in amplified form. He issued a policy directive stating that

> *"In all cases where **traditional** interest in land has not been formally dealt with, the government affirms its willingness to do so and accepts in principle that the **loss** and relinquishment of that interest ought to be compensated."* [16] (emphasis added)

It went on to propose that settlements be negotiated with authorized representatives of each aboriginal group. It is important to stress that what the government was prepared to compensate for under this 1973 policy was the loss suffered, in appropriate cases, of an interest pertaining to "traditional" use and occupation of lands, i.e. hunting, fishing and trapping rights. That was a very important limitation on the intended scope of land claims negotiations.

However, in the hands of an articulate and aggressive native leadership, aided and abetted by an ever-expanding bureaucracy sympathetic to the native cause and a compliant political leadership of varying stripes, the scope of the policy has been greatly expanded over a period of years beyond its original intent. Expanded in 1978, 1981, and again in 1986 and beyond, a recent publication of the federal department now states that:

> *"The comprehensive claims process is intended to lead to agreement **on the special rights Aboriginal peoples will have in the future** with respect to lands and resources. It is not an attempt to define what rights they may have had in the past."* [17]
> (emphasis added)

Thus, what was designed to redress historic wrongs, based on some colour of legal right, has now been expanded to appease the insatiable demands of the native leadership to ever more land and resources. Present-day land claim settlements go far beyond legal entitlement. To the extent that they do, the legal entitlements of the rest of society are diminished. This is unfair and unjust.

The influence of the *Calder* case

What caused the Government to change its mind in 1973? Whenever the legal basis for the 1973 federal land claims policy is articulated by officials of the federal government, and latterly by officials of the B.C. government, reference is made to the 1973 decision of the Supreme Court of Canada in the *Calder* case.[18] In my view, as will be shown, the policy is based on a false interpretation of the import of that decision.

In a document dated March, 1993, published by DIAND and entitled "Federal Policy for the Settlement of Native Claims," these words appear:

> *"The evolution and development of the federal government's land claims policy has been closely linked to court decisions. The first claims policy statement in 1973 was initiated by a decision of the Supreme Court of Canada (the 1973 Calder decision) which acknowledged the existence of Aboriginal title in Canadian law."*

Then, further on in the document, on a page entitled "Background," this statement appears:

> *"The common law concept of Aboriginal rights was addressed in the 1973 decision of the Supreme Court of Canada in the Calder case. Six of the seven Supreme Court justices who heard the case acknowledged the existence of Aboriginal title in Canadian law . . . "*

Those statements do not properly reflect the Supreme Court of Canada's decision in the *Calder* case. The *Calder* case, brought in the late 1960's by the Nisga'a people, claimed that "aboriginal title" over the Nass Valley in B.C. had never been extinguished. At trial, the Supreme Court of British Columbia dismissed the claim. The case was then appealed to the Court of Appeal of British Columbia, a three-man court, which again dismissed the claim, unanimously. The decision was then appealed further by the Nisga'a people, to the Supreme Court of Canada. Again, the appeal was dismissed.

What lawyers call the *ratio* of the case, i.e. the actual basis for the decision, was the finding that the lawsuit was improperly brought because a fiat had not been first sought and obtained from British Columbia as was then required. Four of the seven judges, and thus the majority, took this view. That is the narrow and only finding of the Supreme Court of Canada.[19]

Six of the seven judges did, in their Reasons for Judgment, discuss the question of aboriginal title. Three of the judges in the majority considered that aboriginal title may have existed in the past but that it had been effectively extinguished by the exercise of sovereignty and by colonial actions before B.C. came into Confederation. The three dissenting judges supported the view that aboriginal title existed to the present time.

As a result, the Supreme Court of Canada in the *Calder* case did not decide that aboriginal title exists in Canada today. The Nisga'a appeal was dismissed. There was *no* finding of present-day aboriginal title. Only the three dissenting judges held that view and, in any event, that issue was not essential to the narrow decision made by the Court. Yet in the federal government document, which is the basis for the 1973 claims policy, it is stated and implied that the *Calder* case decided that aboriginal title *exists* in Canada today. It did not.

The mythology surrounding the decision in the *Calder* case is not limited to the policy statements emanating from DIAND. For years many advocates of the concept of aboriginal title have embellished what the *Calder* case decided to support the cause. However, DIAND Minister Ron Irwin recently has taken the mythology to new heights. In answer to a question in the House of Commons on the Nisga'a land claim negotiations he exclaimed, "They won their case in 1973."[20] Such ignorance on the part of the one who represents the interests of all Canadians at the negotiating table on land claims does not build confidence that the outcome will be fair and just.

Even if the *Calder* case had decided that the Nisga'a have aboriginal title over the territories it claimed, which it didn't, it would have been a title far less than full ownership. It was never suggested that it amounted to fee simple ownership. The *Calder* case is no support whatsoever for a land claims policy that sees vast areas of public land transferred in fee simple to native people.

The Royal Proclamation

As well as the *Calder* case, federal officials and others seek support for the comprehensive land claims policy by referring to the Royal Proclamation of 1763. This is a slender reed on which to found a legal entitlement to any aboriginal interest throughout Canada, particularly in B.C.

The Royal Proclamation dealt with the territory in North America ceded to Great Britain from France under the Treaty of Paris. It provided that a large tract of land in the territory covered by the Proclamation be set aside as a hunting reserve for the Indians "with whom we are connected" and "for the present, and until our further pleasure be known." By its terms it did not include the territory of Rupert's Land—that vast territory to the west and north out of which most of present-day Quebec and Ontario, and the whole of what is now Manitoba, Saskatchewan, Alberta, Yukon and the NWT, was carved. Nor, as both B.C. courts found in the *Delgamuukw* case (the subject of Chapter 6), does the Royal Proclamation have any application whatsoever to British Columbia.

Therefore, the Royal Proclamation provides no support for formulating a 20th-century country-wide land claims policy. Nevertheless, this is one of the twin pillars on which the 1973 federal land claims policy was built. The other pillar being the Supreme Court of Canada decision in the *Calder* case which, as we have seen, is on an equally shaky foundation.

Land claim settlements to date

Ten comprehensive claims settlements have been concluded since the establishment of the federal government's claims policy in 1973; two in northern Quebec, four in the Northwest Territories and four in the Yukon.

These agreements are:
1. The James Bay and Northern Quebec Agreement with the Cree and Inuit of northern Quebec (1975).
2. The Northeastern Quebec Agreement with the Naskapi Indian band (1978).
3. The Inuvialuit Final Agreement in the western Arctic (1984).
4. The Gwich'in Agreement over the Mackenzie river delta (1992)
5. The Nunavut Agreement with the Inuit of the eastern Arctic (1993).
6. The Sahtu Dene and Metis Agreement of the Great Bear Lake region (1993).
7. The Vuntut Gwitchin Agreement in the Yukon (1994).
8. The Nacho Nyak Dun Agreement in the Yukon (1994).
9. The Champagne and Aishihik Agreement in the Yukon (1994).
10. The Teslin Tlingit Agreement in the Yukon (1994).

Figure 2 - Land claim agreements to date

Name of Agreement	Date of Agreement	No. of Natives Involved	Financial Compensation	Full Land Ownership	Undersurface Rights	"Traditional" Activities	Royalty Rights	Other Benefits
Quebec James Bay and Northern Quebec Agreement	November 11, 1975	15,932	$225 million (in 1975 $)	14,000 sq. km.		•exclusive fishing, trapping and harvesting rights over 150,000 sq. km.		•participation with Government in environmental and social protection regime; •income security program for hunters and trappers; •self-government under legislation
Northeastern Quebec Agreement	January 31, 1978	465 Naskapi	$9 million (in 1978 $)					
Northwest Territories The Inuvialut Final Agreement	June 5, 1984	2,500 Inuvialut	$152 million (1984 $) and one time payment of $10 million	91,000 sq. km.	91,000 sq.km. includes 11,000sq.km. of sub-surface rights	•wildlife harvesting rights.		•socio-economic measures designed to stimulate economic development. •participation in decision-making processes for wildlife and environmental management.
The Gwich'in Agreement	April 22, 1992	2,200 Gwich'in	Tax-free capital transfer of $75 million over 15 years (1990 $)	22,420 sq.km. in NWT 1,550 sq.km. in Yukon	land ownership includes 6,160 sq.km. of undersurface rights	•wildlife harvesting rights.	•a portion of royalties payable in respect of the Mackenzie River Valley.	•participation in decision-making bodies dealing with renewable resources, land use planning, environmental impact assessment and review, and land and water regulation.
The Nunavut Agreement	May 25, 1993	17,500 Inuit	$580 million (1989 $) over 14 years	350,000 sq. km.		•wildlife harvesting rights.	•share of resource royalties.	•participation in decision-making process dealing with land and environmental management. •self-government.

Name of Agreement	Date of Agreement	No. of Natives Involved	Financial Compensation	Full Land Ownership	Undersurface Rights	"Traditional" Activities	Royalty Rights	Other Benefits
The Sahtu Dene and Metis Agreement	September 6, 1993	1,600 Sahtu Dene and Metis	$75 million over 15 years (1990 $)	41,437 sq. km.	1,813 sq. km. of undersurface rights	•wildlife and harvesting rights. •exclusive trapping rights.	•share of resource royalties.	•participation in decision-making bodies dealing with renewable resources, land use planning, environmental impact assessment and review, and land and water regulation.
Yukon Vuntun Gwitchin Agreement	May 29, 1993	625	$19,161,859 (1989 $)	7,744 sq. km.	7,744 sq. km.	•exclusive or preferential fish, wildlife and trapping rights.	•probable share of future resource royalties.	•exclusive or preferential commercial rights for wilderness, fishing and big game outfitters activities. •special employment and economic development opportunities.
Nacho Nyak Dun Agreement	May 29, 1993	398	$14,554,654 (1989 $)	2,409 sq. km.	2,409 sq. km.	•preferential fish and wildlife rights.	•probable share of future resource royalties.	•representation on Peel River Advisory Committee. •special employment and economic development opportunities.
Champagne and Aishihik Agreement	May 29, 1993	1,035	$27,523,936 (1989 $)	1,230 sq. km.	1,230 sq. km.	•preferential fish and wildlife rights.	•probable share of future resource royalties.	•guaranteed salmon allocation from Alsek River basin. •special employment and economic development opportunities.
Teslin Tlingit Agreement	May 29, 1993	573	$18,655,066 (1989 $)	1,230 sq. km.	1,230 sq. km.	•preferential fish and wildlife rights	•probable share of future resource royalties. •special employment and economic development opportunities.	•veto over game farming or ranching activities.

An overview

The process involved in negotiating these agreements is complex, painstaking and lengthy—some negotiations have been ongoing for over twenty years. They have proved to be a boon to lawyers and consultants, whose fees and expenses on whichever side of the negotiating table they sit are ultimately borne by the taxpayer, and a similar boon to myriads of bureaucrats. It has been estimated that the negotiating costs alone for the land claim settlements in the Yukon started in 1973, and not even as yet fully concluded, reach $90 million.

The end product bears the hallmark of too much legalese. Each of these agreements extend into hundreds of pages and contain thousands of clauses and sub-clauses. If millions of dollars have been spent in negotiating and concluding these agreements, one can well imagine the expenditures that will be incurred in implementing and interpreting them.

Because of the greatly expanded scope of the federal land claims policy brought about by the Mulroney government in 1986, these settlement agreements convey a wide range of rights and benefits far beyond what the land claims policy of 1973 envisaged. They usually include full ownership of large amounts of land; guaranteed wildlife harvesting rights over much larger areas; guaranteed participation in land, water, wildlife and environmental management throughout the larger areas; substantial cash payments; resource revenue sharing; specific measures to stimulate economic development; and a role in the management of heritage resources and parks. Figure 2 shows in summary form the benefits provided by the ten agreements concluded thus far.

The prospect of the creation of still more governments and more bureaucracy is even more frightening, as will be seen in Chapter 3.

Of the greatest import, the rights contained in these land claim agreements are "constitutionally protected," which means they cannot be altered ever in the future except with the concurrence of the native peoples involved or by constitutional amendment. More on this later.

The financial and economic benefits of these land claim settlements to a relatively few native peoples are enormous, prompting the Bank of Montreal to create an aboriginal banking unit complete with its own vice-president, Ron Jamieson, who is quoted as saying:

"The fact is that by the end of the decade, aboriginal people [in Canada] are going to own or control a third of the Canadian land mass and be the recipient of $5 or $6 billion."[21]

Mr. Jamieson's $5 or $6 billion estimate must, by any reckoning, be considered conservative given the prospect of $8 billion to $12 billion for B.C. land claim settlements alone if the present course is followed. Since being hired in the summer of 1992, Mr. Jamieson "has been out pressing the flesh with native groups across the country, in the hope of snagging their business."[22]

Once negotiations are concluded, it has been the practice for the Prime Minister and the Minister of DIAND to visit the territory for a formal signing ceremony with much fanfare and aplomb. Ratification then takes place among the bands involved. Until now, ratification on the Government's part has been through an Act of Parliament. The present federal government has done away with the necessity of bringing future land claim settlements in the Yukon to Parliament at all. In the future they will merely be approved by cabinet order. This, in itself, is a shocking abuse of democratic principles and a disregard for the interests of the Canadian people whose rights and lands are being bartered away without their knowledge.

Recently concluded land claim and other agreements and their passage through Parliament warrant more detailed scrutiny. Space will permit only three of them to be dealt with in detail: the Nunavut deal of the eastern Arctic, the Sahtu and Metis land claim agreement in the Great Bear Lake region of the western Arctic and the four self government agreements settled to date in the Yukon. These are the subject of the next two chapters.

Chapter 1 - Footnotes:

1. Canada, DIAND, *Statement of the Government of Canada on Indian Policy (The White Paper)*, 1969, 6.
2. Ibid., 5.
3. Ibid., 6.
4. Ibid., 11.
5. Quoted in Cumming and Mickenberg, *Native Rights in Canada*, 1972, 2nd edition (Toronto: Indian-Eskimo Association of Canada and General Publishing), 331.
6. In fact, the federal government had met over the previous year with representatives of all 558 Indian bands across Canada and sent questionnaires to all registered Indians seeking their views on amendments to the *Indian Act*.
7. Hansard, *Commons Debates*, June 25, 1969, 10583.
8. Ibid, 10584.
9. *Indian-Eskimo Association of Canada Bulletin*, Vol.10, No.3, July, 1969, 3.
10. Hansard, *Commons Debates*, July 11, 1969, 11128.
11. Quoted in Cumming and Mickenberg, Ibid., 331.
12. Fleras and Elliott, *The Nations Within* (Oxford University Press, 1992), 43-44.
13. Comeau and Santin, *The First Canadians* (James Lorimer & Company, 1990), 18-19.
14. Canada, *Task Force on Program Review (Nielsen Task Force) Improved Program Delivery: Indians and Natives* (Ottawa, Government of Canada, 1985), 31.
15. Comeau and Santin, Ibid., 18.
16. DIAND, 1973. *Statement on Claims of Indian and Inuit People*, Press Release, August, 1973.
17. Submission of DIAND to the Royal Commission on Aboriginal Peoples, March, 1993.
18. Calder vs Attorney General of British Columbia [1973] S.C.R.313.
19. Kenneth Lysyk, *The Indian Title Question in Canada: An Appraisal in the Light of Calder* (The Canadian Bar Review, Vol.51, 1973), 450 at 452.
20. Hansard, *Commons Debates*, February 22, 1995, 9952.
21. John Greenwood, "This Land," *The Financial Post Magazine*, March, 1993, 17.
22. Ibid.

Sacrificing Our Northern Inheritance

"We [meaning the Inuit] start from the premise that we are the rightful occupants and owners of the land. The government should be asking us for permission to occupy our lands and use our resources and should negotiate with us on that basis."   Jack Anawak, MP, 1993 (now Parliamentary Secretary to the Minister of DIAND).

Do not be taken in by the rhetoric of Mr. Anawak. All land in Canada, since the exercise of British sovereignty, is public land owned, in the first instance, by the federal Crown, in the case of the territories; and by the provincial Crown, in the case of the provinces. The Constitution of Canada and every judicial decision that has considered the matter has so found. Unless it has been formally conveyed by Crown grant by the relevant government, it remains Crown property. Even if Crown granted, the underlying title still remains in the Crown.

Land claim agreements in the Northwest Territories

Well might we pause for a moment and reflect on where federal government land claim policy has taken us in relation to the Northwest Territories, a land mass larger in area than either Europe or the sub-continent of India. The total population of the NWT comprises 57,649 persons, of which 22,347 are non-aboriginal.[1] Former Prime Minister John Diefenbaker once described the North as "Canada's last great untouched inheritance." The late Newfoundland Premier Joey Smallwood reflected that view when he angrily reacted to a 1968 proposal of B.C. Premier W.A.C. Bennett that the northern boundaries of the four western provinces be extended northward to the Arctic Sea. "The North belongs to all of us as Canadians," Smallwood exclaimed. And in a real sense he was right.

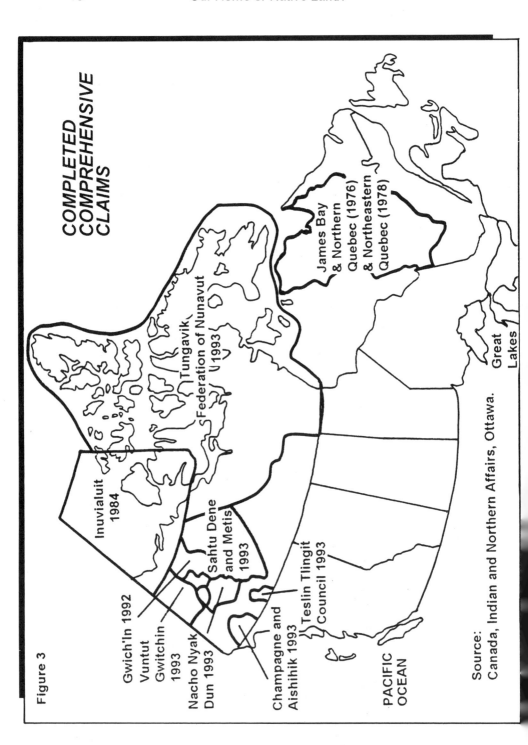

Figure 3

COMPLETED COMPREHENSIVE CLAIMS

Tungavik Federation of Nunavut 1993

James Bay & Northern Quebec (1976) & Northeastern Quebec (1978)

Great Lakes

Inuvialuit 1984

Gwich'In 1992
Vuntut Gwitchin 1993

Nacho Nyak Dun 1993

Sahtu Dene and Metis 1993

Champagne and Aishihik 1993

Teslin Tlingit Council 1993

PACIFIC OCEAN

Source:
Canada, Indian and Northern Affairs, Ottawa.

But, sad to say, successive federal governments in recent years, including the current one, are sacrificing this "inheritance" for all Canadians on the "politically correct" and expedient altar of native land claim agreements. In the NWT alone, the four land claim agreements concluded thus far provide the following combined benefits to just 24,000 people:

- constitutionally entrenched aboriginal fishing, trapping and hunting rights forever over an area of 2.6 million square kilometres—about one-quarter the size of Canada. (Any future third-party use of these areas, such as forest harvest, or mineral and oil and gas development, must go through elaborate new regulatory regimes including, in many cases, native consent.)
- Government cash payments over a number of years, totalling $1.3 billion in estimated 1999 dollars.
- A handsome percentage of the resource royalties from oil, gas and mineral development from within these areas.
- Participation in all decision-making processes dealing with land, water and environmental management with virtual veto power.
- *Outright ownership* of 505,950 square kilometres of land—an area equivalent to over half the size of Ontario—with undersurface rights over portions of it.

In my view, such wholesale give-aways are without justification and are greatly beyond legal entitlement.[2]

Figure 3 shows a map of the land claim agreements completed to date in Quebec, the NWT and Yukon.

Constitutional status of agreements

Few Canadians may realize that the rights contained in land claim agreements such as these, which, in each case number hundreds of pages and literally thousands of provisions, cannot be changed in future—even by federal legislation—unless the aboriginal group which is party to such an agreement agrees. This places land claim agreements on a higher footing than even the charters of Canada's great cities. For example, Vancouver or Toronto, or any other Canadian city you might name, functions under a Charter given it by the provincial government of the province in which it is situated. That provincial government has the legal power to *unilaterally* alter or even abolish that city's charter. The fact that it is not likely to do so is irrelevant. By contrast, the rights contained in land claim agreements are "constitutionally entrenched" because section 35 of the *Constitution Act, 1982* provides that they are constitutionally "recognized and affirmed."

No country's best interests can or should be frozen in time—not even in the frigid north—and yet this is exactly what our government has done. Surely it must be the height of arrogance, to say nothing of myopia, for present-day politicians—aided and abetted by an all too pressing bureaucracy—to assume they are wise enough to put together deals of this magnitude and complexity and, in effect, lock them in place today thus removing them from the ordinary reach of future Parliaments. Suppose a few years down the road it is shown that government has, in some material respect, made a bad error in judgement and significant changes to the rights extended in land claim agreements should be made. Suppose also that the native leadership does not see it that way and opposes such changes. What then? It will matter not that in the greater Canadian interest, it may be deemed to be desirable or even necessary to make amendments which are antithetical to the native interest. Such amendments will be unachievable—at least short of a constitutional amendment.

Whereas in the ordinary course of events specific legislation is powerful enough to override, amend or even rescind a contractual agreement, in the case of these land claim agreements it would not be powerful enough to override them because they are "constitution-alized." Our 1981 constitution-makers' quick fix to assure native peace has now come home to roost! More on this in Chapter 7.

Extinguishment of other rights

It is not by coincidence that these agreements are called "settlements." The original intention of government was that they would, once and for all, settle undefined aboriginal claims and interests and thereby provide certainty for the future. In exchange for the specific rights and privileges set out in the land claim agreement, the band in question would relinquish any undefined aboriginal interest that it might have claimed in other areas not covered by the settlement agreement. Fortunately, such a clause is contained in the Nunavut land claim agreement. Of course, native negotiators have always resisted the inclusion of extinguishment clauses such as these, but successive federal governments until the present one have insisted upon their inclusion.

Apparently, "extinguishment" has now become a dirty word with present DIAND Minister Ron Irwin. It is reported that early in his tenure as Minister, Mr. Irwin sent out a directive to all his ministry personnel to expunge the word from their lexicon. He boasts about

> *"outlawing the scary departmental technical language that natives find so offensive. 'Extinguishment' was the first to go, the word used to describe the federal policy, now being reconsidered, of forcing native groups to give up or 'extinguish' their land rights as a condition of any land claim settlement."* [3]

Little wonder that Mr. Irwin (who, it is reported, acted as a lawyer and negotiator for northern Ontario native groups before entering federal politics)[4] when appointed DIAND Minister caused one national native leader to exclaim, "I think I've died and gone to heaven."[5]

If there are to be no extinguishment clauses in future land claim settlements, one has to question what the *quid pro quo* for governments is in entering into them at all. If finality is not to be achieved, government runs the risk of having to go through the whole process again, at some later date.

Citizenship plus

Even in those land claim agreements where the right to pursue undefined rights in future is to be extinguished, the scope of extinguishment is decidedly limited. One clause provides that nothing in the agreement shall:

> *(a) affect the ability of the Inuit to participate in or benefit from any existing or future constitutional rights for*

aboriginal people which may be applicable to them; or
(b) affect their ability to participate in and benefit from government programs for Inuit or aboriginal people generally, as the case may be; or
(c) affect their rights as Canadian citizens to continue to be entitled to all the rights and benefits of all other citizens applicable to them from time to time.

This kind of clause calls into question the whole rationale for the land claim policy. We have been told that the substantial lands, natural resources, cash payments and other benefits which these agreements provide will break the ties of government dependency and develop a sense of self sufficiency among native people. These are commendable objectives but, in order for the policy to succeed, there should be a corresponding phase-out of ongoing government financial support and native programs to natives covered by these agreements. Good sense, to say nothing of the interest of the overburdened Canadian taxpayer, demands no less. And yet, the very opposite is to be the case because of the right to fully benefit from all other aboriginal programs and, as well, all the rights and benefits provided to Canadian citizens generally. Interestingly, the clause is long on "benefits" and "rights" but makes no mention of "responsibilities."

The "Province" of Nunavut

In addition to land claim agreements, other momentous developments are taking place in the Northwest Territories. A new publicly governed territory to be called Nunavut is being established. This new territory is of staggering proportions comprising more than one-fifth of the country's land mass. At two million square kilometres it will be twice the size of Ontario—Canada's second largest province. The territory covers the area running from the tree line at 60 degrees latitude to the North Pole, embracing the whole of the eastern Arctic and as far west as Great Bear Lake. The federal statute establishing the territory was rushed through Parliament on one afternoon in early June, 1993; it is 67 pages long and calls for Nunavut to come into being on April 1, 1999.

I call the territory a province because the legislation setting it up bears all of the hallmarks of a full-fledged province, including:

- a seat of government or capital;
- an Executive Council (i.e. a Cabinet) presided over by the government leader;
- a Legislative Assembly with power to make laws on a full range of province-like powers including:
  - the administration of justice, including the establishment, maintenance and organization of territorial courts;
  - prisons, jails and lock-ups;
  - municipal and local institutions;
  - hospitals;
  - property and civil rights;
  - agriculture;
  - solemnization of marriage;
  - generally, all matters of a merely local or private nature in Nunavut;
- the establishment of the Court of Appeal of Nunavut;
- the establishment of the Supreme Court of Nunavut.

The Act goes on to entrust in a Commissioner appointed by Ottawa the public lands transferred to Nunavut by Ottawa, with the right to manage, lease or sell the same.

The question that immediately comes to mind is how many people are to be served by this new government with its own seat of government, its own Legislative Assembly with extensive law-making power, its Executive Council with a presiding officer, who will be dubbed "Premier," its Court of Appeal, its Supreme Court and a myriad of boards, commissions and bureaucrats? All of this for less than 22,000 people.

The new bureaucracy and its cost

Apparently fifteen government departments are planned, plus the Executive Council and six government agencies. There will be the usual retinue of policy analysts, public information officers, human resources personnel, program deliverers, deputy ministers, administrators, and even a Commissioner of Official Languages. Who will hold the senior positions in the bureaucracy and in the judiciary? Not likely many Inuit or non-Inuit now living in the territories because 57% of the natives living there are without any secondary schooling. High school graduation rates are getting worse, not better. It is reported that in 1984-85 10% of natives aged 18 had graduated; by 1990-91 the figure had dropped to 6%.[6] But NWT statistics show that only 35 Inuit completed senior matriculation from 1983 to 1993 out of an annual school population of 6,800 Inuit.[7]

John Amagoalik, Chief Commissioner of the Nunavut Implementation Commission and its greatest supporter, now worries that so many government jobs will be created that young Inuit will aspire to nothing else and this could wind up being the most over-administered part of Canada, "with everybody drinking everybody else's bath water and singing patriotic songs."[8]

As for the costs involved in establishing this new bureaucracy, a report submitted to the federal government by Coopers & Lybrand in December, 1992, estimates capital costs for new government buildings etc. for Nunavut at $334 million. It is estimated that $520 million will be spent in operating costs between the start-up date in 1999 and the year 2008. The report goes on to estimate that after 2008 Nunavut will cost $84 million a year more than it costs to service that part of the Arctic now from Yellowknife. The report predicts an additional 930 jobs in the newly established bureaucracy combined with 705 jobs transferred from Yellowknife, bringing the total number of civil servants in the area to 1,635. Virtually all of these costs must be entirely borne by taxpayers from elsewhere in Canada since the consulting firm projects that none of Nunavut's population will contribute any tax revenues for their new government in the foreseeable future. At present only 10-12% is locally generated.

Provincehood disguised

Canadians point to the anomaly of Prince Edward Island with a population of 130,000—a province smaller than many district municipalities—and yet we are about to establish a new "Province" with a population less than one-sixth that of Prince Edward Island. The way out of this utter madness is to suggest that the whole scheme may be unconstitutional because, since 1982, the Canadian Constitution requires that the establishment of new provinces requires the approval not only of Parliament but also of at least seven provincial legislatures having 50% of the population of Canada. If this new territory is not tantamount to establishing a new province without the consent of the other provinces and therefore subverting the constitutional requirement, then I do not know what a new province would look like. If it looks like a duck, quacks like a duck and walks like a duck, the chances are it's a duck.

In fact, subsection 2 of section 23 of the *Nunavut Act* is a tell-tale sign that Nunavut is tantamount to a province, for it provides that the legislature of Nunavut shall not have greater powers than those given to the legislatures of the provinces by sections 92 and 95 of the Constitution Act, 1867. What this means is that the drafters of the legislation were so afraid that they might have given *more* legislative powers to the territory of Nunavut than were given under the Constitution to the provinces of Canada that there had to be a saving clause to ensure this didn't happen. (The fact that there is a somewhat similar clause in the *NWT Act* is irrelevant. The indications of provincehood are less apparent and that Act was passed before there was a constitutional provision requiring the provinces to be involved in the establishment of new provinces.)

Whose brainchild in government was it to establish this "province" in the north and what cost-benefit analyses were undertaken to determine whether this major move is in the best interests of the north and of Canada as a whole? Of course, a majority of the Inuit living in the region voted for the proposal, but who spoke for the government and the people of Canada? DIAND Minister Tom Siddon freely acknowledged that he did. In the truncated debate in the House of Commons on June 4, 1993, discussed in more detail below, Mr. Siddon is quoted in Hansard as saying:

"I remember the night here in Ottawa, I think it was December 15, 1991, when we had a long and fruitful discussion about whether the federal government had the will to make this commitment which we are about to endorse today. I remember

in a sense taking a risk but I did in fact call the Prime Minister and we decided that we could make that commitment . . . "[9]

Is this any way to make public policy of such lasting and costly import?

The question of the possible division of NWT has been considered since 1963. Over the years more and more autonomy has been given to the territorial government, especially since 1967 when Stu Hodgson was the Commissioner. But the concept of dividing the NWT, as the establishment of Nunavut will do, was rejected by two reputable and comprehensive studies that looked into the matter: The Carrothers' Report of 1965 rejected it as did C. M. (Bud) Drury, who was appointed in 1977 by Prime Minister Trudeau to consider the future constitutional development of the NWT.

Gordon Robertson, the much respected former Clerk of the Privy Council—the country's number one bureaucrat—and before that Commissioner of the Northwest Territories and Deputy Minister of Northern Affairs and National Resources, believes that to give provincial status to the North is inadvisable and fiscally unsustainable. He points out that the dependency of the region on high cost resource development and oscillating world resource prices, together with transfer of land and under-surface rights in land claim agreements, will reduce the revenue potential for governments in the region so as to make full provincehood unviable.[10]

It is northern politicians—both native and non-native—that have provided the impetus for territorial division. The rationale for it is more power with other Canadians paying the bills. Northerners have never had to bear the burden of the cost of their government. Today they raise only 10 to 12 cents of every dollar they spend. The rest is granted to them from Ottawa under one program or another. When they run out of money, they call upon Ottawa for more. NWT politicians' salaries and benefits are by far the highest in Canada with the richest pension plan. One study concludes that with allowances and various per diems ordinary MLA's can earn between $81,000 and $114,000 annually and Ministers between $117,000 and $192,000.[11] And there is no outcry from the NWT populace because they don't pay the bill. Nor is there an outcry from the rest of Canada because they know nothing of it.

Signing the Nunavut deal was done with much fanfare. On May 25, 1993, Prime Minister Mulroney with Minister Siddon travelled to Iqaluit. The signing took place at the local high school where several hundred students wearing Nunavut t-shirts cheered wildly in the school's gymnasium. This was to show that the agreement was really for the next generation. One student has recently reported that although it made good television the enthusiasm wasn't exactly authentic. "The teachers made us clap," recalled one student. "They said we'd be in real trouble if we didn't. Most people were just happy to be missing class."[12]

In a recent newspaper account a reporter interviewed more than two dozen young Inuit on Baffin Island between the ages of 14 and 28. He was struck by the generation gap that exists:

"The parents remember their first time at the edge of an ice floe, spear in hand eagerly waiting for a glimpse of a seal; children recall when they first got to pick the cereal of their choice at the local store. But most Inuit youths are uninterested in or even cynical about the new territory. They know little about it, just as many know little of Inuit culture, and tend to think of Nunavut not as something symbolic but simply as a new bureaucracy. 'The bottom line is it's just another territory,' said Eric Ootoovak, 17, a high school student in this hamlet of 1,150. 'It's just more government for a smaller number of people. I don't see as how that will change anything.'"[13]

Sad perhaps, but nonetheless the reality.

Figure 4 – **Map of Nunavut**

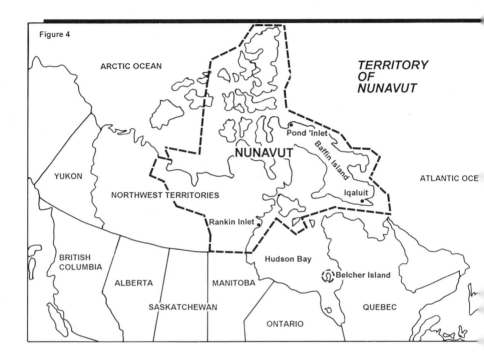

Figure 4

Parliament abused

Both the ratification of the Nunavut land claim agreement and the establishment of the new public territory of Nunavut required parliamentary approval. The legislation was introduced in the House of Commons on May 28, 1993. Bill C-132 was to establish the territory of Nunavut and provide for its government and Bill C-133 was to ratify the Nunavut land claim agreement.

The 287-page land claim agreement, which had been fifteen years in the making, and the legislation to establish the territory of Nunavut formally came to the attention of Parliamentarians for the first time when the Bills were introduced. With virtually little or no time to consider the contents, much less the implications of the whole deal, the government of the day not only brought the matter on for second reading on June 4—one week later—but, quite incredibly, moved a motion that all stages of these bills, including Committee of the Whole, Second and Third reading, be completed on that day! Such a motion requires unanimous consent of all the members. When the motion was called, Deborah Gray (Beaver River), the only Reform party member of the Commons at that time, withheld consent.

Not to be thwarted in their effort to get this matter of great significance through the House in one day, the government House leader then advised the House that the recognized parties, namely the government Conservatives, the official opposition Liberals, and the NDP, had agreed on time allocation under standing order 78(1). This procedure, which is used rarely and is inimical to the concept of parliamentary democracy, is usually applied after an issue has been thoroughly debated in Parliament and the debate has become tedious and repetitious. It is a technique to thwart an opposition filibuster. Here, of course, it was applied *before* any debate had begun.

At this point, the government House leader moved that debate on Bill C-133, establishing the territory of Nunavut be limited to one hour and forty-five minutes for the consideration of all stages of the Bill, including Committee of the Whole. A time allocation such as this does not require the unanimous consent of all members of the House. It only requires approval among the recognized parties. At this time the Reform party did not have sufficient seats to be a recognized party. Deborah Gray's continued resistance to push this thing through the House was therefore a voice crying in the wilderness.

The debate was led off by the Minister Tom Siddon, who spoke for only eighteen minutes outlining the main provisions of the deal but giving no rationale for it. He was followed by Mr. Jack Anawak, the Inuit member for Nunatsiaq, for the Liberal party. He said in part:

"We [meaning the Inuit] start from the premise that we are the rightful occupants and owners of the land. The government should be asking us for permission to occupy our lands and use our resources and should negotiate with us on that basis. Instead the government takes the position that it owns the land and it believes it is being generous by sharing some of our land with us."

He went on:

"I want to say for the record that Inuit do not just assert title to Nunavut. Our title is real. It is the government of Canada that has asserted title to Nunavut. Our title predates any claim by the government whether the government recognizes it or not." [14]

To non-native Canadians, it is not exactly reassuring to know that the man holding these views is now the Parliamentary Secretary to DIAND Minister Irwin. In my view, Mr. Anawak's proposition has no support in either the Canadian Constitution, common law, or in judicial decisions of Canadian courts. Nonetheless, to some it sounds plausible and is accepted unthinkingly even by many in high places.

Mr. Robert Skelly (NDP Comox-Alberni) was next. He showered congratulations all round—to the Inuit and to the government. He also took the tack that these lands belong to the Inuit and that the Inuit are giving up their rights to other Canadians and we ought to be grateful.

Mr. Patrick Nowlan (Independent Member of Parliament from Annapolis Valley, Hants) next spoke and made a scathing attack on how this matter was being dealt with in Parliament:

"If there was ever an example of a dead Parliament doing dangerous things, this bill sadly is it. This bill should not have been brought in in the closing days of Parliament, the last weekend before we rise. . . . The Minister spoke this morning for 18 minutes. Then the government House leader stood up and used standing order 78(1) with the connivance and the

complicity of the opposition who are always railing against allocation of time. . . . We know from the history of this Parliament that this party has had no credibility on constitutional matters. These were the three parties that agreed to Meech Lake some many years ago. In effect, that went down the drain.

"[For] government in its dying days to exercise Standing Order 78(1) to close off debate on something of such magnitude and importance to the people involved is not doing justice to the issue." [15]

Mr. Nowlan then went on to compare the extent of the debate that took place in 1905 when the provinces of Alberta and Saskatchewan were established:

"Just a quick review of the index (of Hansard) in those days when new provinces were being brought into Confederation and being made part of Canada shows that it was not done in the dying days of Parliament. It was not done on a late Friday afternoon or in the dark of night. It was done in open daylight. It had debate at first, second and third readings. There were 84 pages of index of both Bills. I think 52 members participated in debate on one bill and over 52 participated in the other debate. That is what used to happen.

"I say that this is a perversion of the rules and I say it sadly. It is a travesty of Parliament which by its very name, as we all know, means we are supposed to speak." [16]

Mr. Nowlan concluded his compelling and powerful remarks somewhat prophetically:

"I feel strongly that this was the wrong tactic to use on something so fundamentally important for the people affected. It certainly is a poor reflection of the state of this Parliament. The sooner we can have an election and have a variety of parties in this house, the sooner we will not have the conspiracy of silence, the Official Opposition and the NDP agreeing with a government that they usually condemn every day." [17]

Mr. Siddon then in a rejoinder made the point that the agreement in principle had been signed some considerable time previously and that members of the House through parliamentary committees had had a chance to follow the development of this legislative package. However, a check with the Clerk of the Committee shows that there is no record of the Nunavut Bills or the Nunavut land claim agreement ever having been considered by the Standing Committee on Aboriginal and Northern Affairs.

A few minutes later the Bill was read a second time, immediately considered in Committee of the Whole House, reported and read a third time.

An equally speedy passage faced Bill C-132, although the Minister's speech was even shorter than eighteen minutes. Again, the Minister merely paraphrased some of the provisions of the Bill setting up the territory and gave no rationale whatsoever for the need for it, except to say that the Inuit people have long sought after it and that this will bring government closer to the people. Extending congratulatory bouquets to all involved, the Minister then took his seat but not before moving that all stages of debate on this Bill be dealt with that day, to which, at that stage, being 1:45 p.m. on a Friday afternoon, there was unanimous consent among the recognized parties in the House.

With that the two Bills passed the House, moved quickly through the Senate, without so much as a "sober second thought," and received Royal Assent, thereby becoming law.

Sahtu Dene and Metis Land Claim Agreement

One more land claim agreement in the Northwest Territories was to round out the Conservatives' term of office prior to their defeat at the polls in October, 1993. Signed on behalf of the federal government on September 6, 1993, by the new Minister of DIAND, Pauline Browes, the Agreement was with the Sahtu Dene and Metis peoples of the Great Bear Lake region of the western Arctic, embracing the five communities of Colville Lake, Fort Good Hope, Fort Norman, Deline (formerly Fort Franklin) and Norman Wells and surrounding areas; see Figure 5.

As is in the case of the other land claim agreements, the area covered by the Sahtu Agreement is massive in dimension, and its terms comprehensive in scope and far-reaching in consequences—all

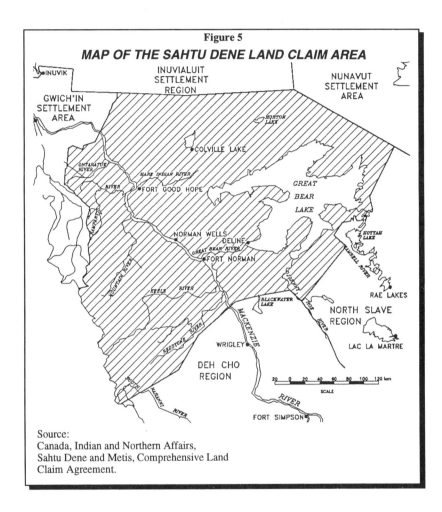

Figure 5

MAP OF THE SAHTU DENE LAND CLAIM AREA

Source:
Canada, Indian and Northern Affairs,
Sahtu Dene and Metis, Comprehensive Land
Claim Agreement.

for a meagre population comprised of 982 adults (829 Dene and 153 Metis) and 773 children, for a total of 1,755. The Sahtu "settlement area"—the area within the NWT covered by the Agreement and where the benefits and terms of the Agreement apply—covers 280,000 sq.kms. (108,200 sq. miles), an area five times the size of Nova Scotia and 30% of the size of British Columbia.

The major benefits extended include:

- Outright ownership to 41,437 sq.km. of land (an area seven times the size of Prince Edward Island, or three-quarters the size of Nova Scotia). These are described as Sahtu lands.
- Undersurface rights (i.e. minerals, oil and gas rights) to 1,813 sq.km. (700 sq.miles).
- A financial contribution from Canada of $75 million in 1990 dollars, which when paid out over 15 years will be approximately $130 million.
- 7.5% of the first $2 million in royalties received annually by the government from within the settlement area plus 1.5% of all royalties above $2 million (no cap).

In addition to the above, the Government is committed to taking measures to support the traditional economy and to assist business development.

Before any oil and gas exploration, development or production activities can take place in the settlement area, the Government must provide the Sahtu Tribal Council (STC) with the opportunity to express its views. Moreover, the operator proposing such activities must consult with the Sahtu Dene and Metis on such issues as environmental impacts and provide Sahtu Dene and Metis with employment opportunities. Similar consultations will be necessary prior to the development of minerals.

The Sahtu Dene and Metis will have exclusive right to harvest wildlife on the Sahtu lands, subject to existing third party harvesting rights. The Sahtu Dene and Metis may permit other people to harvest on their land subject to general legislation on harvesting. Over the larger settlement area, the Sahtu Dene and Metis will have the exclusive right to harvest fur bearers.

Certain traditional harvesting areas which are not included within the settlement lands have been designated "special harvesting areas" with the Sahtu Dene and Metis having exclusive right to harvest in those areas, although other persons may harvest moose there during the fall.

Apart from existing third party rights, in waters overlying Sahtu lands, only the Sahtu Dene and Metis will be licensed to fish commercially. In other waters in the larger settlement area, the Sahtu Dene and Metis have the right to take up half of all new commercial fish licences.

More and more bureaucracy

The provisions of the agreement relating to land, water, resource and wildlife management in the settlement area are extensive and complex. The new bureaucracy to be put in place to administer these provisions is extensive. The agreement authorizes the establishment of the following regulatory bodies:

Renewable Resource Councils
- For each Sahtu community (Colville Lake, Deline, Fort Norman, Fort Good Hope, Norman Wells) to manage the exercise of harvesting rights.

Renewable Resources Board
- To be the main instrument of wildlife management in the settlement area: a six member board: three nominated by government and three by the Sahtu Dene and Metis.

Arbitration Panel
- To settle disputes relating to the Agreement without going to court.

Land Use Planning Board
- To prepare a land use plan providing for the conservation, development and utilization of land, resources and water in the settlement area.
- Sahtu Dene and Metis will nominate 50% of membership.

Land and Water Board
- To regulate all land and water use within the settlement area with 50% Sahtu Dene and Metis membership.
- Once established, this Board will assume the functions of the Northwest Territories Water Board within the area.

Environmental Impact Review Board
- To review impacts of proposed developments in Sahtu lands.

-     When it reviews impacts within the Sahtu settlement area, the Sahtu Tribal Council is entitled to nominate half of the members.

Surface Rights Board

-     To resolve disputes between surface owners and subsurface rights holders over Sahtu land.

These are some but not all of the new boards or regulatory bodies to administer the provisions of this Agreement. Still more bureaucracy will be created when the recently passed *Mackenzie Valley Resource Management Act* comes into force. All of these functions are now being performed either by DIAND or the Government of the NWT. Though the existing regulatory bodies are being supplanted by these new boards they will no doubt continue to function elsewhere but with less work to do.

Who are to staff these new boards and provide the support staff they will require? Over the past 20 years, the people of the North have become what observers call "board junkies." In an economy with few job opportunities for the minimally educated, board appointments are a way to earn handsome per diems, provide frequent travel opportunities and exercise direct political influence. Who is to pay for these new boards and regulatory bodies? Not the Sahtu Dene and Metis, despite the generous cash payments and royalties coming their way. Ottawa will pay 100% of the costs. That means you and me.

Additional benefits

As in the case of other post-1982 land claim settlements, the rights contained in the Sahtu Dene and Metis Agreement are "constitutionally entrenched."

An extinguishment clause, relinquishing any other undefined aboriginal claims to lands and waters anywhere in Canada, save the rights and benefits provided by the Agreement itself, is included. Again this clause is considerably qualified by what I call a "citizens plus" clause similar to the one accompanying the Nunavut deal described above.

Parliament revived

This, the last of the land claim agreements signed by the successive Conservative governments of Prime Ministers Brian

Mulroney and Kim Campbell, was left to the new Liberal administration of Prime Minister Jean Chrétien to finalize by ratification through Parliament. This was not long in coming. Bill C-16 to approve, give effect to, and declare valid the Sahtu Dene and Metis Agreement was introduced in the House of Commons and read a first time on March 10, 1994.

Of course, the political landscape in the House of Commons had drastically changed since the Nunavut Agreement was before the House seven months earlier. A general election had ensued which saw the Conservatives vaporized, the NDP decimated, the Liberals elected with a strong majority of 170 seats out of 295 and the emergence of 54 Bloc Quebecois MPs from Quebec and 52 Reform MPs from British Columbia and Alberta, primarily, but also having representation from Saskatchewan, Manitoba and Ontario.

Obviously, unqualified support for the Bill by the Liberal backbenchers and the NDP rump was predictable, but it was not until second reading debate commenced in the House on April 25, 1994, that it was known how the Bloc and the Reformers would vote. Nor indeed was it apparent that there would be any debate at all, given the reluctance, with one or two exceptions, of past Parliamentarians considering earlier land claim agreements to engage in even a whisper of criticism.

The Bloc immediately declared itself in favour of the deal but Reformers made it known that they had some serious misgivings on which they would seek answers and assurances from the government.

As is customary, the Minister sponsoring the Bill led off the debate. Minister Irwin relied, in part, on the Liberal Red Book used in the election campaign as the impetus for land claim agreements of this kind. He stated:

"We made clear our commitment to address outstanding land claims in 'Creating Opportunity: The Liberal Plan for Canada.' On page 96 of that document there is a very clear and concise statement of this government's intention toward aboriginal people: 'The priority of a Liberal government will be to assist aboriginal communities in their efforts to address the obstacles to their development and to help them marshal the human and physical resources necessary to build and sustain vibrant communities.'

"Comprehensive land claim settlements take us a long way toward accomplishing this goal. By ensuring certainty of land ownership and providing fee simple title to large areas of land they remove some of the most significant obstacles to the economic development and diversification of aboriginal communities." [18]

"These lands and these funds combined with a share of the resource royalties from projects in the Mackenzie Valley will give the Sahtu Dene and Metis the financial resources to support their own economic development initiatives. The money may also be used to support social, cultural, educational and political initiatives." [19]

As Official Opposition, the Bloc's critic on native affairs Mr. Claude Bachand (Saint-Jean) was next to speak. He quickly declared himself and his party in favour of the Bill and the agreement.

By contrast, Mr. John Duncan (North Island-Powell River), the leading spokesman for the Reform Party on native issues, wasted no time in throwing down the gauntlet.

"My primary reasons for speaking in opposition to the bill are threefold. First, there is no legal rationale for this massive fee simple transfer of land. Second, a new bureaucracy is created. Third, the agreement in all its complexity is to be constitutionally entrenched." [20]

After describing the array of benefits the agreement provides, he went on to say:

"I would ask the minister as to the rationale the government has applied in arriving at this huge package of benefits for such a relatively small number. How has the sum of $130 million been arrived at? Is there any indication it is appropriate to the needs of the participants? Will this enormously generous package of benefits result in the regular programs available to native peoples being phased out? There is no indication in the agreement that this is to be so. In fact, the very opposite is said to be the case. . . .

"The area north of the 60th parallel throughout Canada has always been considered to be a part of the public lands of Canada in which all Canadians share an interest . . . It is apparent it is the intention of successive governments of Canada to blanket all of Canada's north with land claim settlements of this kind. One could understand granting to a sparse northern population traditional rights of hunting, fishing and trapping, subject to third party interests. But it is quite another matter to convey the outright ownership of vast territories of land. It is not necessary and my party opposes it." [21]

On the new bureaucracy that the agreement would establish, Mr. Duncan said:

"One has to question the necessity of setting up still another plethora of boards, commissions and instrumentalities within the Northwest Territories . . . Layer of government upon layer of government in the sparsely populated Northwest Territories is not the way to go. We are in danger of turning a sparse population into a bevy of bureaucrats, yet one of the main stated purposes of the agreement is to permit pursuit of a traditional livelihood and way of life." [22]

On the matter of constitutionally entrenching these agreements, he said:

"My second concern is to question the wisdom of entrenching all of the detailed provisions of the agreement until it has been in force for a period of time to consider whether or not it is workable.

"It would be preferable to constitutionalize the land rights and perhaps the other benefits to be paid. All of the administrative and regulatory provisions should not be constitutionally entrenched to ensure flexibility as circumstances dictate.

"Who are we to say we know what is best for future generations in those areas?" [23]

A Liberal backbencher, Mr. Peter Adams (Peterborough), then gave a pat speech in favour of everything about the deal. With all due respect, it appeared that the Member did not know much about the subject for, in having to depart from his written text to answer a question put to him by a Reform MP, he had to take the question under advisement.

Mr. Dave Chatters (Athabasca), another Reform MP having particular responsibilities on native issues, faced head on the often-touted view that agreements of this kind are "to right the injustices of the past." He began:

> "Immediately I have to ask: What injustices are we trying to right? If one is familiar or cares to study the history of the area north of the 60th parallel, one would discover that there is a substantial difference from the history of more southern neighbours.
>
> "To begin with, life for aboriginals in the land north of 60 has traditionally been a subsistence existence, harsh and unforgiving. From the earliest encroachment into this land by European settlement, the federal government has recognized its responsibility to the people living there and made efforts in spite of the vast wilderness and harsh climate to provide, where possible, help through RCMP outposts and local missions.
>
> "I will not accept the popular myth spread by certain self-serving interests that the encroachment of European settlers constitutes an injustice against the aboriginal people here or anywhere else in Canada.
>
> "At the turn of the century western and northern Canada was a vast, mostly uninhabited land in real danger of being annexed to the United States. The aboriginal people living in this vast territory were eager for the technology which the Europeans brought with them, in spite of the problems that came with them.
>
> "It was under these circumstances that the then Government of Canada, through a series of grossly distorted and overly optimistic ads, invited Europeans from all parts of Europe to come to western Canada with the promise of 160 acres or a half square mile of land for the sum of $10 and a freer, richer

lifestyle, but all the time having the real objective of asserting sovereignty over western and northern Canada.

"It was under these circumstances that my grandfather along with thousands of others came to Canada, not to perpetrate an injustice upon the aboriginal people but to accept the opportunity being offered.

"In spite of the great disappointment upon arriving in a bush covered, swampy, fly and mosquito infested homestead in northern Alberta, my grandfather and grandmother built a home with the trees on the land, cleared the land with only an axe and a team of horses, and built a farm in spite of the injustices of hail, frost, depression, injury, disease and government misrepresentation. That is how to build self-esteem and self-worth.

"I cannot and will not be held responsible for the actions of the past political leadership of this country any more than the aboriginal people can be held responsible for their past leadership. Therefore I will not accept the guilt or support compensation for my being here or my helping to develop industries which now support us in the best standard of living in the world. However I would support any agreement or effort to help the aboriginal people of this area to participate and enjoy the benefits of life enjoyed by all other Canadians." [24]

Noting the overly generous financial payment which this agreement provides, Mr. Chatters observed:

"All this is being offered at a time when our country is bankrupt and our most treasured social safety net system is decomposing because of the financial restraints being imposed on it." [25]

Then he put his finger on the nub which motivates so much of the aboriginal agenda:

"Where does this initiative for the land claim settlement come from? In my opinion the initiative comes from the real root of the aboriginal problem in Canada, the insidious parasitic Indian industry. That group of lawyers, consultants, bureaucrats and

Indian leaders year after year swallow up the vast majority of money designated to solve the problems of poverty, illiteracy, substance abuse and suffering among our native people.

"This agreement does nothing to solve that problem and in fact greatly reinforces it. Instead of continuing to feed this selfish parasitic monster, let us break the cycle by making available to aboriginal Canadians programs available to all Canadians and then providing an affordable amount of the $10 billion plus now spent on aboriginal services and programs to grassroots aboriginal people in the form of a guaranteed annual income. . . .

"I ask that members not buy into this guilt trip so skilfully put on us and not enter into another binding contract based solely on racial origin that is to last as long as the sun rises and the rivers flow." [26]

This compelling and moving presentation was all too much for Mr. Jack Anawak, the Inuit member from the Territories and the Parliamentary Secretary to the Minister. He responded as might be expected:

"The attitude of people like the member who just spoke and the other Reform member who spoke earlier, I repeat, is unbelievable. We are not asking him to accept the guilt. All we are doing through this legislation is trying to right the wrongs that were done to the aboriginal people of that area, in this case, the Sahtu. Words fail me because it is too unbelievable to even contemplate the attitude of the Reform Party." [27]

Mrs. Marlene Cowling (Dauphin-Swan River), another Liberal backbencher, delivered a set piece espousing the government line but with no attempt to address any of the legitimate concerns that had been raised. Here again, her ineffectual response to the questions put to her by Reform MPs after her speech indicated a shaky grasp of the essential issues.

Mr. Jay Hill, the Reform member from Prince George-Peace River, made some telling comparisons between what land the Sahtu would have received if Treaty 11, which the Sahtu Dene signed many years earlier, had been fully implemented compared with what they were to receive under this agreement:

> *"Under Treaty 11 people were entitled to 128 acres per person. If the government had fulfilled its lawful obligation under the terms of the treaty even at this late date far less land would have been transferred. Although the Metis would not have received land under the old treaty, including them now means that the Sahtu Dene and Metis beneficiaries would have received just over 900 square kilometres of land with subsurface rights.*
>
> *"In this agreement the government doubled the treaty land entitlement to 1,800 square kilometres. Then it stepped completely outside of the treaty and beyond its lawful obligations and added another 39,000 square kilometres without accompanying subsurface rights. Instead of 128 acres per person the Sahtu have received 20 square kilometres per person. I would call this quite generous.*
>
> *"After doubling the treaty land entitlement and after guaranteeing traditional use rights over the entire settlement area of 280,000 square kilometres, why did the government give the Sahtu fee simple title to 39,000 more kilometres? I would ask the question is this fair and is it a just settlement?"*[28]

On the failure to phase out government programs to Sahtu, in the face of this generous package of benefits, Mr. Hill went on to say:

> *"For all the rights the Sahtu have received, what are their accompanying responsibilities and obligations? Despite the generosity of this agreement, the crown retains responsibility for program delivery and for special economic development programs to encourage self-sufficiency. These programs are in addition to the many government programs the Sahtu and other Canadians are eligible for.*
>
> *"Where is the incentive or the responsibility to become economically self-sufficient if the government is committed to providing programs indefinitely?*

"The crown has gone far beyond its lawful obligations and is not getting any diminishment of its responsibilities in return." [29]

What was the considered response of the Government to the legitimate concerns and questions raised by so many of the Reform members? There was none. Not once did the Minister enter the debate after having made the debate's opening speech. He left it to his Parliamentary Secretary, Jack Anawak, who found it impossible to rise above snide comments and sarcasm. For example, at this point in the debate he said:

"Mr. Speaker, the attitude of the Reform Party reminds me of the story of Rip Van Winkle who slept for so many years that when he woke up things had changed drastically. I think Reformers are still sleeping with the attitude they have.
"Their attitude is surprising when they say how generous the government is. I think the Sahtu Dene and Metis have been pretty generous by giving up 240,000 square kilometres of land to the Government of Canada and only retaining 41,000 square kilometres and 1,800 of subsurface and surface rights. I think that is pretty generous.
"I would like to think that the Reform Party can see reason. However, that might be impossible to ask of such outdated thinking." [30]

This mistaken concept held by native proponents such as Mr. Anawak that land ownership in Canada really belongs to the natives and not the Crown is at the core of the debate on land claims in this country. This is dealt with at length in Chapter 6.

A Liberal backbencher, Mr. Julian Reed (Halton-Peel), picked up on the theme:

"We are not giving the natives anything. It is already theirs. We are simply arriving at a suitable accommodation so that the country can forge ahead." [31]

Native policy based on such an erroneous point of view is on a slippery slope indeed.

The debate on second reading occupied most of the time of the House on April 25, 1994. The debate resumed again on May 2. Mike Scott, Reform MP for Skeena, led off the adjourned debate. In noting that this marked the first time that these kinds of issues were being substantially debated in Parliament, he expressed concern that the media were silent. He said:

"Following the debate on Monday, I eagerly scanned the newspapers and watched television news broadcasts to see how the media treated this issue. Do you know what I discovered, Mr. Speaker? The press totally ignored the issue. I could not find any coverage on Bill C-16 anywhere.

"Admittedly many bills pass through the House that are not very interesting or newsworthy, but this is surely not the case with Bill C-16 which will convey benefits of an enormous piece of land 50 times the size of Prince Edward Island, almost one-third the size of British Columbia, to less than 1,800 aboriginals for all time.

"One would think that with all the remaining land claims yet outstanding the press would be somewhat interested in what is going on here. I know the people in my riding are and I am sure the people in British Columbia and all of Canada are. How is it [sic] that an MP's expense account or the theatrics of question period can remain front page news for days and yet when we see an issue of such profound importance to all Canadians, aboriginal and non-aboriginal alike, being debated the media is [sic] asleep at the switch?

"I have concluded that it is either indifference born out of laziness or a tacit agreement not to provide serious coverage on issues which challenge the Liberal left agenda that has been wholeheartedly adopted and supported by a bunch of the big media in the country." [32]

He commented graphically on the massive benefits being made under the agreement:

"In addition to the outright transfer of over 40,000 square kilometres of land in fee simple, the federal government will pay out approximately $130 million over the next 15 years to

the Sahtu Tribal Council. This equates to more than $130,000
for each adult covered by the agreement.
"Again, to put this into perspective, if every adult Canadian was
given the same amount of money, the government would need
more than $3 trillion in the bank to write out the cheques. Three
trillion dollars is more than four times Canada's total debt of
$700 billion which includes federal, provincial and municipal
government debt." [33]

Reform member Dick Harris (Prince George-Buckley Valley)
focused on the enormous costs of native programs and the lack of
accountability:

"Since 1990 the budget of the Department of Indian Affairs and
Northern Development has increased approximately $400
million a year, the largest increase of any of the ministerial
budgets. In 1994-95 DIAND will spend some $5 billion, of
which 68 per cent or $3.38 billion are grants and contributions
to band and tribal councils, a process which the Auditor
General himself criticized in 1991 as faulty since the
department could not ascertain whether the funds were used
for the purposes intended or managed with due regard to the
economy, to efficiency and to effectiveness.
"Despite this agreement, despite Bill C-16, it is clear that the
Sahtu Dene and the Metis will continue to have access to
every DIAND program that is currently offered. This is in
addition to the settlement terms of this agreement." [34]

Speaker after speaker from the Reform Party hammered their
points home but the government showed no concern. At 3:45 p.m. on
May 2, the Bill was read a second time and referred to the Commons'
Standing Committee on Aboriginal Affairs and Northern Development.

Appearing before the Standing Committee

This Committee, comprised of a government majority but with all-
party representation, dealt with the matter in about five hours over the
course of three days. I was asked to appear before it in Ottawa to give
my views. An hour and a half was allotted to me on the morning of May
31, 1994. I first pointed out that in my view the federal government

based its whole land claim policy on the false premise that the *Calder* case decided that aboriginal title exists in Canada. (My arguments were similar to those which are set out in Chapter 1 of this book.)

I then went on to state that there was no basis found either in judicial decisions or in the Constitution for large land claim settlements that convey outright land in fee simple:

> *"In fact, to my knowledge no court in Canada has found that aboriginal title includes fee simple ownership. Yet in claim agreements such as the one before us today, large areas are being conveyed outright—in this particular case, 41,000 square kilometres, three-quarters the size of Nova Scotia.*
>
> *"In the four settlement agreements thus far north of 60, the total fee simple lands amount to 505,000 square kilometres or about half the size of Ontario.*
>
> *"I'm not talking about the other benefits and the other aboriginal rights that are recognized in the agreement, such as the right to hunt, fish and trap over much larger settlement areas. I don't take great exception to that. What I'm talking about are the fee simple transfers, and I'm merely making the point that these are not supported in any way by the judicial decisions that have been made as to what constitutes aboriginal title.*
>
> *"I suggest that if aboriginal rights do not include total ownership of land in the fee simple meaning of the word, then this committee should be concerned about approving land claim agreements that remove from the public domain vast areas of public lands."* [35]

I then dealt with more specific concerns related to the Sahtu agreement itself:

- the implication of "constitutionalizing" rights in an agreement which runs into hundreds of pages and thousands of clauses;
- the need to clarify whether the Canadian Charter of Rights and Freedoms would apply to future Sahtu-made laws;
- the necessity for governments to have an extinguishment clause of other undefined aboriginal rights in agreements of

this kind; and,

• the wisdom of setting up still more bureaucracy.

Members of the Committee then put some questions to me. Mr. Bachand (Saint-Jean) for the BQ asked me some thought-provoking questions in a civil way which I endeavoured to answer in kind. John Duncan and Dave Chatters of Reform did likewise.

Mr. Elijah Harper, of Meech Lake fame, and now the Liberal Member of Parliament for Churchill, was first off for the Liberals. I had known Mr. Harper previously when he was a member of the NDP government of Manitoba during the federal-provincial-aboriginal round of Conferences from 1983-1987 in which I was involved on behalf of the Province of British Columbia. I had always found him to be soft-spoken, courteous and a worthy spokesman for his cause. This occasion was no exception. He treated me to a history lesson into pre-colonial times (which I didn't particularly agree with but didn't say so) and then he asked me a question on how I viewed the treaties, to which I responded:

"I view them as solemn obligations on both sides towards whatever rights, obligations, and privileges are set out within them. I can't help, however, note that Treaty 11, which has some relevance to this particular case, has always had within it an extinguishment clause that is not unlike the one now contained in this land claim agreement. So I believe in respecting and adhering to the treaties, but in respecting all their terms, including that one. . . . I think the obligations go along with the benefits, and that's one of them. But to the extent that the Crown has ongoing obligations in existing treaties, the terms ought to be honoured and fulfilled, erring on the side of generosity. But the treaties cut both ways and impose obligations in the other direction as well." [36]

Mr. Jack Anawak, the Parliamentary Secretary, was next. His comments continued in the sarcastic tone and offensive way that he had already set during debate in the House. This time to his sarcasm he added vitriol:

> *"My response is very short. I was looking forward to this*
> *particular meeting with you, Mr. Smith. However, on reflection,*
> *having thought about it while being here, I'll say that we Inuit*
> *are hunters and we believe in making sure an animal doesn't*
> *suffer when we're going to kill it. I see the same thing in your*
> *attitude, basically being a dying attitude, in danger of*
> *extinction—the attitudes you have towards aboriginal people or*
> *the people who were first here and so on.*
> *"So my only comment is that rather than prolonging the death*
> *of the attitudes you have, I think it would be better to have a*
> *quick kill, and thus will not respond to any of your*
> *concerns."* [37]

I did not respond. I have always found that personal attacks and offensive comments such as that are evidence of a weak case. Unfortunately, it is the kind of comment that is often forthcoming when anyone questions the aboriginal agenda and where it is leading. It's called intimidation. I kept on answering questions and finished up on a high-note. None of what I said in testimony, of course, made the slightest difference. The Bill was reported back to the House (without amendment) by the Committee later that day.

Third Reading

The Bill returned to the House for third reading on June 13, 1994. Only Reform members Chuck Strahl (Fraser Valley East), John Duncan and Dave Chatters, and Mr. Bachand for the Bloc, engaged in debate.

Mr. Strahl was particularly scathing in his criticism of the process:

> *"This process is worse than Meech Lake. It is shut tight.*
> *Ordinary Canadians are totally excluded. Not even the media*
> *has [sic] access to them. The Sahtu package is presented*
> *before Parliament today as a fait accompli without the benefit*
> *of public discussion beforehand. The Liberal government will*
> *use its majority to ram it through the House, putting its trust in*
> *the continuing silence of the silent majority. . . .*

"It makes a travesty of red book promises. It makes a mockery of the constitutional process. It treats the people of Canada and members of Parliament like children who cannot eat at the table with the big folks. They have to sit at the card table in Parliament and eat the leftovers thrown to them by the negotiators. This is unacceptable." [38]

Expressing disappointment, Mr. Duncan concluded:

"The terms, provisions and conditions have been well canvassed on this side of the House and unfortunately our concerns with bill C-16 still apply. Our pleas, both in the House and in committee, have fallen on deaf ears." [39]

Mr. Chatters had the last word:

"I want to make sure that I and my party go on record opposing this process and this agreement simply because I think it is a huge mistake to be moving Canada toward a system that South Africa is celebrating leaving behind.
"We are imposing ethnic homelands on these people and trapping them in these agreements. That is a terrible precedent to be setting. We should be moving at some point to the equal treatment of all Canadians no matter where they live or what their ethnic or racial background is.
"In closing, when the record is written the Reform Party opposed the agreement and the Liberals pushed it through in spite of the objections of our party and a number of the people involved." [40]

And so, the Bill quickly received Third reading, with only the Reform members voting in the negative. It was then quickly passed by the Senate, again without even a sober second thought, and is now the law of the land.

Still more to come

And the Sahtu Dene and Metis still want more. In a brief prepared by the STC in late 1994 they state:

> *"The Sahtu Dene and Metis will only realize a portion of their aboriginal rights with the signing of their land claim. A major aspiration of the Sahtu Dene and Metis is to govern their own affairs as a distinct cultural identity within the framework of the federated state of Canada. . . . Simply put, any attempt to define our self-government rights must be based on those rights which were traditionally exercised and our history as a sovereign people."*[41]

More special rights, more government, more bureaucracy, and more costs to the taxpayer. And all for 1,700 souls!

The Western Arctic

The preoccupation for still more government in the north continues. Logic would suggest that if the eastern half of the NWT is to be carved off to form the new territory of Nunavut, what remains of the NWT would continue in place and be administered from the present capital of Yellowknife. Instead, major constitutional discussions are now underway to meet the aspirations of the native leadership who would carve up the remaining territory into tribal governments under the mask of "District Orders of Government." The idea is to be found in the report of the Bourque Commission appointed by the NWT government in 1991.

Bourque's million-dollar-plus report proposed that up to 15 new district governments be created and that these would be the first order of government in the NWT. Each district would have its own Legislative Assembly and bureaucracy (possibly including courts) and be responsible for delivering all government programs. The central territorial government would be the lower or second order of government and be responsible for raising taxes and setting standards for program delivery. To reinforce the inferior nature of the central territorial government, all residual powers would go to the district governments. Bourque would have one government spending money that is virtually all raised by other governments—an impossible basis for accountability! Representation without taxation!

Bourque also recommended that it would be up to the district governments to decide who could participate in these district governments and whom they would govern. Bourque proposes that they could be "public, exclusively aboriginal or a combination of both." In other words, district governments would have the power to deny non-native members their most basic civic rights—the right to vote, and run for office, copying what South Africa did when it established Bantu lands under apartheid.

Former Prime Minister Joe Clark has been hired by the federal government to chair a round of Constitutional Conferences to bring people in from all over the Western Arctic. The first was held January 18-22, 1995, in Yellowknife. About two-thirds of the approximately 150 participants were aboriginal. It considered in a preliminary way the Bourque report and other proposals.

This exercise will continue for the next four years with the federal government paying 90% of the cost.

More land claims in the Arctic

As if more systems of government in the Western Arctic aren't enough, there are four more land claims being negotiated in what is left of the western Arctic. These are with the Dogrib, the Metis, the Deh Cho, and the Treaty 8 people. The last obviously already have a treaty as their designation suggests. So much for the suggestion that treaty-making results in finality. The total population of these four groups stands at approximately 12,250.

Chapter 2 - Footnotes:

1. Statistics Canada, *1991 Census* (Ottawa).

2. The Imperial Order in Council of 1870, by which Rupert's Land (which includes the area covered by the present Yukon and NWT) was admitted into Canada, incorporated by reference the terms of an address from the Senate and House of Commons, dated December 1867. The address contained a commitment by the Canadian government to compensate the Indians for any land required for settlement within Rupert's Land. Succeeding Dominion legislation (*Dominion Lands Act, 1883; Dominion Lands Act, 1908;*) contained a provision of similar import. However, this earlier legislation was succeeded further in 1950 with the *Territorial Land Act.* No provision is contained in the 1950 Act to compensate the Indians for land required for purposes of settlement. There would therefore appear to be no longer a *statutory* requirement to enter into treaties in the NWT. In any event, by no stretch of the imagination can it be argued that the cornucopia of benefits to natives contained in the recently concluded treaties in the NWT amount to "compensation" paid to discharge their limited interest, so as to make room for settlement.

3. Canadian Bar Association, *National*, October, 1994, 20.

4. Ibid., 19.

5. Ibid., 20.

6. Jeffrey Simpson, "Paying for self-government. If Nunavut's the model, it's a big tab," *Globe and Mail*, February 11, 1993, A14.

7. NWT Department of Education, *Graduation Statistics*, 1993.

8. Charles Lynch, "Nunavut's John A. knows real native problem," *Ottawa Citizen*, May 19, 1994.

9. Hansard, *Commons Debates*, June 4, 1993, 20393.

10. Gordon Robertson, *Northern Provinces: a mistaken goal* (Montreal: Institute for Research on Public Policy, 1985), 44-48.

11. Don Scott, *Comparison of incomes of NWT and Manitoba MLAs and Ministers, 1995,* (unpublished), Victoria.

12. Scott Feschuk, "Youth don't feel at home in our land," *The Globe and Mail,* July 12, 1994, A4.

13. Ibid.

14. Hansard, *Commons Debates,* June 4, 1993, 20359.

15. Ibid., 20386.

16. Ibid., 20387.

17. Ibid., 20388.

18. Hansard, *Commons Debates*, April 25, 1994, 3420.

19. Ibid., 3421.

20. Ibid., 3427.

21. Ibid., 3428.

22. Ibid., 3428.
23. Ibid., 3429.
24. Ibid., 3433-34.
25. Ibid., 3434.
26. Ibid., 3434-35.
27. Ibid., 3435.
28. Ibid., 3457-58.
29. Ibid., 3458.
30. Ibid., 3458.
31. Ibid., 3459.
32. Hansard, *Commons Debates,* May 2, 1994, 3750.
33. Ibid., 3751.
34. Ibid., 3756.
35. Ibid., 9.
36. Ibid., 20.
37. Ibid.
38. Hansard, *Commons Debates,* June 13, 1994, 5258.
39. Ibid., 5260.
40. Ibid., 5262.
41. Member Group Research Reports, Constitutional Development Steering Committee, NWT, August, 1994.

Carving Up the Yukon

"Having 20-odd public and aboriginal governments [across the North], each with a considerable range of powers, each with a variety of boards and agencies, each with its own costly bureaucracy and each with only a very small economic base, is simply beyond reason. It represents an eternal feast for lawyers and negotiators, and a nightmare for the Canadian taxpayer and anyone who wants to get anything done." Ed Weick, Ottawa-based socio-economic consultant, 1994.

Before the Sahtu Dene and Metis legislation had cleared the House, the Government introduced an even greater package of legislative provisions for natives, this time to approve land claim settlements and self-government agreements in the Yukon. Bill C-33 and Bill C-34, introduced into the Commons on May 31, 1994, represented the culmination of a negotiation process that had been going on between the Council of Yukon Indians and the federal government since 1973. Bill C-33 would give Parliamentary approval to four land claim agreements in the Yukon. Bill C-34 would give similar approval to four corresponding self-government agreements with the same native groups and over the same territory.

By way of background, under the terms of an umbrella agreement signed in May, 1993, the federal and territorial governments and the Council for Yukon Indians agreed to negotiate individual land claim agreements and individual self-government agreements with each of the fourteen "First Nations" in the Yukon. It was agreed that outright ownership would be conveyed to 16,000 sq. miles (41,439 sq.km.) of land in the aggregate to the fourteen "First Nations." Ten thousand sq. miles of this would include the sub-surface rights. The remainder (6,000 sq. miles) would include some but not all sub-surface rights.

Other benefits would include $242.6 million in cash (1989 $), revenues from surface leases, royalties from the development of non-renewable resources and a preferential share in wildlife harvesting; with exclusive harvesting over most of their settlement lands; and 70% of the traplines over much larger adjoining areas. All of this for the 8,000 native population out of a total Yukon population of about 30,000.

As with other land claim agreements, these benefits are to be in addition to those which flow from existing or future constitutional rights for aboriginal people; to all the benefits from government programs for native people; to all the rights and benefits they may be entitled to under the *Indian Act*; and to all the rights, benefits and protections available to all other Canadian citizens.

Although the umbrella agreement sets out the aggregate of benefits to be extended to natives in the Yukon, the process envisages the negotiation of separate land claim agreements with each of the fourteen Yukon "First Nations." Four have been concluded to date with ten more at various stages of negotiation. At the end of the process the whole of the Yukon territory will be blanketed by these agreements. Figure 6 shows roughly the location of the fourteen land claim areas.

Parliament abused again

Although the agreements accompanying Bill C-33 and Bill C-34 were many years in the making, essentially involving closed door negotiations of federal and native bureaucrats, the elected members of Parliament were not considered worthy of being given adequate time to consider the mountainous amount of paper involved. Unbelievably, the two Bills and the agreements accompanying them were introduced into the Commons on May 31, 1994, and called by the government for second reading on the following day! This prompted outrage not only from members of the Reform party this time, but also from members of the Bloc Quebecois who had shown themselves to be in support of the land claim process previously. Mr. Claude Bachand (Saint Jean), the Bloc critic on native affairs, was first to enter the debate after the Minister, Mr. Irwin, made his opening remarks. Mr. Bachand said:

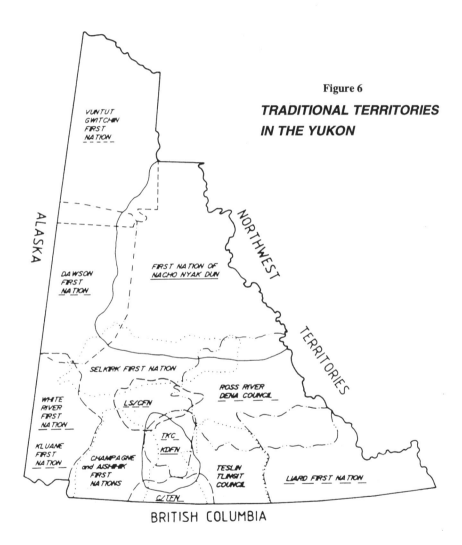

Figure 6

**TRADITIONAL TERRITORIES
IN THE YUKON**

Source:
Canada, Indian and Northern Affairs,
"Yukon First Nations Final Agreement"
Information Bulletin, May, 1993

"First reading took place yesterday morning at 10 o'clock, so you can imagine my surprise, when in the afternoon, a pile of documents, one foot high, appeared on my desk for me to read before today's debate on these two Bills. We are dissatisfied because we worked well into the night and are exhausted." [1]

Mr. Elwin Hermanson (Kindersley-Lloydminster), the House leader for the Reform Party, expressed similar concerns, noting that his colleagues had received a departmental briefing only that morning. He took the matter one step further by moving to adjourn the House at the conclusion of his remarks.[2] It was a procedural matter which, of course, would be voted down by the overwhelming Liberal majority, but the government nevertheless got the message and adjourned the debate one week until June 9.

When debate resumed on June 9th, it ran true to form. The government, supported by the Bloc Quebecois, described both the four land claim agreements and the four self-government agreements in glowing terms and banal phrases without much of an attempt to discuss specifics. Reform Party members, on the other hand, questioned whether pursuing this course of action would likely improve the native condition and expressed serious concerns about specific elements in the package.

Bill C-34 - *Yukon First Nations Self-Government Act*

Before tracing the course of the parliamentary debate, it is essential to describe briefly the contents of these agreements and the two Bills accompanying them. My emphasis will be primarily on Bill C-34 and the four self-government agreements (as distinct from the four land claim agreements accompanying Bill C-33), for these represented a major departure from agreements negotiated previously.

A year previously, on May 29, 1993, the federal government and the Yukon Territorial government signed these agreements with the following: Champagne and Aishihik First Nation, First Nation of Nacho Nyak Dun, Teslin Tlingit Council and the Vuntun Gwitchin First Nation.

The Champagne and Aishihik First Nations are located, primarily, on the east side of the village of Haines Junction. Smaller communities are also established along the Alaska Highway at Champagne and Canyon and along the Haines road at Klukshu. Haines Junction is the first major community northwest of Whitehorse on the Alaska Highway.

There are 1,035 Yukon Indian People enrolled under the Champagne and Aishihik First Nations Final Agreement.

Nacho Nyak Dun First Nation inhabits land in and around the village of Mayo. Mayo is located 407 km north of Whitehorse and the village is situated on the northern bank of the Stewart River. There are 398 Yukon Indian People enrolled under the First Nation of Nacho Nyak Dun Final Agreement.

Teslin Tlingit Council citizens live mainly in the southwest section of the village of Teslin, although with the recent increase of native populations it has expanded into the Fox Point area. There are 573 Yukon Indian People enrolled under the Teslin Tlingit First Nation Final Agreement.

The Vuntut Gwitchin First Nation is located in the community of Old Crow, which is located about 800 km north of Whitehorse, inside the Arctic Circle. It is accessible only by air, or by boat in summer from Fort Yukon, Alaska. The Old Crow area may be one of the earliest settlements in North America. There are 625 Yukon Indian People enrolled under the Vuntut Gwitchin First Nation Final Agreement.

New nations and new citizens

Bill C-34 describes the numerous bands that have entered into these four self-government agreements and the other ten bands who are yet to do so as "First Nations." Similarly, the members of these "First Nations" are described in the Bill as "citizens of First Nations." The Bill provides that these "citizens" shall be determined in accordance with the constitution of the First Nation."

Although Indian tribes historically have sometimes been referred to as "nations," it has long been established by Canadian jurisprudence that Indian treaties were not considered to be treaties between nations in the international meaning of the word.[3] The term "First Nations" has been in common usage generally for about fifteen years within the native community and embraced more recently by others. However, Bill C-34 may be the first time the term has formally appeared in federal legislation. Without putting too fine a point on it, it gives rise to a number of questions such as: Are native people in the Yukon now to have two kinds of citizenship extended to them under Canadian law? If so, are not conflicting allegiances likely to arise? What are the implications, if any, in international law of laws passed by the Parliament of Canada which formally acknowledge the existence within Canada's boundaries of other "nations"? What are the implications of this on the question of self-determination, an issue that is raised regularly in Quebec?

The fact is that there is little support in law for the view that tribal societies that may have existed before the arrival of the white man constituted nationhood.[4] In any event, as numerous judicial decisions have found, native "sovereignty" did not survive the full assertion of sovereignty by colonial authorities. But to acquiesce in the terminology is to concede the debate. That is why I avoid as much as possible using the term "First Nations." (This issue is discussed at greater length in Chapters 6 and 7.)

Native law-making powers

Bill C-34, coupled with the self-government agreements, gives the authority to these "First Nations" to make laws on a broad range of no less than 44 subject matters. On their settlement lands, they will be entitled to make laws on activities such as:

1) licensing and regulation of persons and entities carrying on any business, trade, profession, or other occupation;
2) control or prohibition of public games, sports, races, athletic contests and other amusements (i.e. gambling);
3) construction, repair and demolition of buildings;
4) planning, zoning and land development;
5) control or prohibition of the operation and use of vehicles (this would seem to include licensing of vehicles);
6) control or prohibition of the manufacture, supply, sale, exchange, transportation and consumption of intoxicants (i.e. control of liquor);
7) laws in relation to the administration of justice (this does not come into force until the year 2000);
8) laws relating to public order, peace or safety;
9) laws relating to pollution and protection of the environment;
10) control or prohibition of the use of firearms;
11) any matter coming within the good government of citizens of the "First Nation."

Obviously these law-making powers are far reaching in scope and would include gambling, licensing of motor vehicles, and eventually laws in relation to the administration of justice, which means courts, policing, enforcement, penalties, etc. I have outlined only a few of the powers given. In addition, there are a number of subject matters on which the "First Nations" are empowered to legislate over their members in the Yukon whether or not those members live on settlement lands. For example, they may pass laws applying to all members on the following subjects:

1) Social and welfare services
2) Health care
3) Training programs
4) Adoption
5) Guardianship, custody, care and placement of children
6) Education programs
7) Inheritance, wills, intestacy and administration of estates
8) Solemnization of marriage

The implications of having "First Nation" laws apply to their members who live in parts of the Yukon Territory other than in their settlement lands appears not to have been addressed. Consider what this means. If one of their members lives in downtown Whitehorse or another urban setting, next door to a non-aboriginal Canadian—outside of the settlement land of his "First Nation"—then his rights and the laws that affect him are different from his next door neighbour, because he is an Indian and his next door neighbour is non-native. It is one thing to give law-making powers over a settlement area but this goes far beyond that. It makes laws that are applicable to a native person in an urban setting different from those that are applicable to his non-native neighbour next door. Besides being racist, it is fraught with all sorts of complications.

Coupled with this is the fact that each of the fourteen "First Nations," which will blanket the Yukon when all the self-government agreements are concluded, will have their own legislative powers each with its own capacity to pass different laws from its neighbour. The mish-mash of jurisdictional disputes and inter-governmental wrangling, to say nothing of the bewildered citizen who will be caught up in it all, is too horrible to contemplate.

As for the application of federal and territorial laws, Bill C-34 makes it plain that where a Yukon law and a "First Nation" law conflict, the latter prevails. Only federal laws of general application will remain paramount and will continue to apply to the "First Nation," its citizens and settlement land. Even here, Canada has agreed to enter into negotiations to identify areas where "First Nation" laws may prevail over federal laws.

Native legislatures

What is the nature of the legislative body that will pass these laws? This is left entirely to the constitution of each "First Nation." The Bill says that the constitution of a "First Nation" will provide, among other things, for "the governing bodies of the First Nation and their composition, membership, powers, duties and procedures."

In other words, it is entirely up to the band as to what kind of a governing body it puts in place to pass these laws. Are these governing bodies to be popularly elected every three or four years along democratic lines? Are they to be elected at all or will they be appointed? There is no provision to cover this. What accountability will they have to their members? Will their legislative actions be subject to the Charter of Rights and Freedoms? Admittedly there is a provision that requires the constitution of the "First Nation" to provide for "the recognition and protection of the rights and freedoms" of their members, but that is not to say that whatever provision along those lines is made will be similar to the rights and freedoms provided to other Canadians under the Charter of Rights and Freedoms.

Most fair-minded Canadians would want laws made by aboriginal self-governments to be subject to the Canadian Charter of Rights and Freedoms. The Minister of DIAND has promised that this will be the case, and yet neither Bill C-34, nor the self-government agreements that have been negotiated thus far in the Yukon, impose any requirement in this regard.

In fact, the federal government has been sending mixed signals on the point. Speaking to aboriginal members of the Liberal party, Justice Minister Allan Rock said it was an open question whether the Charter of Rights would apply to legislation passed by aboriginal self-governments. He also is reported to have mused whether Canada's criminal law should continue to apply to natives and suggested it would depend on self-government negotiations.[5]

In my view the Charter probably does not apply to laws made by aboriginal self-governments unless specifically provided for in any self-government agreement or by a constitutional amendment. The question of the application of the Charter of Rights to laws made by native self-governments was sufficiently in doubt at the time of the negotiations of the Charlottetown Accord that a special provision was included in the Accord to provide that the Charter applied to laws passed by aboriginal self-governments. That provision, of course, went the way of the rest of the Charlottetown Accord; the result being that it is highly doubtful that, as things now stand, laws passed by aboriginal self-governments are subject to the Charter.

As if all of the above is not sufficient cause to be concerned about the nature and composition of native legislative bodies being given these sweeping law-making powers, section 9(2) of the Bill must surely eclipse it all. That subsection allows a "First Nation," by its constitution, to delegate its law-making powers "to any other body *or person*" (my emphasis). This open-ended provision would allow the delegation of lawmaking power to the chief or band president acting alone, or any other person that the "First Nation" constitution may designate. So much for representative democracy!

If the federal government had any back-bone at all it would have taken a firm stand on these issues by having safeguards contained in Bill C-34 to ensure democratic principles are followed. But no, these things are left to the vagaries of band government.

Jurisdictional chaos

At present, law-making in the Yukon at the senior level is entrusted to two legislative bodies in Canada: the Parliament of Canada and delegated powers given to the Yukon legislature. When this Bill is passed, and all fourteen self-government agreements are in place, the number of governments having the right to pass laws in the Yukon or parts of Yukon (not including municipal governments) will go from two to sixteen. That is a daunting prospect. More bureaucracy, more taxes, more laws, rules and regulations, uncertainty as to which laws apply to whom, more boards, commissions and councils, and all of this for less than 8,000 native people or about 25% of the population of the Yukon.

Consider the implications of all this for opening up the North. Ed Weick, an Ottawa-based socio-economic consultant, said this:

"The potential for total gridlock is large. Threading a highway or a pipeline (or the protection of a valued ecosystem) through several jurisdictions, each with its own regulatory regime, could pose enormous problems. Disincentives to invest could be substantial: opportunities might be lost if entrepreneurs

*decided that the administrative and regulatory environment
was simply too complex and discouraging."*[6]

And again, speaking of the whole of the North, he said:

*"The notion of three territorial governments with a wide array
of provincial-type powers for a population of 86,000 already
stretches credulity. Having 20-odd public and aboriginal
governments, each with a considerable range of powers, each
with a variety of boards and agencies, each with its own costly
bureaucracy and each with only a very small economic base,
is simply beyond reason. It represents an eternal feast for
lawyers and negotiators, and a nightmare for the Canadian
taxpayer and anyone who wants to get anything done."*[7]

I suspect that to most Canadians the whole idea is
madness—sheer madness. But only a handful of Canadians has any
idea what is going on, and many of the few who do know are part of the
problem.

Who pays for all of this? The self-government agreements provide
that the federal government will enter into financial transfer agreements
to provide the "First Nation" with sufficient financial resources toward
the cost of their "government institutions" and the public services they
will provide. That is so many words for saying that the federal
government, or more correctly the Canadian taxpayer, will foot the bill.
Admittedly, the ability and capacity of each "First Nation" to generate
revenue from its own sources is to be taken into account, but those
prospects appear dim. The fact remains that this will be a very
expensive experiment, financially back-stopped by federal funding.

Appearing again before the Standing Committee

So concerned was I with the import of this Bill that I appeared again
before the Standing Committee on Aboriginal Affairs and Northern
Development, on June 16, 1994, this time by teleconference hookup
from Vancouver to the Committee room in Ottawa. In this new
technology you get to see and interact with the members of the
Committee and they in turn can do the same. I was given about forty
minutes to make a presentation, followed by an extended period of
questions. Preceding me as witnesses on that occasion were a number

of representatives of the Kaska Dena First Nation, whose traditional homelands straddle the B.C.-Yukon border. They had serious concerns about Bill C-33 and C-34 and submitted that their passage "without amendments, will cause irreversible harm to all Kaska people." [8]

Space will only permit a few excerpts from my presentation at that time. I made a couple of general comments before getting into the specifics. I said rather boldly in the course of my opening remarks:

> *"If members do not leave their analytical skills at the door, but would leave perhaps their political affiliations at the door and come to this bill looking at the potential problems it might cause, I feel sure the conclusion of the committee would be that these two bills need more attention and more consideration, and that they ought to be held over for the summer in order to consider, if nothing else, the various concerns that were raised today by the Kaska Dena people in their comprehensive presentation."* [9]

Much had been said about the fact that these agreements had taken many years to fashion. I couldn't let the reference pass:

> *"It has been said that these agreements were 21 years in the making. That's not necessarily a good thing. In fact, I think it is a bad thing. You have successive generations of bureaucrats and others, such as consultants, lawyers, and so on, who have been involved in this process for 21 years and you've got layer upon layer of provisions. I defy anybody to come to this package and work their way through it and fully understand what it means.*
> *"I think it would have been better if the package had only taken 21 days. After all, the U.S. Constitution—that of the most powerful country in the world—fills eight pages."* [10]

On the major abuse of the democratic process contained in Bill C-34 which permits the ratification of the ten future self-government agreements in the Yukon by Cabinet rather than Parliament, I said:

> *"Subclause 5(2) of Bill C-34 permits the bringing into effect of future self-government agreements by cabinet order rather*

than by approval of Parliament. This is a companion provision to the one I already spoke of in Bill C-33. In my view, this is a most undesirable departure from past practice. Agreements of this kind are negotiated essentially behind closed doors and between bureaucrats.

"Inasmuch as these agreements affect the rights of all Canadians they should not be allowed merely to be ratified by cabinet, again, behind closed doors. Scrutiny by Parliament has a salutary effect. That's the history of parliamentary democracy in this country and other countries. We should not jettison the principles of parliamentary scrutiny and democracy by having agreements yet unmade—yet unmade!—approved by this legislation. That to me is an abuse of the parliamentary process. It's far more than just an ordinary delegation of authority that is given in some statutes. This is delegating to the executive the power to make agreements almost unbridled in scope." [11]

On the matter of the right of "First Nations" under Bill C-34 to establish whatever kind of law-making body they saw fit, I had this to say:

"I ask myself the question: what body within the self-governing entity is going to make these laws? Is it going to be a legislative body, fairly constituted, under democratic principles and accountable to its people every three or four years by way of an election? What are the constraints on the legislative body similar to the constraints on the Parliament of Canada as far as the Charter of Rights is concerned? Is this legislative body going to be subject to the Charter of Rights and Freedoms in Canada? I'll get to that in a minute. More particularly, what kind of a legislative body is it going to be?

"You have the answer in clause 8 of Bill C-34. It's going to be whatever kind of body the constitution of the First Nation provides . . . We don't know what the constitutions of these first nations are going to be because they're not written yet; these first nations are not yet in being." [12]

On the right of the "First Nation" to delegate its law-making power to one person provided for in Section 9(2) of the Bill, I said:

"Now, we not only do not know what shape and form these legislative bodies of the first nations will take, but here is a power for those legislative bodies of the first nations to delegate their lawmaking power to one person—to one person. Now, that's a frightening prospect. When you take a look at the powers that these governments are going to have as set out in schedule II to the bill, one person may be . . . making laws for the First Nation. This isn't a delegation of power to administer law. This isn't something that has to do with carrying laws into effect. The words are "including a power to enact laws." You're going to give that to one person? Come on. Don't let that go by, Mr. Chairman." [13]

I concluded by saying:

"The whole history of Canada—indeed, the bywords of the Canadian Constitution and the way of doing things—are peace, order and good government. I want to suggest to the committee if these bills go forward they will not enhance the benefit and the interests of peace, order and good government in Canada; they will result in friction, confusion and uncertain government.
"For goodness' sake, if I may say so with all the passion I have—and I'm here as an independent person: I don't have to testify before the committee, but I've been involved in matters constitutional and legal for all of my career and I want to see what's best be done for the native people and all Canadians—let's not push this thing through unduly. Let's have more consideration so at the end of it everybody can be happy and say yes, this has been an honourable settlement that advances the peace, order and good government of Canada and all of its citizens." [14]

Dialogue with the deaf

In recounting my appearance before the Standing Committee on Bills C-33 and C-34, I've leap-frogged in time over much of the Second

Reading debates in the House of Commons of Bills C-33 and C-34. On June 9, 1994, the House resumed its debate on Second reading of Bill C-34. It was apparent from the outset that Reform party members were going to pull all stops in an effort to have passage delayed until after the summer recess so that greater public input could be forthcoming and the implications of the package could be more fully assessed. Mr. Bill Gilmour, Reform MP for Comox Alberni, summed up his party's mood:

> *"I simply cannot understand why the government is attempting to ram the legislation through the House in the same manner as the Conservatives did in 1993 with similar legislation regarding the Nunavut deal, Bill C-132. . . .*
> *"Where is the new style of government the Liberals promised in the red book? For example, section 5 (2) allows the other land claim agreements to be ratified by cabinet rather than by Parliament. Again it means it will be behind closed doors, not in the House as we are doing today. It means Parliament will no longer be involved. Again where will it be? It will be behind closed doors. So much for the open government promised by the Liberals."* [15]

For his part, Minister Irwin, who took part in the debate at this stage, inferred that consultation had been sufficient because the legislation had the support of the Government of the Yukon, the Yukon Chamber of Commerce and the mining association plus "all of the Liberals in this House, by the Bloc, by the Conservative Party of two, and by the NDP." Shades of the Charlottetown Accord!

The debate on Bill C-34 and Bill C-33 raged on most of June 9 and was adjourned at 5:50 p.m. until another day. That day came on June 14 when the House voted 185 to 44 in favour of the Second reading of Bill C-34. The Second reading of a Bill does not by any means present the last opportunity to debate it. The Report stage and the Third Reading stage are two further opportunities which permit debate.

Clearly by now the government had had enough of the debate. With the summer recess fast approaching the government secured the support of the Bloc Quebecois to limit further debate at the Report stage to one hour and a similar limitation at Third Reading. The motion was immediately put to a vote and was passed. Only Reform members opposed.

Burning the midnight oil

The Bill came back before the Standing Committee at 3:30 p.m. on Thursday June 16 in what proved to be a marathon session. The Reformers were determined to keep the Bill before the Committee long enough to prevent its passage by Parliament before the summer recess. After the presentations by teleconferencing from Vancouver by the Kaska Dena First Nation and by me, previously described, DIAND officials and other governmental officials gave evidence.

Following that, the Committee commenced clause by clause consideration of the Bill.

Mr. Dick Harris, Reform MP (Prince George-Bulkley Valley), moved that the Committee adjourn its deliberations over the summer months and reconvene in the fall to determine the progress that had been made to deal with the concerns that had been expressed by the Kaska Dena. The motion was defeated 6:2.

The Reformers proposed three amendments to Bill C-34. The first was to provide that the laws passed by "First Nation" governments would be subject to the Canadian Charter of Rights and Freedoms. The second was to remove the potential for "First Nations" to delegate their law-making powers to one person. The third was to require that the ten further land claim agreements and self-government agreements for the Yukon come back to Parliament rather than be approved by Cabinet order. The Committee continued its deliberations, without other than a very short break, until 6:30 a.m. the next morning. Motion after motion were put by the Reformers to make amendments of one kind or another or to challenge the rulings of the chair, but in all cases they were defeated. Almost always by a 6:2 majority.

During that long night of sometimes acrimonious debate, no less than 79 motions were put to the committee. In all of them the Liberals, BQ, and NDP lined up on one side of the issue and the Reform MPs on the other.

Had the Reformers been able to keep the debate going until 12 noon the next day, there was a good prospect that the Bills could not have proceeded through the House before the scheduled summer recess. As it was, after 15 hours of continuous debate, the exhausted Reformers ran out of steam at 6:30 a.m. and the Committee, by a vote of 6:2, agreed to report the Bill to the House without amendment.

Quick dispatch in the House

It was a bitter blow for the Reformers. Mr. John Duncan (North Island-Powell River), the lead critic for Reform on native issues, said that the handling of this Bill "speaks volumes about the Liberal government commitment to governing with integrity."

He stated further: "I quote from their famous red ink book that 'people are irritated with governments that do not consult them or disregard their views or that try to conduct key parts of the public business behind closed doors. Open government will be the watchword of the Liberal program.'" [16]

The reference to "behind closed doors" was precisely what was being set in place, for Bill-34 would allow the other ten Yukon agreements yet to be concluded to be approved by Cabinet Order and not come to Parliament at all.

Debate on Third Reading took place the following day, June 22. In the limited time allotted, Reform members mustered all their arguments and efforts to have the legislation held over until the fall. Especially since the government had acknowledged that this legislation could not come into force until the passage of certain Yukon surface and subsurface legislation which had not yet even been introduced in Parliament. But all to no avail. The legislation was read a third time and passed on Wednesday, June 22, 1994.

Sober second thoughts in the Senate

Hastily the Bills were hustled on to the Senate for quick passage. Interestingly enough, it seems that many of the Senators had concerns similar to those that had been raised in the Commons by members of the Reform party. In any event, on the day Bill C-34 was introduced into the Senate, Senator Royce Frith, an influential Liberal member, asked some probing questions. It was then referred to the Senate Standing Committee on Aboriginal Peoples.

The Committee raised concerns about the new kind of citizenship that Bill C-34 would provide and that the dual citizenship issue would be confusing to Canadians. Senator Andreychuk stated: "Many members of our Committee felt that it was an inopportune time to create a new category of citizen and a new definition which may not be supported by international law, and certainly would not be understood elsewhere." [17]

Apparently the Committee asked government officials how to distinguish this type of citizenship from the traditional type of Canadian citizenship. The answer given was—through education. Senator Andreychuk found this answer unsatisfactory.

The senator said that the Yukon Tribal Council had the impression that these Bills would be passed the previous week and that the Senate process "would be swift, if not superficial." The Senate Committee took umbrage at such a suggestion and was unanimous in noting that this is not the way to handle significant pieces of legislation. Senator Andreychuk said: "Our deliberations are necessary, and the process must be changed." [18]

The Senate Committee was particularly concerned about Bill C-34 going ahead in the face of the opposition of the Kaska Dena. Accordingly, it asked that negotiations be accelerated between the government and Kaska Dena representatives and requested the Minister or departmental officials to update the Committee in the fall on how these negotiations were proceeding. The Committee made it plain that, in its view, these Bills should not have been passed by the Commons until the Kaska Dena concerns had been dealt with, but since they had been passed, they recommended that they should not be proclaimed until efforts to successfully negotiate with the Kaska Dena over the next few months had been concluded.

The Committee presented its report to the full Senate on July 6 and its chairman, Senator Andreychuk, advised the Senate that the Committee was unanimous "in some of our concerns, as well as our support for Bill C-33 and Bill C-34."

Apparently the Committee had been convinced by departmental officials that the deal was unique to the Yukon and would not likely set a precedent for other land claim and self-government agreement negotiations. How this conclusion was reached was difficult to discern but, in any event, the Committee was satisfied on that issue and that sufficient consultation had taken place between all levels of government and "all groups." No mention was made of the citizens of Canada or the elected members of Parliament.

Senator Andreychuk expressed further concerns:

"Bill C-33 and Bill C-34 seem to have moved rather quickly, particularly Bill C-34. The committee believes that Bill C-33 is similar to other land claims agreements and there was nothing

*unusual or different about it. However, the committee feels that
Bill C-34 is the first time that self-government has entered into
an agreement with aboriginal peoples in such a forceful
manner. There are concerns as to whether this is a complete
negotiation or whether this will lead to further negotiations.* "[19]

In Third Reading debate, Senator Royce Frith was more
outspoken. In alluding to righting a history of wrongs concerning the
aboriginal people, he said that in his view those wrongs were the result
of a wrong principle, namely treating aboriginal peoples differently and
badly because of their race; that is, basing status and rights on
ethnicity or race. He then went on to say that this Bill perpetuates the
same wrong principle that led to the very wrongs it seeks to right:

*"We are awarding rights not enjoyed by all Canadians to a
certain group of Canadians, based on the qualification of race.
Race will determine who will enjoy these privileges, however
deserved they are.*
*"That is not a principle with which I can agree. I feel that status
and rights based on race are constitutionally and
jurisprudentially pernicious, though I support the end reached
here, namely the attempt to right a long history of wrongs and
to establish what we must accept is an exciting new concept;
that is, self-government for the aboriginal peoples, a concept
and a construction that will eventually put us as Canadians in
the forefront of nations who treat their aboriginal peoples with
justice. Therefore, although I support the end result here, I
believe that the means, status and rights based on race will be
seen, in the long run, to have spawned unanticipated,
undesirable results in other contexts, and for other races.* "[20]

With all due respect, Senator Frith was proposing to square the
circle. Native self-government by its very nature is based on race. The
two are inseparable. At the end of the day the Senate passed both
Bills.

Parenthetically, we castigate the Senate from time to time because
Senators are appointed, and therefore not accountable to the Canadian
people through elections, and because many of them receive their
appointments for past political favours. Ironically, however, in very short

order the Senate in this case caught on to the import and the serious implications of what this legislation provided. Although in the end it passed the Bills, it did so with obvious reluctance. What a contrast to the position of the government and other opposition parties, other than Reform, in the House of Commons who, in spite of lengthy rational debate, would not concede that there was one iota of concern worthy of amendment in these two Bills and the voluminous agreements that accompanied them.

Lessons to be learned

The passage of Bill C-34 provides the observer with some lessons for the future on matters of this kind. These are:

- No matter how meritorious the concerns and questions, if it is an issue involving native people, those concerns will be considered by the native leadership, the Indian industry, and "politically correct" opinion to be anti-native. In such an intellectual climate, it seems impossible to discuss this subject on its merits.
- Any and all concessions to the native people are blindly considered to be desirable, regardless of their cost, or their probable future consequences to native or non-native Canadians.
- Meaningful public debate of land claim agreements cannot take place after these deals are signed and ratified by the interested parties. At that stage, it is too late. Any serious questioning of what has been done is wheel spinning.
- Because the native and government leadership and particular interest groups approve the deal that should not be considered to be sufficient. The implications of these deals must be clearly and fairly spelled out to the Canadian people as a whole. That is what Parliament is supposed to do, but sadly the process in Parliament is ineffective. But, instead of the Parliamentary process being improved upon, it is going to be side-stepped so that future land agreements in the Yukon will not even come to Parliament.
- To its shame, the national media will rarely cover any aspect of this issue for fear of being considered to be anti-native. During protracted debates on the Sahtu Dene and Metis and Yukon agreements, which occupied much of Parliament's timetable in May and June, 1994, virtually no media coverage of any kind was provided by television, radio, newspaper or national magazines.

Chapter 3 - Footnotes:

1. Hansard, *Commons Debates,* June 1, 1994, 4718.
2. Ibid., 4722.
3. *Regina vs. White and Bob,* 52 WWR.193 (B.C.C.A.), affirmed by S.C.C. (1966) 52 DLR (2d), 481.
4. See Dickerson and Flanagan, An Introduction to Government and Politics: A Conceptual Approach, 3rd edition (Nelson Canada, Scarborough, Ontario, 1990), 39-40.
5. "Charter will apply to natives, Rock says," *Vancouver Sun,* May 13, 1994, A9.
6. Ed Weick, "Why pour more cash into the Arctic Ocean?," *Financial Post,* March 12, 1994.
7. Ibid.
8. *Proceedings of the Standing Committee on Aboriginal Affairs and Northern Development,* Issue No.10, June 16, 1994, 29.
9. Ibid., 53.
10. Ibid., 53-54.
11. Ibid., 56.
12. Ibid., 57.
13. Ibid., 58.
14. Ibid., 60.
15. Hansard, *Commons Debates,* June 9, 1994, 5085.
16. Hansard, *Commons Debates,* June 21, 1994, 5700.
17. *Senate Debates,* July 6, 1994, 786.
18. Ibid., 787.
19. Ibid., 787.
20. Ibid., 785.

Land Claims in
British Columbia

"We are the true owners of British Columbia. The Indians
across the province own everything—the rivers, the trees,
the bugs, the animals. You name it. Subsurface rights, the
air, the rain, the whole shot. That's what we mean when we
say we have aboriginal title to the land." James Gosnell,
Chairman, Nisga'a Tribal Council, 1984.[1]

Such are the words of the late distinguished Chief of the Nisga'a
who was the leading spokesman for B.C. Indians at the Aboriginal
Constitutional Conferences held between 1983 and 1987. The words
may make good philosophy, ideology, or even religion but they make
very poor law. There is no judicial support in Canada for such an idea
and yet the current provincial government has unreservedly accepted
the concept of "aboriginal title." But by whose definition? Chief
Gosnell's or someone else's? Government spokesmen have never
answered.

Colonial policy toward the Indians

It is beyond the scope of this book to attempt to outline in detail the
complex history of the Indian land question of this Province from
colonial days onward. That history was examined in a painstaking way
by Chief Justice McEachern in the *Delgamuukw* case. Eighty six
pages of his judgment are devoted to it.

For our purposes, a brief review begins with British efforts to
colonize Vancouver Island. In 1849, the Colony of Vancouver Island
was established and a Royal grant of the Island was conveyed to the
Hudson's Bay Company. The grant reserved to the Crown the right to
revoke it after five years if the Company failed to establish a viable
colonial settlement. No mention was made in the grant of Indian title.[2]

James Douglas, the Chief Factor for the Company was, in 1851, also appointed Governor of the Island colony. By instructions from his Company's head office, Douglas was advised "to consider the natives as the rightful possessors of such lands **only as they occupy by cultivation or had houses built on** at the time when the Island came under the undivided sovereignty of Great Britain in 1846. All other land is to be regarded as waste, and applicable for the purposes of civilization. . . "[3] (emphasis added)

No doubt to ensure friendly relations with the natives, who far outnumbered the handful of white settlers, Douglas went beyond his instructions and began to purchase the "native interest" in certain lands around Victoria, Saanich, Fort Rupert and Nanaimo. Over a six year period, Douglas entered into 14 such agreements. The agreements preserved to the Indians only their village sites and farmlands and permitted them to continue hunting and fishing in unoccupied areas. Even though these conveyances were expressly made by the Company, subsequent judicial interpretations have found them to be treaties between the Crown and the tribes involved. They are known as the "Douglas" Treaties. Douglas's requests to London for funds to enter into still more agreements of this kind were rebuffed and he then discontinued the practice. Apart from a portion of the Peace River which is included in Treaty 8 negotiated by the federal government in 1899, these are the only treaties that exist in British Columbia.

Although abandoning treaty-making as such, Douglas by no means forsook dealing with the native interest. As an alternative, he embarked upon a vigorous policy of establishing Indian reserves. This was a most significant development for it established a direction in white-native relations in this Province which is distinct from early government policy in the rest of Canada. Supporters of modern-day treaty-making are quick to commend Douglas for his early treaty-making efforts, but are inclined to ignore his even more significant efforts at establishing reserves.

By 1858, the province's non-native population was swelling in the wake of a gold rush. Demand boomed for quality land in good locations for white settlers. Douglas, by now Governor of both the Island and Mainland colonies, responded by establishing Indian reserves. With input from the Indians, he allotted land for band villages, burial grounds, cultivation, and hunting. Indians were also entitled to the free use of all unoccupied lands until taken up by settlers by pre-emption or homesteading. Until 1866 Indians had equal rights with all others to pre-empt lands for cultivation.

In 1870, Joseph W. Trutch, then Commissioner of Land and Works for the Colony and Surveyor-General, later to become the first Lieutenant-Governor of the Province and one of the colony's principal negotiators of the terms of British Columbia's entry into Confederation in 1871, reviewed and summed up the colonial Indian policy in this way:

> ". . . for the past ten years at least, during which I have resided in this Colony, the Government appears to me to have striven to the extent of its power to protect and befriend the Native race, and its declared policy has been that the Aborigines should, in all material respects, be on the same footing in the eye of the law as people of European descent, and that they should be encouraged to live amongst the white settlers in the country, and so, by their example, be induced to adopt the habits of civilization . . .

> "This policy towards the Indians has been consistently carried out, so far as I am aware, by successive Governors, and under it the Indians have assuredly . . . 'been made amenable to English laws', . . .

> "The Indians have, in fact, been held to be the special wards of the Crown, and in the exercise of this guardianship Government has, in all cases where it has been desirable for the interests of the Indians, set apart such portions of the Crown lands as were deemed proportionate to, and amply sufficient for, the requirements of each tribe; and these Indian Reserves are held by Government, in trust, for the exclusive use and benefit of the Indians resident thereon.

> "**But the title of the Indians in the fee of the public lands, or of any portion thereof, has never been acknowledged by Government, but, on the contrary, is distinctly denied.** In no case has any special agreement been made with any of the tribes of the Mainland for the extinction of their claims of possession; but these claims have been held to have been fully satisfied by securing to each tribe, as the progress of the settlement of the country seemed to require, the use of sufficient tracts of land for their wants for agricultural and pastoral purposes."[4] (emphasis added)

Interestingly enough, counsel for the native cause in the *Delgamuukw* case, which is discussed at greater length in Chapter 6, attempted to discredit Trutch's summary of colonial policy, calling it "a perversion of history." However, relying on several historians, including perhaps British Columbia's greatest historian, Dr. Margaret Ormsby, the Chief Justice in the *Delgamuukw* case sagely observed, "Historians have not generally treated Trutch as unkindly as plaintiffs' counsel."[5]

In any event, by the time the united Colony of B.C. entered Confederation in 1871, 120 Indian reserves had been established throughout the Colony.[6] But this was only the beginning. Today, of 2,323 Indian reserves throughout the whole of Canada, 1,634 of them are located in B.C.[7] The practice of establishing Indian reserves without entering into treaties, sets B.C. apart from the rest of Canada in dealing with the Indian interest.

Critics have made much of the fact that the reserves established in B.C., although many in number, are small in comparison to the much fewer but larger reserves established on the Prairies as part of treaty-making. This is due in part to the differences in the topography of the two regions and also due to varying habits, wants and pursuits of the Indians themselves.

British Columbia has been described as a "sea of mountains." On the coast at least, large blocks of agricultural land are in short supply. Moreover, the coastal Indian economy was mainly derived from the products of the sea. Hence coastal reserves tended to include pocket-size settlements in valley bottoms and fishing sites along the coast or along river banks. In the B.C. interior, reserves were somewhat larger to provide for some measure of future farming and ranching.

By contrast, the Prairies were blessed with semi-open plains of vast proportions. The federal government could afford to be generous in allocating reserves and still have adequate land for settlers.

That said, the per capita difference is not all that great. The total area of reserves in Canada is 2.68 million hectares. In B.C., the total area of reserves 344 thousand hectares or 13% of the total for Canada.[8] B.C. has 17% of Canada's status Indians.

Confederation changes the relationship

When B.C. entered Confederation in 1871, Ottawa assumed legislative responsibility for its "Indians and Lands reserved for Indians" under the terms of the *British North America Act, 1867*.

Article 13 of B.C.'s Terms of Union with Canada placed other obligations on Ottawa. It reads:

"The charge of the Indians and the trusteeship and management of the lands reserved for their use and benefit, shall be assumed by the Dominion Government, and a policy as liberal as that hitherto pursued by the British Columbia Government, shall be continued by the Dominion Government after the Union." (emphasis added)

Article 13 goes on to impose an obligation on the Province to provide tracts of land to the federal government for the establishment of additional Indian reserves "of such extent as it has hitherto been the practice of the British Columbia Government to appropriate for that purpose."

In sum, the expressed constitutional obligation of the Province was to provide lands for more reserves. Nothing more. Any and all other constitutional obligations to the native people rested on Ottawa's shoulders.

No mention was made in the Terms of Union of "Indian title." This was no mere oversight. Just a year earlier—1870—the legislation which constituted Manitoba as a province specifically mentioned unextinguished Indian title and how it would impact on land conveyances. It is inconceivable that the question of Indian title, so fresh in the mind of federal authorities in 1870 in respect of Manitoba, would be overlooked only one year later when B.C.'s entry to Canada was under consideration. The better view is that there was a recognition by federal authorities in 1871 that B.C. was dealing with the Indian matter differently, i.e. by the establishment of reserves.

An Allotment Commission was established in 1876 which for many years travelled throughout the Province setting out reserves. More than 1,000 reserves were established over the period. In many instances the Province did not agree with the allotments. The matter came to a head in 1912 with the McKenna-McBride Agreement. Signed by Dr. J.A.J. McKenna, a Special Commission appointed by Canada, and Sir Richard McBride, Premier of B.C., it provided for the establishment of a 5-man commission to:

- cut-off acreage from existing reserves where there was considered to be more land than was reasonably required,
- add land to existing reserves where more was reasonably required,

- create new reserves where necessary, and
- confirm the boundaries of existing reserves if the acreage was adequate.

The Commission sat continuously from 1913 to 1916 and visited all the tribes in the province. Its report was published in four volumes in 1916.[9] The Commission recommended the cut-off of 47,000 acres of existing reserves but would have added a further 87,000 acres of new reserve land, for a net increase of 40,000 acres. Debate arose with the Indians on some of the specific recommendations of the McKenna-McBride Commission and, as a consequence, the Ditchburn-Clark Committee—a committee of two senior federal and provincial officials—spent a further three years making adjustments to the McKenna-McBride recommendations to everyone's satisfaction. At last the way was paved to settle the issue.

B.C.'s obligations discharged

By the passage of Order in Council PC.1265, dated July 19, 1924, the federal government formally acknowledged that B.C. had satisfied all the obligations of Article 13 of the Terms of Union respecting the furnishing of lands for Indian reserves and described the process as a "full and final settlement of all differences between the governments of the Dominion and the Province." Such an acknowledgement by the federal government is support for the long-held provincial position that B.C. had fully discharged its obligations to its Indians even though it had done so differently from the rest of Canada.

The claim for aboriginal title persists

The Province considered the establishment of reserves to more than satisfy any claims which the Indians might have over their traditional territories in British Columbia. Without question, in the minds of the provincial government of the day, and for many years subsequently, the aboriginal interest had been effectively dealt with.

Native pressure on land claims

Neither the Indians nor, to some degree, later federal governments, however, considered the establishment of reserves to be a substitute for negotiating the question of native title. On at least two occasions shortly after the turn of the century, Indian delegations directed their grievance to King Edward VII. The first, in 1906, saw three Indian chiefs petition the King directly who responded that this was a matter to be dealt with by Canadian authorities.[10]

B.C.'s Indians did not give up easily. Political pressure continued to be directed at Ottawa. In 1910 a British Columbia citizens' group, supportive of the native cause, urged Prime Minister Wilfred Laurier to refer a series of questions to the Supreme Court of Canada designed to seek answers on whether aboriginal title existed in British Columbia and, if so, its scope and extent. Because Premier McBride demurred, Prime Minister Laurier did not proceed.[11]

In 1913 the Nisga'a formally laid claim to the Nass Valley, based on their traditional use and occupancy, and petitioned Ottawa for redress. Two years later, a native political activist group called the Allied Tribes was formed and, in 1920, published, "A Half Century of Injustice Toward the Indians of British Columbia," in which it charged the federal government with treating natives worse than the province of B.C. ever did. Persistent lobbying succeeded in having a Special Joint Committee of Parliament struck to consider their demands. After hearing witnesses on all sides of the issue, the committee concluded unanimously "that the petitioners have not established any claim to the lands of British Columbia based on aboriginal or other title."[12]

Fed up with persistent lobbying by B.C. Indians and satisfied that the Parliamentary Committee had given the final word, in 1927, the federal government amended the *Indian Act* to prohibit the collection of funds for pro-land claims activities. This effectively terminated Indian political activity on land claims until the law was repealed in 1951.

More modern times

When the federal government established its land claims policy in 1973 with Jean Chrétien as Minister, it anticipated that the NDP government of Premier Dave Barrett would be a willing partner. After all, Frank Calder, the chief of the Nisga'a was a Minister Without Portfolio in the Barrett Cabinet. However, it soon became clear that Premier Barrett was not about to acquiesce or enter into land claim negotiations unless Ottawa first acknowledged its exclusive responsibility for settling land claims and assuming their cost. Such an acknowledgement never came. In 1976, Ottawa went ahead and opened talks with the Nisga'a on its own.

The Social Credit government of Bill Bennett, which won the 1975 election, maintained B.C.'s longstanding resistance to being drawn into land claim negotiations. Stated Premier Bennett in 1978:

"The provincial government does not recognize the existence of an unextinguished aboriginal title to lands in the province,

nor does it recognize claims relating to aboriginal title which give rise to other interests in lands based on the traditional use and occupancy of land. The position of the province is that if any aboriginal title or interest may once have existed, that title or interest was extinguished prior to the union of British Columbia with Canada in 1871."

The Socreds take a second look

Such was the Province's position until 1987. In March of that year, the Social Credit government of Premier Bill Vander Zalm created a Native Affairs Secretariat to handle the growing clamour to meet native demands. By July, 1988, this had evolved into a full fledged Ministry of Native Affairs with Jack Weisgerber as minister.

About a year later the Premier's Advisory Council on Native Affairs, comprised of a number of native and non-native British Columbians, was established to provide advice to the Cabinet and the Premier on native policy issues. Ostensibly, the Council's mandate was limited to assessing government economic and social policies to assist the further development of the province's native people.

But it was naive of the Vander Zalm government to think it could make these moves without having to squarely face very quickly the issue of its position on aboriginal title and aboriginal rights. The increased visibility given to native affairs by the establishment of a separate Ministry and an Advisory Council; an enlarging bureaucracy sympathetic to the native cause; and heightened expectations among the native leadership—all combined to put the Premier in the role of the boy with his finger in the dike unable to hold back the largely self-generated rising tide.

On August 8, 1990, at a Cabinet meeting at Harrison Hot Springs, the government announced that it would accept all the recommendations of the Advisory Council presented to the government a month earlier. It agreed "to assist the Government of Canada in its responsibilities to negotiate and settle outstanding land claims in British Columbia."[13]

Note the careful wording. It **does not** say that the province would join in the talks as an equal partner but would be only involved for the purpose of "assisting" the federal government to discharge its obligations in regard to land claims and "to protect the interests of British Columbians in any negotiations."[14] This was the Socreds' middle ground; they would sit at the table without recognizing aboriginal title and maintain that the primary responsibility lay with the federal government.

The province's involvement was to be limited further by significant caveats. "The ultimate financial responsibilities must rest with the federal government" and that "Canada must compensate both Native people and the province"[15] for any settlements arrived at. Most importantly, the new policy specifically rejected "the existence of an undefined aboriginal title which purports to give Indian people ownership of the entire province, 'lock, stock and barrel'."[16]

The reaction to the new policy was mixed. For the most part the media considered it to be an "historic watershed"[17] and, in many ways, it was although the caveats, which were formidable indeed, were inclined to be overlooked or downplayed. The native reaction was the exact opposite.[18] Saul Terry, president of the Union of B.C. Indian Chiefs, and Ernie Crey, vice-president of the United Native Nations, focused on the caveats, saying there was nothing new in the Premier's statement. Don Ryan, speaking for the Gitksan and Wet'suwet'en hereditary chiefs, dismissed it out of hand. It was a classic case of one side seeing the glass half full and the other side seeing it half empty.

Premier Vander Zalm justified the policy shift by asserting that the province had a "strong moral obligation to set the historical record right in our dealings with Indian people"[19] and an obligation to represent the interests of British Columbians at talks affecting so much of B.C.'s land, resources, and economy. He may also have been influenced by a public opinion poll at the time indicating that most British Columbians wanted these matters settled.[20]

The politics of confrontation

What also prodded the Vander Zalm government was a growing wave of road and rail blockades, protests, and court actions in the cause of aboriginal rights. Control of resource development on "traditional territory" was often the spark that lit a powder-keg. On several occasions, Indian bands managed to win interim court injunctions against logging on "traditional lands," pending the resolution of the issue of whether or not title existed, which would be determined at a full trial.[21]

At the same time, some militant bands turned to illegal and confrontational blockades. Gitksan-Wet'suwet'en Indians, confident that their law suit (*Delgamuukw*) would go in their favour, began challenging the authority of the provincial government over their traditional territory by blockading railways, highways and even occupying a sawmill that had closed for lack of fibre. The Gitwangak band demanded that loggers "donate" one truckload of logs each per week since the trees, they claimed, were on their territory. "Indian people have already become a third order of government, and that's the reality . . ."[22] explained Gitksan-Wet'suwet'en spokesman Don Ryan.

Putting the new policy into practice

The Vander Zalm government was not long in putting its new-found land claim policy into practice. On October 3, 1990, the government announced that it would join the land claim negotiations that had already been underway between the federal government and the Nisga'a Tribal Council for some 18 years. The Premier attempted to keep his caveats intact when he stated in his Government's press release of that day:

"Following our recent and historic commitment to facilitate the resolution of land claims in B.C. **by the Government of Canada**, *I am pleased to announce that we will fully join the Nisga'a land claims negotiations which have been under way between the Nisga'a and Government of Canada for many, many years."* [23] (emphasis added)

With another party at the table, the talks focused on the development of a Framework Agreement on the topics to be negotiated and the timetables and procedures to be followed. Such an agreement was signed by the three parties—Nisga'a, Canada and British Columbia on March 29, 1991. It provided that:

- every effort would be made to conclude an agreement in principle within two years;
- lands, renewable and non-renewable resources, environmental issues, cultural artifacts and heritage, economic development, Nisga'a government, compensation, direct and indirect taxation, would be on the bargaining table;
- British Columbia would review the fisheries element of the agreement which had been under negotiation since 1982;
- Canada and British Columbia would attempt to settle "their respective participation in the cost of settlement" before signing an agreement in principle;

- the parties acknowledged the need for the public and interested groups to be informed in a general way on the nature and progress of the negotiations including having public information meetings.
- details of positions and documents exchanged or developed during negotiations were to be confidential, unless otherwise agreed to by the parties.
- Canada would fund the Nisga'a their costs of the land claim negotiations.

The province capitulates

The content of this Framework Agreement represented a total capitulation from the qualified support the province had given to land claim negotiations the previous August. Instead of the province "assisting" the federal government in the settlement of land claims, it had become a full partner. Instead of the province holding to its position that it would not recognize aboriginal title, it was now prepared to negotiate on a wide range of issues that go to the broadest definition of the term. Moreover, instead of the province holding to its position that the federal government must pay the total cost of land claim settlements, including compensating the province for Crown land taken, it now proposed to negotiate the matter with Ottawa.

This capitulation, before substantive negotiations had begun, was even more astonishing in light of an event which took place eight days before the signing of this Framework Agreement. On March 8, 1991, Chief Justice McEachern brought down his judgment in the *Delgamuukw* case which native aspirants had anticipated would settle once and for all in their favour the question of aboriginal title, inherent legislative jurisdiction and land ownership. Instead, the Chief Justice categorically dismissed such claims. In effect, the judgment reaffirmed what had been up to then the longstanding position of the province on land claims.

One would have thought that this historic case would have caused Ottawa and Victoria to pause and ponder whether their land claims policy was well-founded. The very opposite proved to be the case. Governments at both levels did not bat an eye in their zeal to "settle land claims" on the most generous of terms. It was as though these governments had **lost** the law suit rather than won it.

Not only did the province rush to sign the Framework Agreement with the Nisga'a, but the provincial bureaucracy in the full-fledged Ministry of Native Affairs geared up in a major way.[24] A Land Claims

Implementation Group and a Native Claims Registry were established. Up to now all land claims throughout Canada were filed with the native claims registry of DIAND in Ottawa. To have a provincial registry tended to show that the provincial government was taking charge of the land claims process. Bureaucratic committees were formed "to expedite the exchange of information and to develop comprehensive programs and policies relating to general Native issues."[25] The provincial budget for 1991-1992 added nearly $5 million for new programs. With this flurry of activity one would have thought that native affairs was a provincial responsibility instead of a federal one.

On January 31, 1991, Native Affairs Minister Jack Weisgerber unveiled the principles that would guide the province in future land claims negotiations.[26] These included:

- settlements should be fair, consistent, affordable, final and binding;
- settlements should respect the property interests of others;
- settlements should include a framework for natural resource conservation and management;
- settlements should provide that all British Columbians enjoy comparable levels of government services on the basis of comparable levels of taxation.

The Government also established a Third Party Advisory Committee (TAC) consisting of representatives of major organizations whose members have a direct interest in the resolution of native land claims. The major resource sectors, unions, business organizations, municipalities, outdoor recreation, tourism, and environmental groups were to be represented.

The province's capitulation on the issue continued. In the May, 1991, Speech from the Throne, it committed itself to paying its "fair and proper share" of land claim settlements.

The B.C. Claims Task Force

Meanwhile the Federal Government, the Province, and the First Nations' Congress representing B.C.'s Indians, established a 6-month task force to define the scope of land claim negotiations, including the time frames, the need and value of interim measures and public education.

The seven members of the Task Force included three aboriginal leaders—Chief Edward John of the Tl'azt'en Nation and the Carrier-Sekani Tribal Council, Chief Joe Mathias of the Squamish Nation, and Chief Miles Richardson of the Haida Nation—and three representing government—Tony Sheridan, the assistant deputy minister of B.C.'s Native Affairs Ministry, Audrey Stewart, director of B.C. claims for DIAND, and Allan Williams, QC, former provincial Attorney-General. The chairman was brought in from Nova Scotia, Murray Coolican, a businessman and former chairman of a federal task force on Comprehensive Land Claims Policy, which had previously supported native self-government in the broadest sense.

Released in June, 1991, the B.C. Claims Task Force Report rewrites the aboriginal history of B.C. The Report maintained that the *Calder* case was "a major turning point"[27] because the Supreme Court of Canada "ruled" that the Nisga'a had held aboriginal title in pre-colonial times. The Court did no such thing. The only thing that the majority of the judges, and therefore the Court, "ruled" was that the case had been improperly brought.

In its review of relevant litigation, the Task Force totally ignored the most important decision of all—the judgment of Chief Justice McEachern in the *Delgamuukw* case which had come down three and a half months earlier. The *Delgamuukw* case gave a very different description of the state of affairs of aboriginal society in pre-colonial times than that contained in the Task Force Report. Moreover, the *Delgamuukw* judgment kicked the props out from under the legal basis for entertaining land claim settlements on so broad a scale. It was more convenient for the Task Force, therefore, to omit any reference to the *Delgamuukw* judgment than to attempt to explain its way around it. These omissions of significant recent events bring to mind a quote from George Orwell about totalitarianism in *Nineteen Eighty-Four*—"Who controls the past controls the future."[28] The seven member Task Force was definitely "controlling" this past.

"Treaty negotiations in British Columbia provide an opportunity to recognize First Nation governments on their **traditional territories**," said the Task Force. "Traditional territories" are not Indian reserves but lands which natives "claim" are theirs: the lands that make up the 42 claims that have since been put forward covering 111% of the province (including Vancouver and lower Vancouver Island.)[29]

The past practice of having undefined aboriginal rights extinguished in exchange for a treaty settlement was to be discouraged. In my view, such extinguishment clauses are the *quid pro quo* for governments to enter into land claim agreements in the first place: to **settle** matters.

Alluding to the view that "First Nations," in "exercising their sovereign authority"[30] had concluded treaties in the past, the Task Force called for B.C. treaties to cover the widest possible range of rights and benefits. The magnitude of the subjects which the Task Force proposed to be negotiated is set out in Figure 7.

Figure 7 - Subject matters proposed to be included in B.C. treaties

Lands/territory
Environmental issues
Funding
Direct and indirect taxation
First Nations government
Language, culture, archaeology and heritage
Renewable and non-renewable resources (including wildlife, flora and fisheries)
Social development
Traditional activities: hunting, fishing, trapping, gathering
Government programs
Economic development
Compensation
Interim Protection Measures
Eligibility and initial enrolment procedure
Offshore areas and ocean management
Constitutional matters
Certainty and Finality
Beneficiary Organizations

Source: Appendix 5, British Columbia Claims Task Force Report, June 28, 1991.

The Task Force recommended that a B.C. Treaty Commission be established to manage the treaty-making process with commissioners appointed by Canada, the Province and the "First Nations" overseeing a six-stage process for negotiating treaties. It called for a "new relationship" in which "recognition and respect for first nations as self-determining and distinct nations with their own spiritual values, histories, languages, territories, political institutions and ways of life must be the hallmark."[31]

The report called on the parties to consider "a financial component to recognize past use of land and resources and First nations' ongoing interests, and to provide capital for community and economic development."[32] The report also called on the province to open the door to the negotiation of "a new fiscal relationship," and to "recognize first nations governments on their traditional territories." In sum, the Task Force had steered the province in one direction: native self-government, aboriginal title, and ongoing financial support for natives. In short, perpetual separation from the mainstream of Canadian society—all based on race or ethnic origin.

The provincial government of Premier Rita Johnston received the Task Force's report on July 3, 1991. Premier Johnston stated that the recommendations would require detailed study before bringing them to cabinet. However, with unseemly haste, given the gravity of the Task Force's recommendations, the B.C. Cabinet accepted the major recommendation—the establishment of an independent Treaty Commission only eight days later.

The "Age of Enlightenment"

If B.C.'s Indians had any doubts that the provincial government was committed to settling land claims, those doubts must have ended with the election of the NDP in October 1991. As Aboriginal Affairs Minister Andrew Petter declared, "One hundred years of policies aimed at denying aboriginal peoples their historic rights are at an end."[33] The Harcourt government took the final step in abandoning the province's historical position by unconditionally supporting aboriginal title and self-government, without defining them.

Chief Joe Mathias of the Squamish Band had no illusions about what this meant: "What we're talking about is nation-to-nation, government-to-government negotiations. . . . We're not coming there picking up crumbs on our knees. We're coming there as equals." [34]

The new NDP government was quick to accept all the recommendations of the Claims Task Force Report and on September 21, 1992, the Squamish Indian reserve in North Vancouver was the site of a ceremony commemorating the launch of the B.C. Treaty Commission. Draped with traditional Indian garb and standing on sacred blankets, Prime Minister Brian Mulroney and Premier Mike Harcourt signed a deal that committed Canada and British Columbia to settle all Indian land claims in British Columbia by the year 2000.

The importance of the moment was punctuated by the rhetoric. "The time has come for all Canadians . . . to say . . . yes, a solid generous yes to the native peoples of Canada," proclaimed Prime

Minister Mulroney. "It is long overdue."[35] A statement by the First Nations Summit read, "On this day, B.C. First Nations remember all of their past leaders and ancestors who struggled so hard over the years."[36] Summit Grand Chief Edward John added that the signing marked "the end of 125 years of denial by governments . . . and the beginning of a new relationship."[37]

This "new relationship" was proposed to be centred around recognition of undefined "aboriginal rights" and "aboriginal title"—concepts that had been rejected by successive B.C. governments for 120 years and which have received only a most modest meaning from the Courts.

The Chief Commissioner, selected by the unanimous consent of B.C., Canada and the First Nations Summit, was Charles J. (Chuck) Connaghan, a respected Vancouver management consultant. The Summit appointed two of the remaining four members and the federal and provincial governments selected one member each. Thus a laborious negotiating process, expected to continue for several years, which will see a period of bargaining between individual Indian bands on one side, and the federal and provincial governments on the other, was launched.

The goal is to ensure that the relationship between B.C.'s Indians and the federal and provincial governments would in the future be governed by treaties. But, unlike the relatively simple and few issues dealt with in the earlier treaties negotiated elsewhere in Canada, treaty-making in B.C. is at present designed not only to settle land claims, but also to deal with the host of other crucial subjects set out in the preceding table.

The politics of exclusion

The process does not provide for the interests of "third parties"—landowners, resource companies, ranchers, farmers and all others holding some form of tenure from government likely to be affected by land claim settlements—to be represented at the negotiating table. These stakeholders are expected to rely on senior governments to represent their interests.

Third party interests

True, there is some measure of consultation through a 31-member Treaty Negotiation Advisory Committee but this consultation contemplates its members vaguely "liaising" with government negotiators. Even here members swear oaths of confidentiality which hinder them from passing on to the members they represent any hard information about the negotiations. There is no provision for third parties to have any direct input or impact on the negotiations.

Local governments are somewhat better off on the matter of consultation as a result of a Memorandum of Understanding signed in the Spring of 1993 between the Union of B.C. Municipalities and the Provincial government. It recognizes that the land claim negotiation and settlement process "must be fair, open, principled and community based, and the process must be democratic, efficient, inclusive and acceptable to all parties."[38] To ensure these objectives, the agreement provides that affected municipalities are to be "represented in the process of negotiating treaties as respected advisers" and may, in certain cases, have a seat at the negotiating table. It remains to be seen whether promised consultation with municipalities will measure up to advance billing.

Ordinary citizens' interests

So much for "third-party" interests and the interests of municipalities, but what about the interests of ordinary British Columbians? After all, when all is said and done, it will be they who pick up the tab, or a good part of it. "Public consultation" is promised but how has it worked out in practice?

Events at Stewart, B.C., may provide the answer. Stewart is a District Municipality comprised, in these resource-depressed times, of some 700 souls. Tucked away in the northwest corner of the province close to the Alaska Panhandle, the rugged and spectacular terrain and the rigours of coping with measureless winter snows has produced in its citizens a resolve to endure hardship and to carve out a niche for themselves and their community of which they can be justly proud. Stewart falls within the land claim of the Nisga'a whose traditional territory comprises a vast area of 25,000 square kilometres. Obviously, the people of Stewart have a great deal at stake in this land claim negotiation, which has been conducted behind closed doors for 17 years and is now said to be close to settlement.

On the evening of May 25, 1993, the good people of Stewart were served up a "public information" meeting that can only be described as a farce. Jointly sponsored by the two senior governments and the Nisga'a Tribal Council, it attracted almost a quarter of the population of Stewart, some visitors, a bevy of about 20 bureaucrats and a chartered helicopter load of members of the Nisga'a Tribal Council. After introductions, the gathering was treated to a slide presentation by the federal team. So general was it in scope, and without any direct bearing on the Nisga'a claim, that the presentation was largely meaningless.

After the 15-minute slide show, one would have expected the parties to report on the state of the negotiations, followed by questions from the floor. After all, this was the first and possibly the only time the people of Stewart would get to question the main parties to the negotiations face to face. No such luck. The meeting was promptly adjourned for coffee and doughnuts and the citizens were advised that if they had any questions they could raise them with individual members of the negotiating teams on a one-on-one basis. There was no opportunity to express concerns or elicit information. That was it. End of meeting. The task of informing the citizens of what was going on behind closed doors and what were the implications of the Nisga'a land claim negotiations were not advanced one jot or tittle that evening.

Frustration continued to build in those north western B.C. communities affected by the Nisga'a claim—Smithers, Terrace, Kitimat, Prince Rupert—because no information on specifics is available to the public. Reform MP Mike Scott conducted a series of informational meetings in the Skeena riding in an attempt to include the public in a meaningful dialogue and solicit opinions and views. "All negotiations are taking place behind closed doors and in secret. The land and resources are publicly owned and the public must have a say," said Scott.

On August 10, 1994, more than 300 people attended a meeting in Smithers anxious to know what was going on behind closed doors and demanded the government tell them how their land and livelihoods would be affected. Reform MPs Dick Harris and John Duncan joined Scott in addressing the audience.

Scott's similar meeting in Prince Rupert was "highjacked by the Nisga'a" according to headlines in the *Prince Rupert Daily News.*[39] Nisga'a Chief Joe Gosnell and a large number of band members attended and voiced strong objections to the public forum. The manager of the Watson Island Pulp Mill advised the meeting that 800 pulp mill jobs could be lost if the mill's fibre supply was threatened.

The meeting in Terrace was attended by 450 people many of whom expressed their deep distrust of government on this issue. They clearly felt alienated from the process and had little or no confidence that their interests were being represented at the negotiating table.

The promise of openness

This pent-up public frustration did not go unnoticed by the B.C. Treaty Commission. In its first Annual Report released September 1, 1994, it stated:

"The Commission also has concern about the response of the Principals to their obligation to inform the public about the historic need for treaty making in British Columbia and about the ways in which this need is being addressed. In the view of the Commission, the three Principals have been slow to proceed in this regard. It is clear that the absence of accurate information from the Principals has led, and will continue to lead, to apprehension and resistance from interest groups and the public." [40]

The message was beginning to get through to the provincial government. On September 20, 1994, the Premier held a news conference in Victoria in which he committed himself to an "open land claim process" for all British Columbians. He set out five principles:

- open negotiations must be the rule, not the exception;
- all British Columbians must have the opportunity to provide meaningful input;
- B.C.'s negotiating mandate will be made public;
- B.C. will pursue the most effective means of sharing information about the negotiating sessions;
- the legislature will "sign off" treaty settlements.

Whether this new-found promise of openness is genuine remains to be seen. Certainly it appears to have had no impact on the way the Nisga'a negotiations are being conducted even though the Nisga'a Framework Agreement imposes an obligation on the governments to ensure the public, and all others having an interest, are well informed on the progress of the negotiations. B.C.'s negotiating mandate has never been made public as promised.

The extent of land claims

To date, 42 "First Nations" in B.C. have filed intentions to negotiate treaties. The 38 of these that have been made public are set out in Figure 8. Entire rainforests, mountain ranges, fields, lakes, rivers, and even urban areas have been placed on the negotiating table. The total

Figure 8 - Statements of Intent filed with B.C. Treaty Commission

	Name of First Nation	Name of People	Number of People	Description of Area covered
1.	Ktunaxa Nation	Ktunaxa, Kinbasket Bands: Columbia Lake, Lower Kootenay, Shuswap, St. Mary's and Tobacco Plains	Approx. 1,000	Big Bend of Columbia River, including all of the Kootenay Sinuosishes to Missoula, Montana to Bonner's Ferry, Idaho to Upper Arrow Lakes
2.	Sliammon Indian Band	Sliammon Indian Band	750 members	Lasqueti Island and Texada Island, Welcome Pass, Todd Inlet, Cortes Island, Comox, parts of Denman Island
3.	Songhees Indian Band	Songhees Indian Band	314 members	overlapping claims with Esquimalt Indian Band and Beecher Bay Indian Band, South End Vancouver Island and fishing areas on the Fraser River
4.	Yale First Nation	Yale People part of the Tait People	Approx. 112	Cascade Mountains, Manning Provincial Park, Spatsum
5.	Burrard Indian Band	Tslul Waututh People	291	Port Moody, Vancouver, Granite Falls, Diamond Head
6.	Cariboo Tribal Council	People of Canim Lake, Canoe Creek, Soda Creek, Williams Lake First Nation	1,644	Williams Lake, Mt Stevenson, Wells, Bridge Lake
7.	Carrier Sekani Tribal Council	Carrier Sekani Tribal Council: Sustut'enke (Sekani), Saschojan l'l'azt'en, Wetsut'en, K'oo Dene, Sai K'uz Whet'en, Na ole t'en Tsu Yaz to t'en	12,000	Same as set out in Carrier Sekani 1982 Comprehensive Claim
8.	Ditidaht First Nation	Ditidaht People	457	Traditional Territory extends seaward to where Vancouver Island is no longer visible from a canoe, Carmanah, Cowichan Lake
9.	Esketemc Nation	Esketemc Shuswap People	650+	Straddles Fraser River from Taseko Lakes on west to Timothy Mountain on east
10.	Gitanyow Hereditary Chiefs	Four Traditional Wolf Houses and Four Frog Houses	714	Cranberry River, Nass River, White River
11.	Haisla Nation	Haisla (Kitamaat) and Henaaksilal (Kitlope) People	1,200	Description of area unclear
12.	Heiltsuk Nation	Wuyalitxu, Yisdaitxu, Wuthiteu, Quaquayaitxu, Xixis, Kuiatxu	2,500+	Bella Bella, Calvert Island

	Name of First Nation	Name of People	Number of People	Description of Area covered
13.	In-shuck-ch	Communities of Douglas, Skookumchuck and Samahquam	701	All lands generally drained by Lillooet Lake and Harrison Lake
14.	Kaska Dena Council	Kaska Nation	800-1,200	Lower Post, Rabbit River, Stone Mountain Park, Rocky Mountains (parts)
15.	Katzie Indian Band	Katzie Indian People	370	Pitt Lake, Pitt River, Golden Ears Park, Surrey, Langley & New Westminster
16.	Ka·'yu·'k't'h'/che: Kitles Tet'h' Nation	Ka·'yu·'k't'h'/che: Kitles Tet'h' Nation (Kyuquot Nation) (Tribe)	Approx. 350	Checleset Bay, Union Island, Kashett Inlet
17.	Lheit-Lit'en Nation	Carrier Indians-Lheit-Lit'en People	210	Pelican Lake, Blackwater River, 10 Mile Lake, Moose Lake, Great Beaver Lake, Bedrestl Lake
18.	Musqueam, adapted from Xw'muthk'i'um	Xw'muthk'i'um People	890	Spanish Banks, Iona Island, Capilano Creek, Tsawwassen, Canoe Pass
19.	Nanoose First Nation	Nanoose First Nation	Approx. 189	Piper's Lagoon, Alberni Inlet, Columbia Beach Islands, Bellinas, Gerald Islands
20.	Nuu Chah Nulth Tribal Council	Nuu Chah Nulth 13 Bands	6,350	West Coast of Vancouver Island
21.	Oweekeno Nation	Membership of Oweekeno Nation	207	Oweekeno Lake, Rivers Inlet, Dawsons Landing (Map)
22.	Squamish Nation	Squamish Membership	2,552	Lower Mainland, Point Grey to Roberts Creek, Elaho River, Green Rivers, Whistler, Port Moody
23.	Tsimshian Tribal Council	Gidzalaal, Ginaxangiik, Gisp'ax, P'ots, Gitantoyko, Gitlan, Gilutsau, Gittsis, Gitwilquots, Gitga'ata, Kitsumkalum	10,000	The area "defined by our First Nations"
24.	Champagne and Alshihik First Nation	Southern Tutchone and Tlingit descent	Approx. 11,000	Nothern B.C. entirely encompasses the Tatshenshini and Alsek drainage Haines Road to the Takhini River drainage
25.	Treaty 8 Tribal Association	Blueberry River, Doig River, Fort Nelson, Halfway River, Prophet River, Saulteaux and West Moberly First Nation	Approx. 2,200	Northern B.C., northwestern Alberta, southwestern NWT and south portions of Yukon

	Name of First Nation	Name of People	Number of People	Description of Area covered
26.	Xaxli'p	Xaxli'p People	700+	No description provided
27.	Sechelt Indian Band	Sechelt First Nation	900	Sechelt in south, Sechelt Peninsula, portion of Texada Island, both sides of Jervis Inlet
28.	Gitksan Hereditary Chiefs	Gitksan	8,500	Area of north central B.C. claimed by Gitksan in Delgamuukw case.
29.	Tsawwassen	Coast Salish	Approx. 250	Fraser River delta, Point Roberts (USA), Boundary Bay, Roberts Bank and adjacent sea areas
30.	Hul'qumi'num	Cowichan tribes, Chemainus, Lyackson, Penelakut, Halait, Malahant, Lake Cowichan bands	5,016	Cowichan & Chemainus valleys. Dodds Narrows in north, Goldstream Park in south, Cowichan Lake in west, Gulf Island in east
31.	Homalco Indian Band	Homalco Band	350	An area surrounding Bute Inlet, west of Chilko Lake
32.	Pavilion Indian Band	Pavilion Band, Stl'atl'imx	387	Undefined except for "1,050 sq.miles"
33.	Teslin Tlingit Council	Tlingit	Approx. 750	Drainage system of Teslin Lake (northern B.C.)
34.	Tsay keh Dene Band	Tsay keh Dene	277	Mt. Trace in North, South Pass Peak in west, Nation River in south, Mt. Laurier in east
35.	Wet'suwet'en Nation	Wet'suwet'en	2,800	Area of north central B.C. claimed by Wet'suwet'en Nation in Delgamuukw case including Burns Lake, Morice River
36.	Westbank	Westbank (Okanagan)	500	Central Okanagan Valley
37.	Haida Nation	Haida	7,000	Entire Haida Gwaii (Queen Charlotte Islands), the surrounding waters, the air space, the Kaigainaa Archipelago-waters inc. Dixon Entrance, half of the Hecate Straits, halfway to Vancouver Island and westward into the "abyssal ocean depths."
38.	Te'Mexw	Beecher Bay, Nanoose, Songhees, T'Sou-ke	849	"See map for each First Nation"

land area under claim exceeds 111% of the province, because of overlapping claims. Virtually every corner of the province is covered. Traditional territories under claim include the entire lower mainland including the City of Vancouver (overlapping claims by several bands), most of Vancouver Island (claimed by the Nuu-chah-nulth Tribal Council), the Queen Charlotte Islands (the Haida nation), most of the Kootenays (the Kootenay Area Indian Council), and all of the north and northwest of the province (several bands). Even some bands that signed the Douglas Treaties have now returned and said that those weren't generous enough. The Nanaimo band, for instance, has laid claim to 79 acres of prime land in Nanaimo.[41]

Wendy Grant, B.C. representative to the national Assembly of First Nations states:

> "We can claim downtown Vancouver. It is ours. There is nothing in anybody's laws saying that it is no longer belonging to Musqueam or Squamish or Capilano or Tsawwassen. This is the bottom line. Yes, there's a whole province under claim because there's a whole province that hasn't been paid for, hasn't been negotiated, and hasn't had any kind of joint-venture possibility."[42]

Although this statement has little **legal** merit, Aboriginal Affairs Minister John Cashore isn't so sure. "Most of this tax base rests on Crown land **which was never legally obtained**, by treaty or by war, from the aboriginal people who occupied it for centuries before European settlement," he says.[43] (emphasis added) By so saying, the Minister has accepted the plausible line espoused by the native leadership. As we shall see in Chapter 6, it is a line that has been categorically rejected by the Courts. Never before has a Minister of the Crown put into question the underlying ownership of Crown land.

Cost of settlements

The likely cost of final settlements is a mystery. If governments know, it is a secret. The NDP government has agreed to parity of compensation: whatever one B.C. band gets, the rest get nothing less. According to one columnist, NDP Aboriginal Affairs Minister, John Cashore, says "to talk money [now] would not be helpful" and refuses to discuss estimated costs.[44]

But cash is only one element. On the table is Crown land, timber harvesting rights, wildlife harvesting rights, subsurface rights, fishing rights, resource royalties, and control over land-use decisions. Other costs include continuing government social and economic development programs, native self-government, and paying compensation to Indians for private property interests within their traditional territory. The same Mr. Cashore is reported to have said that cash will be relatively insignificant . "The big thing will be land and self-government."[45]

Joseph Gosnell, Nisga'a Tribal Council president, adds,

"These negotiations are not about generosity. This is not charity. This is a debt, unpaid for 150 years and rising . . . We know that the people of Canada do not have the cash to pay the back rent, that is, the money properly owed to us for the seizure of our land and the plunder of its natural resources without consent or compensation. But we are not about to settle for the 20th-century equivalent of trinkets and beads."[46]

A provincial insider, who does not wish to be named, recently confided that the total cost may go as high as $15 billion. Some trinkets, some beads!

Despite assurances to the contrary, private property may indeed be at stake. Minister John Cashore concedes that the potential scope of claims may include expropriations of private interests: "It may be necessary to purchase interests held by persons other than Canada, British Columbia or the First Nations. The types of interests which might have to be purchased would include fishing vessels and licenses, forest tenures, traplines, mining interests and other tenures. . . . I can say that anyone whose legal interest is expropriated will be fairly compensated."[47]

Who is to pay for all this? Previous B.C. governments have maintained that the cost should be borne by the federal government and thus shared by taxpayers across the country. Ottawa, of course, disagreed pressing for a 50-50 split. Despite the uncertainty over the eventual cost of settlements, in June 1993, Ottawa and Victoria agreed to a complex cost-sharing formula. B.C. and Canadian taxpayers will share cash payouts to natives based on a land/cash ratio while all of the land transferred to natives will come from provincial Crown land.[48]

The federal government says it will pay the province for lost resource revenues. These lost revenues could be enormous. A Price Waterhouse study concluded that the lands claimed, even as early as 1992, encompassed resource industries generating 200,000 jobs and $17.5 billion in yearly revenues.

Moreover, the province has agreed to pay 50% of the cost of compensating dispossessed Crown land lease-holders in claim areas. The federal government will pay the other half. This could mean covering half of everything from a rancher's cattle to lost revenues from mines and sawmills.

Interim measures agreements

Negotiations to conclude permanent treaties of the scope presently contemplated is a laborious process which will take many years. Indian bands had complained for decades that they were being robbed of the timber and mineral royalties reaped by government from land they claimed as their traditional territory. This had led to frequent blockades and confrontations where Indians demanded a say over land use.

Interim measures agreements are designed to provide natives with some assurance that resources or interests in land which ultimately might be negotiated in their favour would not, in the interim, be extracted without their interests being protected.

On August 20, 1993, the Government of British Columbia entered into a Protocol with the First Nations Summit to govern the procedure for entering into these interim agreements. Instead of a modest framework agreement setting out the procedures to be followed, the Government, in the preamble to the Protocol, made three whopping concessions.

In the first preamble the Government states that it recognizes aboriginal title. What does "aboriginal title" mean in this context? Does it have the highly restricted meaning which the Court of Appeal in *Delgamuukw* has given it or is it the expansive meaning held by the late Chief Gosnell or others among the native leadership? Actions by provincial negotiators indicate that the government gives it the expansive meaning.

The second preamble recognizes the "inherent right of First Nations to self-government in Canada." I deal with this concept in detail in Chapter 7. This is a fanciful idea without, in my view, any legal or constitutional support. In fact, it has been specifically rejected by every court that has been asked to deal with it, the latest being the B.C. Court of Appeal in the *Delgamuukw* case. I ask then, what right has the government of British Columbia to recognize "the inherent right of First Nations to self-government" in the light of the highest judicial authority in this province dismissing the concept?

In the third preamble the parties agree that "a government-to-government relationship exists between First Nations and the Government of British Columbia." What does this "government-to-government relationship" mean? By what constitutional or legal authority is it established? Talk of negotiating with bands, on a "government-to-government basis" is a total misnomer; is prejudicial to the interests of the provincial government; and, worse still, unduly raises the expectations of the native people. Such is the basis on which interim measures agreements are being negotiated.

Premier Harcourt startled most observers when he let it slip out at a news conference in September 1994 that the province had already signed perhaps as many as 100 of these agreements based on the principles set out in the Protocol. In mid-November, 1994, the government released a batch of 42 interim agreements signed up to that time—all negotiated behind closed doors and all released because of demands under the *Freedom of Information Act*.

The Clayoquot Sound Agreement

One of the most significant of these interim measures agreements is the one relating to Clayoquot Sound. This remote 260,000-hectare region on the west coast of Vancouver Island has been the subject of intense emotional debate between environmentalists demanding its complete preservation, and pro-logging advocates who promote its limited resource use. At the same time, five Indian bands—the Hesquiaht, Toquaht, Ucluelet, Ahousaht and Tlaoquiaht (known as the Central Region First Nations of the Nuu-chah-nulth Tribal Council) claim the land in question.

The Clayoquot agreement provides for a variety of things including the establishment of a board composed of representatives of the province and the five Indian bands to jointly advise in the management of this vast area. The board's mandate is all-embracing, including the review of all land-use plans for the area such as forest tenures, logging, mining, water resources, wildlife management, recreation and parks.

The agreement provides that the board "will accept, propose modifications to, or recommend rejection of" any plans, decisions, recommendations or reports involving land use and resource extraction in Clayoquot Sound. This includes policy decisions related to logging and logging practices such as clear-cutting and road-building, reforestation and ecological restoration, land tenure, aquaculture, wildlife management, public recreation activities, and the setting of park boundaries and its management, and mining. The board will also hear public complaints about land-use activities and monitor these activities. All government ministries and agencies must submit their plans for the region to the board for approval.

Decisions of the board, to be effective, will require a double-majority of aboriginal representatives. That means the natives have a veto. In effect, if a large corporation such as MacMillan Bloedel wanted to build a logging road or undertake logging, it would have to get the approval of the five native bands. One MacMillan Bloedel spokesman said, "We're at the mercy of politics. But we have to support land-use decisions because we will indeed require the approval of the First nations before we log in the future."[49]

Concerning the Clayoquot Sound agreement, *Vancouver Sun* columnist Vaughn Palmer wrote:

". . . more than any other concrete act by the Harcourt government, it represents a break with history in treatment of the aboriginal people. . . . Now, here and for the first time, a B.C. government, acting on its lonesome, has surrendered control of a vast region of the province to a joint management board. . . . And the board will become the chief arbiter of the fate of the Clayoquot. . . . the New Democrats clearly intend this agreement as a model, not just for the management of the Clayoquot, but for every area subject to land claims—which is to say virtually all of B.C. "[50]

Although Premier Harcourt is quoted as saying the decisions of the board may be overturned by Cabinet, a plain reading of the agreement shows the only role the Cabinet has under the deal is to **implement** decisions made by the board if not implemented otherwise by government or its agencies within 30 days.

Abdication by government

Meaningful consultation is one thing, but when efforts by governments to accommodate the demands of a particular interest group go beyond genuine consultation into the realm of joint decision-making, governments have abdicated their obligation to govern. Such is what has happened with the Clayoquot interim agreement. But such a move is entirely consistent with the Government's ill-found intention to deal with bands on a "government-to-government" basis.

For their part, the aboriginal leadership in B.C. must, in private, stand in awe at what it has been able to achieve in furtherance of the aboriginal agenda. Time and time again their leadership asserts its demands upon government only to discover they are acquiesced to willingly. Like pushing a door ajar, the lack of resistance from within invites further entry.

Other interim measures agreements

Another interim agreement involves fourteen northern Vancouver Island bands that gives them a virtual veto over aquaculture and fisheries from Denman Island to the north end of Vancouver Island including Johnstone and Queen Charlotte Straits. Any fish farms, commercial fishing lodges, and logging activities that might affect fisheries must be referred to the 14 "First Nations." The agreement was sparked by Indian anger over the intrusion of the thriving commercial fish farm industry in areas of traditional native fishing.

Likewise, the NDP and the Nemiah Valley Indian Band signed a "government-to-government" agreement over the Chilko Lake area. The agreement established that any aboriginal title that is eventually negotiated takes precedence over the creation of a provincial park. The Lheit Lit'en Nation near Prince George was handed "jurisdiction and authority" over 200,000 hectares of land.

Entire government bureaucracies have been issued guidelines on aboriginal consultation. The environment ministry, for example, was ordered to recognize the native right to "sustenance use" of resources within traditional territory. The natives, of course, are left to define for themselves what "sustenance" means, even if it means hunting out of season. The province has ignored warnings that ill-defined agreements over wildlife resources such as these could lead to disaster. Overharvesting of resources or other illegal activities by natives are not automatically punished—on the contrary, enforcement officers first evaluate whether an "appropriate level of consultation" took place with native authorities and only then give the matter to prosecutors who explore "reasonable alternatives" to prosecution.[51]

Third party interests ignored

Again, in the case of interim measures agreements, third party interests and the interests of ordinary British Columbians are not being heard. This blatant lack of consultation boiled over with a volcanic-like eruption over an interim agreement that had been negotiated and was about to be signed between the Harcourt government and the Council of the Haida Nation. Called to a meeting in Queen Charlotte City on August 3, 1994, sport fishing operators and related organizations, said to represent the majority of over 400,000 recreational fishermen in the province, were presented with a *fait accompli* by provincial bureaucrats. The draft agreement concluded that there was a need for improvements to the recreational fisheries on the Charlottes and that it was the Haidas, and the governments, and they alone, that would settle these issues. Restrictions on the growth of the industry and effective control by the Haida was contemplated. All of this without the knowledge of, or consultation with, recreational fishing operators who have invested millions of dollars in their Charlotte operations and who have developed an exceptionally productive use of the resource in terms of jobs, conservation, tourism, and economic returns.

Under the leadership of the Sport Fishing Institute of B.C., the sport fishing interests and organizations such as the B.C. Wildlife Federation, the Fisheries Council of B.C. and the B.C. Business Council went on red alert. Letters bombarded the Premier's office, a public awareness campaign was launched with the publication in newspapers throughout the province of a large advertisement deploring the action and calling the Premier to account. The ad features a naked light bulb with the caption "Mike Harcourt, How long are you going to keep 97% of B.C. citizens in the dark?" and goes on to describe the backroom deal in the Charlottes. A hastily arranged meeting was convened by senior officials in the Premier's office and senior bureaucrats from relevant ministries. At the meeting, the recreational fisheries representatives threw down the gauntlet, demanded that the agreement be scrapped, and, for good measure, unveiled copies of even more graphic newspaper advertisements which the Sport Fishing Institute and its supporters were intending to run. Within 48 hours, the deputy minister in charge advised that the deal would be scrapped with the assurance that "your organization will be fully consulted prior to concluding any interim agreement" with the Haida.

This incident rocked the government to the core on its public consultation policy on land claims. A month later, the Premier announced his new-found commitment to openness in land claim negotiations previously described. However, to prove that this is genuine, the government should apply it to the negotiation of interim agreements as well. Otherwise, British Columbians run the risk of having another batch of these agreements being dumped on their lap in a year's time or so without having had any chance for input.

More recently, the Council of Forest Industries of B.C. (COFI) has examined the interim measures agreements negotiated up to February 1995, which by that time had grown to 54 in number. COFI concluded that at least 20 of them that pertain to land and resources "promote false perceptions of aboriginal jurisdiction over asserted traditional territory [and] generate non-achievable expectations of industry and government."[52] COFI has asked that all negotiations on future interim measures agreements be put on hold "until consistent, workable and public-supported government policy is in place."[53]

The Indian minority

What is most striking is the relatively small number of people who will directly benefit from land claims agreements in B.C. According to the 1991 census, status Indians in B.C. number 94,006 (2.7% of B.C.'s population). Only 49,756 of them (1.4% of B.C.'s population) live on reserves.[54] It is only the seventh largest ethnic group in the province. For example, the Haida natives who wish to govern the Queen Charlotte Islands and control recreational fisheries in the Islands total 2,915 located in two villages. The Nisga'a, who likely will be the first B.C. Indian band to settle a land claim and will presumably control the Nass Valley and a good portion of the Nass Valley fishery, total 4,078. The Nuu-chah-nulth (Nootka), who now control Clayoquot Sound and all of its forest resources, number 5,745.[55] About half of these natives do not live on reserves and may not even reside in their respective territory.

All status Indians, whether or not they live on reserves, are slated to receive the rich benefits that flow from these agreements. For B.C.'s relatively few Indians, the upcoming treaties promise a bonanza in cash, property and economic opportunity.

Conclusions

The outcome of these treaty negotiations, as presently contemplated, with the self-government arrangements which are likely to follow, could re-shape the economic, social, and political face of British Columbia. If this process goes ahead, at the end of the day, B.C. may create dozens of fiefdoms, or so-called "First Nations," each with their own law-making body, territory, justice system and economy.

In process and in substance the present B.C. treaty-making process is ill-conceived, unworkable, unaffordable and unjust. It must be substantially modified.

Chapter 4 - Footnotes:

1. *Globe and Mail*, April 30, 1984.
2. A reference is made in one of the preamble paragraphs of the Royal grant that colonization would result in "the protection and welfare of the native Indians residing" in the area.
3. Letter from A. Barclay, Secty, Hudson's Bay Company to James Douglas, Chief Factor, Fort Victoria, dated December 1849. (Ex 1039-21) *Delgamuukw Case.*
4. Quoted at pages 131 and 132 of Chief Justice McEachern's judgement in *Delgamuukw vs. B.C.* (N.B. The page numbers referred to are those of the bound volume of the Reasons for Judgment released on March 8, 1991, and widely distributed.)
5. McEachern, C.J. in *Delgamuukw vs. B.C.,* 131-132.
6. *Indian Reserves in the Colony,* B.C. Legislature Sessional Papers, Victoria, January 13, 1873.
7. *The Aboriginal Peoples of British Columbia: A Profile* (Victoria: Ministry of Aboriginal Affairs, 1992), 1.
8. DIAND, Schedule of Indian Bands, Reserves and Settlements, December 1990.
9. Report of the Royal Commission on Indian Affairs for the Province of British Columbia, (McKenna-McBride Commission), 1916.
10. Paul Tennant, *Aboriginal Peoples and Politics* (Vancouver: U.B.C. Press, 1990), 85.
11. Ibid.
12. Parliament of Canada, Special Joint Committee of Senate and House of Commons, 1926-27, x.
13. *Communique,* Government of British Columbia, August 8, 1990.
14. Ibid.
15. Ibid.
16. Ibid.
17. Vaughn Palmer, "B.C. takes historic step on land claims," *Vancouver Sun,* August 10, 1990.
18. "Nothing new in premier's land-claim talk, Indians say", *Vancouver Sun,* August 10, 1990, B.1.
19. *Communique,* Government of British Columbia, August 8, 1990.
20. Subsequent polls have shown that when the cost and implications of land claims are understood, public support is far less forthcoming. (Angus Reid Focus Group Research, *Attitudes towards Land Claims,* August, 1994.)
21. Most of these cases have not yet gone to trial.
22. "Nothing new in premier's land-claim talk, Indians say," *Vancouver Sun,* August 10, 1990, B1.

23. News Release, "B.C. Opens Land Claim Talks," Province of B.C., October 3, 1990.
24. Information Update, Ministry of Native Affairs, November, 1990.
25. Ibid.
26. News Release, "Province Announces Principles for Land Claim Negotiations and Establishes Third Party Advisory Committee," Ministry of Native Affairs, January 31, 1991.
27. *The Report of the British Columbia Claims Task Force*, June 28, 1991, 12.
28. George Orwell, *Nineteen Eighty-Four* (1949; rpt. Penguin, 1980), 199.
29. "Staking Claim," *Vancouver Sun*, April 1, 1995, 1.
30. *The Report of the British Columbia Claims Task Force*, 17.
31. Ibid., 16.
32. Ibid., 26.
33. "B.C. NDP recognizes aboriginal land title," *Globe and Mail*, December 11, 1991, A1.
34. Ibid.
35. "Mulroney, Harcourt sign historic treaty with natives," *Vancouver Sun*, September 22, 1992, B1.
36. *Kahtou News '92*, October 1, 1992, 6.
37. *Vancouver Sun*, September 22, 1992.
38. Memorandum of Understanding between British Columbia and Union of B.C. Municipalities, March 22, 1993.
39. "Nisga'a highjack Scott's forum," *Prince Rupert Daily News*, October 5, 1994.
40. Shortly thereafter Mr. Chuck Connaghan, Chief Commissioner, announced his intention to resign from the Commission, effective December 31, 1994.
41. Dave Cunningham, "Betting on their version of history," *British Columbia Report*, March 1, 1993, 26.
42. "Land claims drawing attention of business," *Vancouver Sun*, September 10, 1994, C1.
43. "Responses to Questions from Mike Scott, MP, submitted by Jack Weisgerber, MLA, to Minister John Cashore for reply," (1994), 3.
44. Jim Hume, "Hush-hush land-claim cost may spook the taxpayers," *Times-Colonist*, January 21, 1995, A5.
45. Ibid.
46. Joseph Gosnell, "Pricing a land-claims backlash," *Vancouver Sun*, November 1, 1994.
47. "Response to Questions from Mike Scott, MP," Ibid., 4.
48. *Memorandum of Understanding Between Canada and British Columbia Respecting the Sharing of Pre-Treaty Costs, Settlement Costs, Implementation Costs and The Costs of Self-Government*, June 21, 1993.

49. Robin Brunet, "A convenient time for a sellout," *British Columbia Report*, April 4, 1994, 19.

50. "Clayoquot deal a first for First Nations," *Vancouver Sun*, December 13, 1993, A8.

51. Tom McFeely, "Conservation takes a back seat," *British Columbia Report*, December 28, 1992, 7.

52. "Agreeing to exclude third parties." *B.C. Report,* April 10, 1995, 17.

53. Ibid.

54. Statistics Canada, *The Daily,* March 30, 1993, 2.

55. DIAND, *Indian Register Population by Sex and Residence 1991* (Ottawa: Queen's Printer, 1992).

"Topping Up" Existing Treaties and Other Largesse

"The government believes that treaty settlements will end the years of uncertainty surrounding land entitlements."
Honourable John Cashore,
B.C. Minister of Aboriginal Affairs.[1]

Consider Mr. Cashore's assurances in the light of the events of this chapter.

Thus far I have dealt exclusively with one kind of land claim negotiation taking place at the present time in parts of Canada, that is, negotiating treaties over areas where none now exist. These are known as "comprehensive land claims." There is another kind of negotiation going on throughout the country known as "specific claims."

Specific claims[2]

Specific claims arise from alleged non-fulfilment by government of existing treaty or other obligations, or claims arising from the alleged improper administration of lands, including Indian Reserves, and other assets held in trust under the *Indian Act*. As will be seen, the settlement of these alleged grievances has become a bonanza for natives to hundreds of millions of dollars, large tracts of land and sundry other benefits.

The process of addressing these alleged grievances began in 1973 through the Office of Native Claims established in the DIAND. For starters, the government waived the statute of limitations which prohibits other Canadians from taking a claim before the courts after a certain length of time (usually 6 years) and also waived the doctrine of *laches,* a common law rule whereby a court may refuse to hear a claim if it considers the claimant has waited too long to bring it forward. By 1981, over 70 such claims had been submitted but only 12 had been settled. Native leaders complained that the process was too slow and the acceptance criteria by government was "overly restrictive." Government responded to the criticisms, changed the rules, eventually established a Specific Claims Commission and speeded up the process. This opened the floodgates.

According to information supplied by the DIAND, by 1994, 632 specific claims had been received; of this total, 258 were under review and 91 were in negotiation. The remaining 283 had been resolved as follows: 117 through settlements; 55 rejected; 69 closed; 20 in litigation and 22 referred for administrative resolution. Most of them relate to alleged events which took place many years ago—some more than 100 years ago—long after the people involved have died and many of the records have been discarded.

Some examples of specific claim settlements are as follows:-

1. Treaty No.7 Bands, Alberta. Failure to meet provisions of Treaty No.7 concerning the provision of ammunition. First put forward in 1960. Settled in December 1974 for $250,000.

2. Penticton Band, British Columbia. Compensation for lands cut off from Reserves in 1920. Settled in March, 1982 for $14,217,118 and 12,243 acres of land.

3. Oromocto Band, New Brunswick. Compensation for alleged improper surrender of 29 hectares in 1953 for use by the National Defence Department (Camp Gagetown). Settled in July 1983 for $2,550,000.

4. Six Nations, Ontario. Alleged faulty expropriation of land for railway purposes. Settled in December, 1985 for $1,000,000.

5. Westbank Band, British Columbia. Compensation for lands cut off from Reserves in 1920. Settled in November 1983 for $8,273,886 and 56 acres of land.

6. Blackfoot (Siksika), Alberta. Treaty livestock entitlement. Settled in April 1984 for $1,675,000.

7. Garden River Band, Ontario. Band alleged that Squirrel Island, adjacent to reserve was incorrectly surrendered in 1859. Settled in March 1987 for $2,530,000.

8. Big Cove Band, New Brunswick. Band alleged a breach of land sale conditions in 1879. Settled August 1988 for $3,216,000.

9. Kawacatoose Band, Saskatchewan. Band alleges their surrender of land to Soldiers Settlement Board in 1918 was not valid and price paid to them inadequate. Settled October 1991 for $3,020,000.

10. Kitigan Zibi Anishinabeg Band, Quebec. Alleged illegal alienation of 200 acres of reserve land in 1868. Settled November 9, 1988 for $2,686,187.
11. Sakimay Band, Saskatchewan. Alleged wrongful surrender of 6,000 acres in 1907. Settled March 1992 for $3,940,000.
12. Cowichan Band, British Columbia. Alleged wrongful taking of 700 acres of band land in 1886. Settled December 2, 1992 for $552,000.
13. Stanjkoming Band, Ontario. Band alleged an interest in Rainy Lake Indian Reserve No.18B. Settled July, 1990 for $2,789,231.
14. Nanaimo Band, British Columbia. Band claimed 2.76 acres used for railway right of way since 1883 had been improperly acquired. Settled January 12, 1994 for $1,835,000.
15. Piapot Band, Saskatchewan. Band alleged 1918 and 1919 land surrenders under Soldiers Settlement Board were invalid. Settled March 25, 1993 for $12,100,000.
16. Sechelt Band, British Columbia. Seven claims by band dating back to 1891 alleging improper surrenders and nonfeasance by government. Settled January 1992 for $4,410,000.[3]

This list represents only 16 of the 117 settled specific claims to date. Amazingly, no less than 40 of them relate to bands in British Columbia. They range from claims for lands cut-off certain reserves by the federal government in 1920 without band consent, to compensation for railway and road rights of way allegedly improperly taken many years ago. And we in B.C. thought we hadn't settled any land claims yet!

Up to the end of 1992, the federal government had contributed $169 million and provinces $39 million to this kind of specific claim since the process began in 1973. About 350 such claims remain to be dealt with and new claims are still coming forward. But this was only the beginning. Treaty land entitlements were next.

Treaty Land Entitlements[4]

Claims, known as "Treaty Land Entitlements" have become such a major part of specific claims that the federal government has set up a special Treaty Land Entitlement Division just to handle them. Of these claims, one DIAND official put it, "They're big they're expensive and there's lots of them."

Between 1871 and 1923, the federal government concluded the eleven "numbered" post-Confederation treaties with Indians which covered northern Ontario, all of Manitoba, Saskatchewan and Alberta, the Peace River block of B.C. and portions of the territories. Their purpose was to "open up for settlement, immigration, trade . . . and other purposes" lands to which the treaty applied. It also sought to ensure that there would be "peace and goodwill" between the Indians and the Crown. The Indians were to release and surrender all their "rights, titles and privileges" and assume certain obligations such as to maintain peace and good order between themselves, other tribes, and "Her Majesty's other subjects."

The benefits extended to the Indians by the early treaties called for reserves to be established equivalent in size, in most cases, to one square mile for a family of five. They were to be held by the government for the collective benefit of the band and not subject to sale or other disposition. Other benefits included annual cash payments of $25 to each chief; $15 to each headman; and $12 to each Indian. Schools were promised and agricultural implements, livestock, seed and supplies were provided. For these and the other benefits specified, the band surrendered all its interest (whatever that might be, in law) to its surrounding territory. The band retained its right to hunt, fish and trap in that territory under government regulation until the land was required for settlement or for mining.

Shortly after signing these treaties, the government started setting up reserves. The process of determining the number of Indians and then surveying the actual reserve took place at the time of "first survey". In southern Saskatchewan surveys began in 1875 and most were completed by 1885. Once families had reserve land set aside for them, they had no claim to further land, despite the fact the families continued to grow. At the time, it wasn't uncommon for the government to add an extra 10% to 30% more land because it was thought that some members of the band might be on extended hunts or be visiting other reserves. Sometimes these Indians never materialized or they settled on other reserves.

At times, individuals were missed and this could be determined by researching paylists which were developed to keep track of yearly treaty payments. On these lists, the Indian agent would note when new Indians were added, why they hadn't been included before, and how far back treaty money was paid. If it was not paid from the time of first survey, that indicated that the individual may have been missed when the reserve was set up. At other times, reserves were set up anticipating people would move or bands would amalgamate but which did not happen. Sometimes, Indians "took treaty" after reserves were established but the size of reserves was not increased.

The Government of Canada transferred to each of the three Prairie provinces, under the *Natural Resources Transfer Agreement* of 1930, ownership and jurisdiction over Crown lands and natural resources within their respective provinces. Although it was considered that the reserve allotment process within the Prairie provinces was essentially complete by 1930, the Transfer Agreement required that each of the three provinces would provide unoccupied Crown lands "necessary to enable Canada to fulfil its obligations under the treaties with the Indians of the province."

Nothing much transpired until the mid 1970s when pressure from the Federation of Saskatchewan Indians asserted that 30 out of 72 Saskatchewan bands had a "shortfall"—an amount of land alleged to be owed to them but not included in their reserves. Moreover, the native leadership argued that the "shortfall" should be calculated on the basis of the latest band membership and not membership at the time of the treaty. Amazingly, the governments agreed.[5]

Meanwhile Bill C-31, which was passed in 1985, significantly increased the number of treaty Indians. This bill gave "status" to Indian women (and their minor children) who had married non-Indians. The bands wanted these new population numbers taken into account in calculating shortfalls of treaty lands. Again, the governments agreed.

The Saskatchewan experience[6]

In 1976, Saskatchewan agreed to negotiate the issue of "shortfalls" with the Federation of Saskatchewan Indians provided that the Federation could bind all bands pursuing such claims. The Province was prepared to negotiate on the basis of "present population times 128 (acres per person) less land already received." "Present population" meant the population as of December 31, 1976. To satisfy claims in southern Saskatchewan, the Province agreed it would do its best to provide unoccupied Crown land. However, because most of the land in the south had already been alienated by the federal government prior to *The Natural Resources Transfer Agreement* of 1930, the Saskatchewan government took the position that any band that was unhappy with a southern allocation of land must look to the federal government for satisfaction.

The Saskatchewan formula

Based on this formula, the 15 bands in Saskatchewan known in 1976 to have treaty land entitlements, would be provided with 946,532 acres in settlement. Problems associated with the implementation of the Saskatchewan formula soon arose. First and foremost was the shortage of suitable unoccupied Crown land in the vicinity of many existing reserves. The problem became even more acute when the number of entitlement bands doubled from 15 to 30 between 1978 and 1984 for a total of some 1.3 million acres due under the new formula.

Holders of longstanding permits to areas of pastureland under the Federal Prairie Farm Rehabilitation Administration found themselves threatened by the intention to add large areas of Crown land to existing reserves. Likewise rural municipalities became alarmed because once federal or provincial Crown lands within those municipalities became reserve lands, taxes paid on those lands would end since Indian Reserves are not taxable. Moreover, the Saskatchewan Wildlife Federation claimed that more wildlife habitat would be destroyed if more and larger Indian reserves were established.

Some senior DIAND officials began to have second thoughts about the Saskatchewan formula. They considered it was too generous and put some bands in a "windfall" position. One such example which was often cited was the Oxford band in Manitoba where negotiations were following along similar lines in that province. Oxford had a shortfall of just 15 acres but under the Saskatchewan formula it would have been eligible for over 20,000 acres.

There was also the possibility that the bands without a shortfall would consider the deal unfair. The Government was essentially giving lands to all members of the bands who allegedly had been shortchanged including the heirs of those families that had previously received land. Since the government was giving these families a second allotment of land, could this be considered fair to those families that only received one allotment?

Three northern bands successfully settled their claim based on the Saskatchewan formula and received 69,785 acres. This was because there was sufficient unused Crown land in the north of the province to make such a settlement without undue interruption to third party and other interests.

By 1989 both the Saskatchewan and Federal government refused to proceed with any further agreements based on the Saskatchewan formula and cast around for an acceptable alternative.

Office of the Treaty Commissioner[7]

In an effort to resolve the impasse, the Federation of Saskatchewan Indian Nations and the province of Saskatchewan established the "Office of the Treaty Commissioner" in 1989 as an independent office designed to resolve outstanding issues and to make recommendations.

The "equity formula"

The Commission considered a number of formulae but in the end proposed one which took a proportion of the band's present population equivalent to the percentage of individuals or families for whom no land was first surveyed, as a fair and equitable construction of the treaty land entitlement obligation. In other words, if ten percent of the band population had been overlooked at the time of first survey, then ten percent of the band's current population would be considered to have suffered a shortfall and that would be the basis for calculating how much additional land the band would now be entitled to. This would mean that the descendants of those families which were not included in the original survey would now be accounted for, while the decedents of those families which were included in that survey would not. This became known as the "equity formula."

The Commission then applied the new formula to the claims of the 27 bands who had claimed Treaty land entitlement. At that time it would have meant that the total number of acres to be awarded would be 841,419 if the settlement took place forthwith. Because band populations are increasing at the rate of about 3% per year, the number of acres could be expected to increase up to the date of the various settlements.

The Commissioner in his report went on to recognize that there were insufficient amounts of suitable and available Crown land in many parts of the survey districts of the province to meet the Treaty land entitlement. In order to resolve this dilemma, it was proposed that the bands be paid cash equivalent to the value of the acreage to which they were entitled. They could then go on to the open market and purchase their land entitlement directly. A value of $262.19 per acre was proposed as the appropriate value and the total estimated cost of this proposal would amount to $220,611,648.

The "honour payment"

Not content to put forward this most generous formula which went far and beyond the formula based on first survey, the Commissioner went one step further. He made much of the fact that in 1976/77 the overly generous Saskatchewan formula was agreed to between the federal and provincial governments and the Federation of Saskatchewan Indians and that to go back on this formula by replacing it with the new one would amount to a breach of faith with the Indians.

The Commissioner recommended that provision be made to make-up the difference from the Saskatchewan formula or "for generations to come the elders will relate how Canada and Saskatchewan broke their promise and cheated the Indians. A legacy of mistrust and bitterness will thus be transmitted. This legacy would be as a poison to Indian/non-Indian relations;" [8]

Accordingly, the Commissioner recommended that for every band which would receive less land under the equity formula than it would have received under the earlier Saskatchewan formula, a dollar value be assigned for each acre of the difference and a cash payment be made accordingly. Because the net difference in acreage between the application of the two formulas amounted to 524,583 acres, the Commissioner calculated that an additional amount of $74,340,064 would be required for this purpose. This additional dollar amount, which is dubbed an "honour payment", would top up the $220,611,648 due under the equity formula.

When this sum is added to the earlier figure, the Commission estimated the total cost of the equity formula model to be $294,951,712. As we shall see, this amount proved to be $150 million too little. It was proposed that the sum be paid over a period of 7-10 years based on a complicated cost-sharing formula between the federal and provincial government.

As a further addition, the Commission then recommended a payment of up to $50,000 per year for two years be made to assist each band in the "implementation of this proposed settlement."

Saskatchewan Treaty Land Entitlement Framework Agreement

On September 22, 1992, a Saskatchewan Treaty Land Entitlement Framework Agreement, which accepted the recommendations set out above, was entered into between the Government of Canada, the

Government of Saskatchewan, and the Federation of Saskatchewan Indian Nations.

Thus governments committed themselves in Saskatchewan alone to an amount which has grown because of still further claims to $446,404,164.03 in entitlement money to 26 bands over a 12 year period. These monies would enable entitlement bands to purchase up to 1,576,851.63 acres of land in Saskatchewan.

Pause for a moment to consider the implications of this. It means that 26 Indian bands in Saskatchewan have now been given the right and the money to buy up land all over Saskatchewan equivalent in area, in the aggregate, to the size of 1,500 Stanley Parks! The land need not be contiguous to existing reserves. Once it is purchased, it is given reserve status which means two things. First, the property comes off the municipal or provincial tax role. Secondly, because it becomes an Indian reserve, all income generated on the reserve is non-taxable and services provided to the reserve are also non-taxable. Whether the good people of Saskatchewan have yet realized it or not, over the next dozen years there is a potential for hundreds of new reserves to sprout up like mushrooms all over Saskatchewan with a corresponding erosion of the tax base. Figure 9 summarizes what treaty land entitlements in Saskatchewan are costing the Canadian and Saskatchewan taxpayer. Bear in mind that reserves had already been given to these bands shortly after the date of treaty, 75 or more years ago.

How this will work out in specific cases is illuminating. Turtleford MLA Lloyd Johnson views the framework agreement as "a most positive step" for three bands in his constituency. His newsletter, dated April 1994, shows:-

The Witchekan Lake Band

- In 1916, although not under treaty, a reserve of 4,237 acres was set up based on a band membership of 32.
- In 1950, the band adhered to Treaty 6; population, 58 people. Subsequently, 37 people joined the band bringing the band membership to 95.
- The band's claim is that only 32 of 95 of their number (i.e. 35%) were allocated land.
- But the band membership now numbers 389.
- Under treaty land entitlement, this band will receive an additional 32,443 acres.

Figure 9 - Treaty land entitlements
of 26 bands under the Saskatchewan Framework Agreement

Band	Actual Shortfall in acres	(a) Additional Acreage under Equity Formula	(b) Cash equivalent of Column (a)	(c) Additional "Honour Payment"	Total cash (b) + (c)
Beardy's	11,648	71,138	$19,175,704.20		$19,175,704.20
Canoe Lake	6,885	49,973	$13,412,333.40		$13,412,333.40
English River	13,041	37,647	$10,457,408.20		$10,457,408.20
Flying Dust	6,788	33,910	$9,196,342.56		$9,196,342.56
Joseph Bighead	3,615	16,435	$4,471,781.19	$1,739,862.00	$6,211,643.19
Keeseekoose	7,552	48,677	$13,102,397.77	$4,895,741.73	$17,998,139.50
Little Pine	30,720	92,870	$25,732,066.50		$25,732,066.50
Moosomin	24,960	75,355	$20,880,639.80		$20,880,639.80
Mosquito	20,096	33,153	$9,596,792.38		$9,596,792.38
Muskeg Lake	3,072	13,386	$3,647,814.97	$4,994,413.88	$8,642,228.85
Muskowekwan	18,121	51,556	$14,332,798.30		$14,332,798.30
Nut L./ Yellow Quill	11,802	101,471	$27,135,653.73	$2,241,077.37	$29,376,731.10
Ochapowace	44,928	54,160	$16,222,124.10		$16,222,124.10
Okanese	6,906	14,337	$4,069,921.10		$4,069,921.10
One Arrow	10,752	58,616	$15,852,313.20		$15,852,313.20
Onion Lake	25,984	108,551	$29,630,152.00		$29,630,152.00
Pelican Lake	5,962	35,715	$9,632,302.71		$9,632,302.71
Peter Ballantyne	22,466	234,249	$62,428,657.00		$62,428,657.00
Piapot	39,073	81,081	$23,017,020.50		$23,017,020.50
Poundmaker	13,824	47,687	$13,125,250.40		$13,125,250.40
Red Pheasant	20,118	72,332	$19,869,976.50		$19,869,976.50
Saulteaux	16,845	56,144	$15,478,470.80		$15,478,470.80
Starblanket	4,672	11,236	$3,156,095.85		$3,156,095.85
Sweetgrass	8,192	23,914	$6,638,656.96		$6,638,656.96
Thunderchild	38,464	120,816	$33,407,734.60		$33,407,734.60
Witchekan Lake	7,923	32,443	$8,862,660.29		$8,862,660.29
Totals:	424,408	1,576,852	$432,533,069.10	$13,871,094.99	$446,404,164.03

The Pelican Lake Band

- Reserve lands of 8,481 acres was established in 1917 for the band members covered by treaty.
- 59 additional Indians "took treaty" in 1949 and 1950 without additional reserved lands being given.
- The band's claim is that only 59% of band's earlier membership received land.
- But the band membership now numbers 683.
- Under treaty land entitlement, this band will receive an additional 35,715 acres.

The Thunderchild Band

- Accepted the terms of Treaty 6 in 1874.
- The band numbered 185 people at first survey in 1881 and 21,440 acres was reserved.
- Transfers from other bands and adherence to treaty brought earlier number of band members up to 468 without increase in reserve land.
- The band claims that only 36% of earlier band membership received land.
- But the band membership now numbers 1,470.
- Under treaty land entitlement the band is entitled to another 120,816 acres—120 times the size of Stanley Park!

These three bands are typical of what is happening all over Saskatchewan. Frankly, I consider the largesse being meted out under this program to border on the obscene. Persons unborn at the time these Prairie treaties were entered into 75 or more years ago are included in the calculations for these large amounts of land. No regard is given to whether these people need the land in pursuit of an agricultural lifestyle. In fact only 44% of the 33,000 people which make up the membership of these 26 bands in Saskatchewan live on reserves.[9]

Manitoba Treaty Land Entitlements[10]

Manitoba's negotiations have been following Saskatchewan's lead. In October, 1993, a protocol on Treaty land entitlements was signed by the Indian chiefs of Manitoba and the federal and provincial governments. To date 26 bands have put forward claims.

Alberta Treaty Land Entitlements[11]

Alberta is prepared to settle these kind of specific claims but on a band-by-band basis, contending there are too many differences to reach a package deal. The province is of the view that it needs to get directly involved in negotiations to defend its interests. As one provincial official said, "since the federal government acts as a trustee for the Indians it has an obligation to act in the best interests of the beneficiaries of their trust."

By using genealogical records such as church lists, the province of Alberta discovered that up to 20% of those claimed as being missed at first survey were not eligible because they, or previous generations, had received land at other reserves.

Ontario Treaty Land Entitlements

A status report on native land claims in Ontario recently compiled by the Ontario Federation of Anglers and Hunters paints a daunting picture. No less than 114 claims have been submitted and are under active review. At least 100 of them fall into the category of specific claims including claims for treaty land entitlement. The rest are comprehensive land claims to areas over which there have never been treaties or land claim settlements. British Columbians have been encouraged to believe that their province is the only one that hasn't entered into treaties with their native peoples. The fact is that there are significant portions of Ontario, and Quebec as well, not covered by treaty.[12]

Counting the cost

Figure 10 prepared from information gleaned from various sources shows that federal and provincial governments have paid or have agreed to pay $754,756,797 in specific claims and treaty land entitlements to date and to give 355,620 acres of land in settlement of these claims. This, of course, is entirely separate from the massive fiscal obligation which the federal government has assumed for comprehensive land claims settled in the NWT and the Yukon and which governments are likely to assume in the future in B.C., Quebec, Ontario, and elsewhere.

Figure 10 - Cost of specific claim settlements to 1994

	Treaty land entitlements	Other specific claims	Totals Acreage	Totals Cash
B.C.				
Acreage		36,937	**36,937**	
Cash		$55,909,089		**$ 55,909,089**
Alberta				
Acreage	85,582	11,950	**97,532**	
Cash	$127,126,577	$43,125,000		**$170,251,577**
Sask				
Acreage	97,112	23,170	**120,282**	
Cash	$454,368,157	$38,627,536		**$492,995,693**
Man				
Acreage	100,000	378	**100,378**	
Cash	$9,000,000	$2,656,107		**$ 11,656,107**
Ont				
Acreage		493	**493**	
Cash		$12,575,697		**$ 12,575,697**
Que				
Acreage		0	**0**	
Cash		$2,686,187		**$ 2,686,187**
Yukon				
Acreage		0	**0**	
Cash		$1,716,447		**$ 1,716,447**
Maritimes				
Acreage		0	**0**	
Cash		$6,966,000		**$ 6,966,000**
Acreage	**282,694**	**72,928**	**355,622**	
Cash	**$590,494,734**	**$164,262,063**		**$754,756,797**

It is reported that the 1994 Public Accounts of Canada show $8.3 billion in contingent liabilities attributed to DIAND. The report says that a major part of this is made up of specific claims and so-called "treaty obligations" of the kind dealt with in this chapter. What is even more disconcerting is that the report goes on to state that there are another 460 specific native claims and lawsuits that haven't been tallied up and don't form any part of the contingent liabilities shown in the report.[13]

Observations and conclusions

The Specifics Claim process is an ongoing saga with many such claims still to be finalized. This holds true as well for the particular kind of specific claim known as treaty land entitlements. What the final cost will be, if indeed finality can ever be achieved, remains to be seen.

Surely all reasonable persons who have endured reading about the litany of largesse described in this chapter must conclude that the process of addressing alleged grievances has gone very seriously awry and should be substantially modified.

It is no coincidence that our jurisprudence has established strict time limits and other evidenciary rules that determine whether claims are legitimate. People pass off the scene, evidence is lost or discarded, and recollection of events become dim with the passage of time. To allow the specific claims described in the earlier part of this chapter to be advanced now after the passage of scores of years—and in some cases over a hundred years—is a travesty of all that Canadians know to be fair and just. No other class of Canadians is similarly privileged either in the courts or in their dealings with governments.

As far as treaty land entitlements are concerned, there is some doubt whether there were any significant shortfalls of land at all on a tribe-by-tribe basis (rather than a band-by-band basis within a tribe). One DIAND official, knowledgeable on these matters, acknowledged that, there were no doubt "shortfalls" to some bands, but if you took the lands given at first survey to the tribe as a whole, then shortfalls to some bands would, in many cases, be more than offset by excess lands given to other bands.

This litany of largesse also raises general questions about the strict adherence to treaty obligations. How is it that when it comes to invoking treaties, the native people demand every jot and tittle of compliance—even to the extent of pressing hundred year old grievances. On the other hand, governments for their part have extended benefits to all Canadians, especially natives, far and beyond anything ever contemplated by the terms of any treaty: medicare, welfare, economic assistance, higher education, housing, pensions, tax exemptions, etc. Surely it is not unreasonable for governments to say that they have more than "paid in full" any and all obligations arising under these old treaties and, from here on, treaty Indians will be dealt with on the same basis as ordinary Canadians.

A final lesson to be learned has to do with the matter of finality and certainty. Present land claim policy is being sold to the Canadian people by Mr. Cashore and others on the basis that the settlement of outstanding claims will bring finality and certainty for natives, non-natives and governments. If the relatively short and simple provisions of the earlier treaties has given rise now to the outlandish specific claims and treaty land entitlements described in this chapter, then the infinitely more complicated modern day land claim agreements recently concluded and presently contemplated will give rise to endless rancour and claims of non-fulfilment "as long as the sun shines and the rivers flow."

Chapter 5 - Footnotes:

1.   Memorandum of John Cashore, Minister of Aboriginal Affairs, *Questions from Mike Scott, M.P.,* Province of B.C., July 7, 1994.

2.   DIAND, *Federal Policy for the Settlement of Native Claims* (Government of Canada, March, 1993).

3.   From Summaries and Working Documents prepared by DIAND.

4.   DIAND, Ibid.

5.   Office of the Treaty Commissioner of Saskatchewan, Explanatory Paper on Treaty Land Entitlement, Saskatoon, (undated).

6.   Office of the Treaty Commissioner of Saskatchewan, Report and Recommendations on Treaty Land Entitlement, May, 1990.

7.   Ibid.

8.   *Saskatchewan Treaty Commission Report,* 53-54.

9.   Indian and Northern Affairs, Canada, *Indian Register, Population by Sex and Residence, 1993,* 32-39.

10.   From information supplied by Manitoba Department of Northern Affairs.

11.   From information supplied by the Provincial negotiator's office, Alberta Native Land Claims.

12.   *Status Report on Native Land Claims in Ontario,* The Ontario Federation of Anglers and Hunters, August, 1994.

13.   "Taxpayers face $8B tab for native land claims," *Ottawa Citizen,* October 21, 1994.

The Mother of all Trials

"Aboriginal persons and commentators often mention the fact that the Indians of this province were never conquered by force of arms, nor have they entered into treaties with the Crown. Unfair as it may seem to Indians or others on philosophical grounds, these are not relevant considerations. The events of the last 200 years are far more significant than any military conquest or treaties would have been. The reality of Crown ownership of the soil of all the lands of the province is not open to question. . . . "
Chief Justice Allan McEachern, *Delgamuukw* Case, 1991.

Anticipating a result that would strengthen their hand in future land claim negotiations, 35 Gitksan and 13 Wet'suwet'en Chiefs commenced litigation on October 23, 1984 by filing a Writ of Summons and Statement of Claim in the Supreme Court of British Columbia. They alleged that, from time immemorial, they and their ancestors occupied 22,000 square miles in British Columbia and claimed they were entitled to a judgment declaring:

(a) that they own the territory;

(b) that they are entitled to govern the territory
by aboriginal laws which supersede the laws of
British Columbia; and

(c) that they are entitled to compensation for all
resources removed from the territory from 1858
to date.

The territory claimed in northwestern British Columbia is almost equivalent in size to New Brunswick and encompasses the towns of Hazelton, Smithers, Houston, and Burns Lake.

The law suit was brought against the Attorney General in right of British Columbia (the B.C. government) and the Province successfully moved to add the Attorney General of Canada as a co-defendant. The case came to be known as the *Delgamuukw* case, after the first named of the chiefs in the court documents.

From the plaintiffs' perspective, this was to be the judicial determination which, once and for all, would settle in their favour, and by logical extension to other bands in the province, the outright ownership of their so-called "traditional territories." It would also give them the right to govern themselves by aboriginal laws passed in aboriginal legislative bodies to the exclusion of provincial laws. In some respects this was to be the lawsuit long sought by the native leadership in this province as far back as 1910.

The legal resources engaged on the case alone were enormous. There were no less than nine legal counsel for the natives; eight for the Province and five for the Attorney General of Canada. No full accounting has ever been made of the legal costs of this trial and its subsequent appeal to the Court of Appeal.

From figures disclosed under the *Access to Information Act,* from 1980 to 1992, the Government of Canada paid in excess of $12 million to lawyers acting for native bands involved in litigation of various kinds **against** the B.C. Government. Of this, it appears that over $8 million was paid to counsel representing the natives in this case.[1] This, of course, does not include the fees of those lawyers on the government side (both federal and provincial)—also paid by the taxpayer—which could well be of equal amount or more. That is just legal and expert witness fees. It does not include the untold cost of bureaucrats' time at both the federal and provincial level in researching archival and other material nor the cost of official reporters and court personnel engaged in administrative support of all kinds.

Despite the high costs involved, in my view, it was essential to obtain the judicial determination which a decision in this case would and did provide on the subject of aboriginal title.

Conducted before Chief Justice Allan McEachern, the trial proved to be the "mother of all trials" in the annals of British Columbia judicial history. It lasted 374 days between May 11, 1987 and June 30, 1990. A good portion of the trial took place at Smithers, smack in the middle of the territory claimed; the balance of the trial in Vancouver.

The magnitude of the task is best described in the Chief Justice's own words:

> "A total of 61 witnesses gave evidence at trial, many using translators from their native Gitksan or Wet'suwet'en language; "Word Spellers" to assist the Official Reporters were required for many witnesses; a further 15 witnesses gave their evidence

on Commission; 53 Territorial Affidavits were filed; 30 deponents were cross-examined out of Court; there are 23,503 pages of transcript evidence at trial; 5,898 pages of transcript of argument; 3,039 pages of commission evidence and 2,553 pages of cross examination on affidavits (all evidence and oral arguments are conveniently preserved in hard copy and on diskettes); about 9,200 exhibits were filed at trial comprising, I estimate, well over 50,000 pages; the plaintiffs' draft outline of argument comprises 3,250 pages, the provinces' 1,975 pages, and Canada's over 1,000 pages; there are 5,977 pages of transcript of argument in hard copy and on diskettes. All parties filed some excerpts from the exhibits they referred to in argument. The province alone submitted 28 huge binders of such documents. At least 15 binders of Reply Argument were left with me during that stage of the trial.

"The Plaintiffs filed 23 large binders of authorities. The province supplemented this with 8 additional volumes, and Canada added 1 volume..." [2]

To familiarize himself with the area the Chief Justice took a 3-day helicopter and highway view of the area and took automobile trips into the territory during many of the evenings of the 50 days he sat in Smithers. The evidence adduced was intensely detailed and involved a painstaking and exhaustive examination of oral history, genealogy, sociology, anthropology, conventional history, and relevant law. From the conclusion of the hearing it took the Chief Justice almost a year of deliberations before pronouncing judgment and issuing his reasons for judgment of some 394 pages on March 8, 1991.

The findings of the Chief Justice

The judgment of the Chief Justice was unequivocal. It dismissed outright the natives' claims to full ownership of the territory and legislative jurisdiction (or self-government) over it. It also dismissed their claim for damages. Moreover, through a careful scrutiny of the legislative history of the Colony of British Columbia, the powers entrusted to the Colony's governors, and the land law regime of the Colony, the Chief Justice concluded that Colonial actions exhibited a clear and plain intention to extinguish aboriginal interests to all the lands within the Colony thereby allowing the Crown to give an unburdened title to settlers. In short, he concluded that the aboriginal rights which may have existed in the Colony, including the territory of the plaintiffs, were extinguished, by operation of law, by the time B.C. entered Confederation in 1871. This extinguishment finding did not extend to rights in reserve lands or fishing rights.

On the question of ownership

The Chief Justice relied on the common law as enunciated by numerous judicial authorities by which he was bound. First among them was the nineteenth century decision in the *St. Catherine's Milling* case. Although essentially a dispute between Canada and Ontario as to which level of government had proprietary ownership over 32,000 sq. miles of territory in Ontario ceded by treaty to the Ojibway Indians in 1873, the case is of fundamental importance in its findings as to the nature of aboriginal rights. In those days, Canada's highest court was the Privy Council in London. It is illuminating to set out the views of Mr. Justice Taschereau, who gave one of the majority judgments of the Supreme Court of Canada, which heard the case before the appeal to London. He found that the practice of the Crown in entering into treaties was not a recognition of Indian title but was done as a matter of goodwill and not legal necessity.

Justice Taschereau states at p.647:

"It was further argued for the appellants that the principles which have always guided the Crown since the cession in its dealing with the Indians amount to a recognition of their title to a beneficiary interest in the soil. There is, in my opinion, no foundation for this contention. For obvious political reasons and motives of humanity and benevolence, it has, no doubt, been the general policy of the Crown, as it had been at the times of the French authorities, to respect the claims of the Indians. But this, though it unquestionably gives them a title to the favourable consideration of the Government, does not give them any title in law, any title that a Court of justice can recognize as against the Crown."[3]

To find otherwise, the learned Justice said, would be to deduce:

"... that all progress of civilization and development in this country is and always has been at the mercy of the Indian race. Some of the writers cited by the appellants, influenced by sentimental and philanthropic considerations, do not hesitate to go as far. But legal and constitutional principles are in direct antagonism with their theories. (pp.647-9)"[4]

The Supreme Court of Canada concluded that, at the time of Confederation some six years **before** the Treaty, these were Crown lands which, by virtue of S.109 and 117 of the *BNA Act, 1867*, belonged to Ontario rather than Canada.

On appeal, the Privy Council upheld the decision of the Supreme Court of Canada with Lord Watson describing the rights which the Indians acquired under the Royal Proclamation of 1763, as not being proprietary or property interests at all but rather "a personal and usufructuary right, dependent on the goodwill of the sovereign." Lord Watson went on to say: "The Crown has all along had a present proprietary estate in the land, upon which the Indian title was a mere burden."[5]

Concerning the *St. Catherine's Milling* case, Chief Justice McEachern said:

> "...the description of being a "burden" on the Crown's title is hardly descriptive of a proprietary interest in the Indians. Standing alone, *St. Catherine's Milling* is authority against aboriginal ownership and jurisdiction and it establishes that aboriginal rights exist "at the pleasure of the Crown." Those are judicial pronouncements of fundamental importance."[6]

After reviewing other judicial decisions from throughout the Commonwealth and in the United States, the Chief Justice in *Delgamuukw* summed up the law on the question of ownership as follows:

> "In my view, it is part of the law of nations, which has become part of the common law, that discovery and occupation of the lands of this continent by European nations, or occupation and settlement, gave rise to a right of sovereignty. Such sovereignty in North America was established in part by Royal grant as with the Hudson's Bay Company in 1670; by conquest, as in Quebec in 1759; by treaty with other sovereign nations, as with the United States settling the International border; by occupation, as in many parts of Canada, particularly the prairies and British Columbia; and partly by the exercise of sovereignty by the British Crown in British Columbia through the creation of Crown Colonies on Vancouver Island and the mainland.

> "Aboriginal persons and commentators often mention the fact that the Indians of this province were never conquered by force

of arms, nor have they entered into treaties with the Crown. Unfair as it may seem to Indians or others on philosophical grounds, these are not relevant considerations. The events of the last 200 years are far more significant than any military conquest or treaties would have been. The reality of Crown ownership of the soil of all the lands of the province is not open to question and actual dominion for such a long period is far more pervasive than the outcome of a battle or a war could ever be. The law recognises Crown ownership of the territory in a federal state now known as Canada pursuant to its Constitution and laws.

"In my judgement, the foregoing propositions are absolute. The real question is whether, within that constitutional framework, the plaintiffs have any aboriginal interests which the law recognizes as a burden upon the title of the Crown."[7]

On the question of self-government

Having categorically dismissed the natives' claim to ownership, the Chief Justice was equally firm in rejecting their claim to a right to pass their own laws over the territory of the Gitksan and Wet'suwet'en people to the exclusion of the laws of British Columbia. The Chief Justice's finding has the effect of totally demolishing the much touted doctrine of the inherent right to self-government, for if there had been some constitutional or legal basis for that doctrine the learned justice would have been obliged to recognize it. Instead, as the Chief Justice said:

"...neither this nor any Court has the jurisdiction to undo the establishment of the Colony, Confederation, or the constitutional arrangements which are now in place. Separate sovereignty or legislative authority, as a matter of law, is beyond the authority of any Court to award...

"The plaintiffs must understand that Canada and the provinces, as a matter of law, are sovereign, each in their own jurisdictions, which makes it impossible for aboriginal peoples unilaterally to achieve the independent or separate status some of them seek. In the language of the street, and in the contemplation of the law, the plaintiffs are subject to the same law and the same Constitution as everyone else. The Constitution can only be changed in the manner provided by the Constitution itself."[8]

On the nature of aboriginal rights

Having dismissed their claims to ownership and jurisdiction, the Chief Justice went on to deal with the nature of aboriginal rights. Since aboriginal rights do not consist of ownership and jurisdiction, what do they consist of? The Chief Justice held that they included all those sustenance practices and the gathering of all those products of the land and waters of the territory which the ancestors of the Indians practised before the arrival of European civilisation, including wood, food and clothing, and products of their culture for ornamentation—in short, what their ancestors obtained from the land and waters for their aboriginal life.[9]

It is equally important to note what the Chief Justice did not include within the definition of aboriginal rights. He states that aboriginal rights "do not include commercial activities, even those related to land or water resource gathering, except in compliance with the general law of the province." In short he found there is no aboriginal right to conduct commercial activities even those related to the soil.

On the question of extinguishment

The Chief Justice found that aboriginal rights exist at the pleasure of the Crown and may be extinguished when the intention of the Crown is clear and plain. He then reviewed the legislative history of the colony and concluded that there was a clear and plain intention to extinguish such aboriginal rights. The Chief Justice stated:

> "I find the constitutional and legal arrangements put in place in the colony were totally inconsistent with aboriginal rights the continuation of which would have prevented the Crown from the settlement and development of the colony. As the intention of the Crown must be ascertained objectively from a consideration of all the circumstances in their historical setting, I find the Crown clearly and plainly intended to, and did, extinguish aboriginal rights in the colony by the arrangements it made for the development of the colony including provision of conveying titles and tenures unencumbered by any aboriginal rights and by the other arrangements it made for Indians."[10]

Having ruled out land ownership, jurisdiction and now other aboriginal rights, the Chief Justice did not totally rule out certain limited native interests. He found that the history of the colony supported the view that the native people were promised the right to those areas reserved to them, namely their villages, agricultural lands and fishing sites. Beyond this he found that the native people had the right to fish and hunt for sustenance purposes on unoccupied Crown lands. He found that this remains "until such time as the land is dedicated to another purpose" and that this is sufficient to impose a fiduciary obligation on the Crown to continue to extend these rights. Note however, that these rights were to be exercised for subsistence purposes only and subject to the general laws of the province and exercised on Crown land only until dedicated to another purpose.

Government reaction to McEachern's judgment

Of all of the matters constitutional which preoccupied British Columbians during 1991, and there were many, without doubt the most significant was the judgment of the Chief Justice in this case delivered on March 8. Although it was an unqualified victory for the provincial and federal governments, when the decision came down the reaction on the Court House steps among provincial officials was sombre—almost crestfallen. One exclaimed that the province certainly did not expect **that** outcome!

The fact is that in some parts of the bureaucracy in Victoria the hard-line legal position taken by counsel for the Province in the law suit was not strongly supported. Government lawyers involved in the case, who assisted outside counsel, did a superb job in advancing the interests of the province but the policy-makers, particularly in the Ministry of Native Affairs, held different views.

As a result, when the decision came down, the Attorney General of the day, Russell Fraser, no doubt influenced by the policy-makers, adopted weasel words by way of government response. He is quoted as saying: "Let's not consider this to be a win-lose situation, but an opportunity. The government is committed to working with natives throughout the province to resolve their legitimate differences."[11] "Legitimate differences" in whose eyes he did not say. In the eyes of those who had lost the case, resolving their legitimate differences meant nothing short of ownership and jurisdiction—the very things they had lost in the law suit. Premier Vander Zalm took a slightly different tack. He said "We'll continue to meet and negotiate with native people in order to provide them with social and economic programs and opportunities."[12]

The judgment ought to have had a profound effect on the direction of public policy at both the federal and provincial level on the whole question of aboriginal rights, including land claims. But alas, the decision was largely ignored. Worse still, since then governments at both levels have not batted an eye in their zealous desire to "settle land claims". The decision, which was to mean so much, has been expunged from the lexicon of all those pressing for land claim settlements. Incredibly the report of the B.C. Claims Task Force released three months after the McEachern judgment ignores the case and recites a history of the aboriginal people in this province that is greatly at variance with that found by the Chief Justice.

Switching counsel

October 1991 saw the election of an NDP government in British Columbia. By this time the *Delgamuukw* case was on its way to the Court of Appeal but would not be heard for several months. In March 1992 the NDP fired the team of five lawyers from the Vancouver firm of Russell and DuMoulin that secured the province's Supreme Court victory and replaced it with Swinton & Company's Bryan Williams who, it is reported, had previously advised natives in land use disputes.[13] At the time, Attorney General Colin Gabelmann is reported to have said he was approving the change in lead counsel "to seek a fresh perspective" on the government's legal argument. Bryan Williams was chosen to provide that fresh perspective because, Gabelmann is reported to have said, he was a well-known lawyer considered sympathetic to aboriginal claims.[14]

Provincial Minister of Aboriginal Affairs, Andrew Petter, saw the province's shift in legal position as a way to have the Court of Appeal "move the issues on to the negotiating table."[15] Clearly the NDP government hoped that the Court of Appeal would give legal approbation to its previously ill-founded support for the concept of the inherent right to aboriginal title and native self-government.

There being no longer any party involved in the appeal that was prepared to uphold many of the findings of the Chief Justice's judgment, since the province had substantially shifted its ground, the Court took the rare step of appointing Russell and DuMoulin—previously Counsel for the province—as "friends of the Court."

Decision of the Court of Appeal

A five member panel of the Court of Appeal comprised of Justices Taggart, Lambert, Hutcheon, Macfarlane and Wallace heard the appeal over a two month period from May to July, 1992, sitting in Vancouver. By this time the number of legal counsel engaged in the case had expanded to over 40. This was largely because a great number of intervenors were added to the lawsuit and allowed to make submissions. Some of the intervenors represented native interests while others represented industry associations and similar interests.

The hearing concluded on July 3, 1992, but judgment was not forthcoming until June 25th the following year. The majority judgments were written by Justices Macfarlane and Wallace. Mr. Justice Taggart gave no reasons, but concurred with Macfarlane. The remaining two Justices, Lambert and Hutcheon, wrote their own reasons dissenting from the majority in varying degrees.

The law then, arising out of this case, can be said to be that pronounced by Mr. Justice Macfarlane and, where applicable, supported by Mr. Justice Wallace. The dissenting judgments are beyond the scope of this consideration.

The decision of the Court of Appeal on the main issues is as follows:

On the question of ownership

The Court supported the finding of the trial judge that the plaintiffs had not established a claim to ownership over the vast territory in question except in locations already within reserves.

On the question of self-government

Likewise the Court of Appeal supported the finding of the trial judge rejecting the plaintiffs' claim to jurisdiction, or the right to pass their own laws over the territory and thereby superseding federal and provincial laws. The Court held, as every court in Canada that has examined the issue to date has held, that sections 91 and 92 of the *Constitution Act, 1867* exhaustively distributed legislative power in Canada to either the Parliament of Canada or the legislatures of the provinces.

On this point Mr. Justice Macfarlane states:

"With respect, I think that the trial judge was correct in his view that when the Crown imposed English law on all the inhabitants of the colony and, in particular, when British Columbia entered Confederation, the Indians became subject to the legislative authorities in Canada and their laws. In 1871, two levels of

government were established in British Columbia. The division of governmental powers between Canada and the Provinces left no room for a third order of government."

"Any doubt that aboriginal people are subject to this distribution is eliminated by s.91(24), which awards legislative competence in relation to Indians to Parliament." [16]

This finding strikes the death knell to the much touted concept of the inherent right to native self-government and yet our politicians at both levels continue to spout the idea as having some validity. It doesn't.

On the question of extinguishment

All five judges of the Court of Appeal overturned the decision of the trial judge on the issue of extinguishment, holding that **limited** aboriginal rights continued to exist and were not extinguished before 1871.

On the nature of the aboriginal rights not extinguished

The view of the majority—and thus the law established by the decision—is expressed by Mr. Justice Macfarlane who held that the nature and content of aboriginal rights are determined by asking what the ancestors of the claimants regarded as practices or activities which were "an integral part of their distinctive culture" at the time British sovereignty was asserted in 1846. This is similar to how the trial judge characterized aboriginal rights.

Put another way, the Court characterized aboriginal rights as the aboriginal community's "right" to engage in those practices and activities associated with the use of the land they occupied that were traditional, integral and distinctive to their society and way of life at the time sovereignty was exercised by the Crown. This is a most important finding for it effectively limits the scope of aboriginal rights to those which are related to traditional activities.

The Court went on to find that the nature of those rights possessed by a particular aboriginal community were fact and site specific and could only be determined by an understanding of the history of that community, the location of its traditional territories, and the type of activity pursued within those territories prior to European contact.

The Court held that practices which arose because of "European influences" do not qualify for protection as aboriginal rights. This would include commercial trapping, commercial forestry activities, commercial fishing, and presumably most mining except for surface mining of shale, argillite and other stones integral to the aboriginal society.

To sum up, the findings of the Court of Appeal, not unlike the trial judge, were exceedingly modest in comparison to what the plaintiffs had sought. The Court found no ownership rights, no rights to inherent self-government, no expansive definition of aboriginal rights or title, and what limited aboriginal rights it did find does not include the right to engage in commercial activities. At best it found a right to engage in those traditional activities for sustenance and ceremonial purposes, which were distinctive to the particular aboriginal society prior to colonial contact. This, the court found, is the sum and substance of aboriginal title and rights related to land in British Columbia.

Import of judgment

Due pause is necessary at this point to consider the full import of the Court of Appeal judgment, for it knocks away the props from much of the aboriginal agenda being pursued by the native leadership with such acquiesence on the part of politicians now in power both federally and provincially. The first point to stress is that the Court of Appeal's findings are the law of the land. This is not just one other opinion or point of view to be given equal weight to the opinions of philosophers, sociologists, consultants, advisers, politicians and sundry soothsayers. This is the law on the nature of aboriginal interests on land in B.C.[17]

Aboriginal rights are not a proprietary land right at all. This means that the current land claim process begun at the federal level in 1973, described in such detail earlier in this book and now being pursued in British Columbia and elsewhere, which sees the ownership of vast areas of land being conveyed to the natives, is entirely without legal support. It bears repeating that in the NWT and the Yukon, recently concluded land claim agreements have seen the outright ownership of land, in the aggregate, amounting to an area larger than half of Ontario, conveyed to less than 25,000 people.

Does a similar fate await British Columbians when one considers that outright ownership of land is part of the claims being advanced by more than 40 bands representing a similarly small percentage of the population? One such claim by the Musqueam Band covers the City of Vancouver. That band numbers 850 persons.

Admittedly these are "claims" and have not yet been subject to negotiation, but can ordinary British Columbians be confident in the ability of their governments—both federal and provincial—to represent their interests in these forthcoming negotiations? Citizens ought to be assured that governments will not put on the negotiating table benefits greater than those which the courts have found constitute aboriginal rights.

Appeal to the Supreme Court of Canada

On October 22, 1993, the Gitksan and Wet'suwet'en filed an appeal in the *Delgamuukw* case to the Supreme Court of Canada. The Court granted leave to appeal on March 9, 1994. Such an appeal would take months to prepare and a hearing date could not be expected until 1995. Suddenly on June 13, 1994, the parties announced the signing of an agreement to adjourn their litigation so as to pursue a negotiated settlement instead.

As we have seen, the gains achieved by the natives in this law suit thus far have been modest compared to the claims put forward. This modest result corresponds with other litigation of this nature put forward in other parts of Canada such as the Bear Island case in Ontario.[18] The Bear Island case can be said to be to Ontario what the *Delgamuukw* case is to B.C. The case, with an array of 20 lawyers, representing the parties and many intervenors, dealt with issues strikingly similar to those in the *Delgamuukw* case. Both the Supreme Court of Ontario and the Court of Appeal of Ontario ruled against the natives, finding that if there ever had been any aboriginal rights, they had been effectively extinguished. The Supreme Court of Canada on August 15, 1991, dismissed the aboriginal appeal with a brief 2-page judgment supporting the substantial findings of fact of the trial judge, which were in many respects similar to Chief Justice McEachern's in the *Delgamuukw* case.

No small wonder then that the Gitksan and Wet'suwet'en have now pulled back from pursuing their appeal further in the *Delgamuukw* case to the Supreme Court of Canada. They would prefer to pursue a negotiated settlement with the Harcourt government and Ottawa.

Normally, any move to settle a matter out of court rather than to pursue costly litigation is a commendable development but there are several aspects to this arrangement that give cause for concern. First and foremost is the question of what principles will guide the provincial government as it enters upon these negotiations, particularly around the ownership of land. By all means negotiate the scope and dimension of the traditional aboriginal rights that the Courts have said these native people are entitled to, but to go beyond that is to bargain away the public assets of all British Columbians for which any government in power is only the present custodian for future generations.

A second troubling feature of this deal is that the government has agreed, once the adjournment is formally granted by the Court, to issue a joint statement regarding "mutual respect for the histories, the laws, customs and institutions of Gitksan and Wet'suwet'en societies and of the laws of British Columbia." The meaning of that is ominous. The findings of the Chief Justice at trial, undisturbed by the Court of Appeal, in effect has found that the histories, laws, customs and institutions of the Gitksan and Wet'suwet'en societies do not supersede the law making power of the legislature of British Columbia. It is to be hoped that what the Courts have found in this regard will not be conceded away.

Another troubling feature is the willingness of the Province to apparently negotiate these matters without the involvement of the federal government. The law and the Constitution are clear—the federal government must be a party—and perhaps the only government party—to treaties with Indian peoples.

Implementing the *Delgamuukw* Case

The decision of the Court of Appeal contemplates that processes will be established to determine, in a systematic and objective way, whether the modest kind of aboriginal rights it recognized, exist in specific situations. And, if so, whether those rights can be reconciled with other uses to which Crown land might be put.

Unless handled properly this case by case determination could become a complex and lengthy process. The process of the provincial government determining whether to grant timber licences, mineral claims, grazing permits, or Crown grants, in the light of a potential aboriginal interest, must be undertaken in a practical, reasonable and timely way. Unless properly handled, such a process is a recipe to grind B.C.'s resource-based economy to a halt, in a province where 92% of the territory is Crown land, most of which is under some form of tenure or another.

And yet this is precisely the direction that the present provincial government seems to be headed. In a major policy directive dated January 25, 1995[19] all government administrators engaged in granting land and resource tenures on Crown land are obliged to first make a determination if there are likely to be aboriginal rights affected. If there are, the land administrator is required to determine the implication that granting the resource interest would have on those rights and whether the resource interest can co-exist with the aboriginal right. This is a difficult task to impose on beleaguered bureaucrats responsible for making decisions on land and resource tenures. If the aboriginal peoples that might be affected are not willing to consult, then the policy paper says that this does not give the Province justification to go ahead. Such deference!

Three recent examples of the application of this overly rigid new Crown land policy underscore the difficulty:

• The good people of the Miocene and Spokin Lake area near Williams Lake wanted a fire hall to serve their district and approved it in a referendum in November 1993. A free Crown grant to 1.2 hectares was verbally promised by local provincial land administrators, as is the usual practice for such facilities. B.C. 21 even provided $75,000 in funding with the rest of the cost being borne by local taxpayers. The fire hall is built, but the word has now come from Victoria that the cabinet has turned down the issuance of a free Crown grant. Instead it will issue a 30-year lease at a one-time cost of $3,916. The difficulty is that the lease would provide that the improvements on the land, i.e., the fire hall, belong to the province. Apparently the reason for this last-minute change of heart is that aboriginal sources have said cases of this kind "may prejudice future [land-claim] negotiations."

• Near Penticton, Apex Resort has spent $1 million installing a water line and intake that would draw annually a modest amount of available water from Nickel Plate Lake. The water would more than meet Apex's future needs for residential, snowmaking and fire-prevention purposes. Apex proceeded in accordance with its 1990 development agreement with the province and sought and received approval from the Similkameen Improvement District, which has already received substantial benefits from Apex for the project, with more to come. All interim approvals were obtained and Apex is now ready to turn on the tap. Now the province says the matter must first go before the Seven Peaks Joint Technical Group, composed of equal representation from local native bands and government officials. This committee sprang into being under an agreement signed in December, 1994, between the province and the so-called Okanagan Nation comprising three Indian bands. In that agreement the province formally accepts the principle that the Okanagan Nation is "for all time protectors of the lands, waters and resources of the Okanagan traditional territory."

• Private-property owners are not immune. One would-be purchaser wishes to build a house on private land near Olalla. The subdivision has been completed, with all the normal approvals for the province having been obtained, including successful percolation tests. The purchaser has now applied for approval to install a septic tank. Provincial officials have advised him that the issue will have to be referred to the local Indian band for its consideration. The closest Indian reserve is 12 kms away!

Suggested approach

The only way the granting of Crown tenures will not totally bog down is if three criteria are adhered to:

1. The onus should be on the aboriginal group rather than on the province to make a reasonable effort to establish that there is an aboriginal right that would be seriously impaired by the proposed tenure. Instead, the policy paper puts the onus on the province.

2. The inquiry must be limited to the kind of aboriginal rights recognized by the Court of Appeal in the *Delgamuukw* case and **not** the more expansive category of aboriginal rights sought by the natives. It is the traditional activities and practices performed by aboriginal societies before the arrival of the white man—and these alone—that need to be reconciled with other tenures. Mr. Justice Macfarlane gave some examples:

   "Two or more interests in land less than fee simple can co-exist. A right of way for power lines may be reconciled with an aboriginal right to hunt over the same land, although a wildlife reserve might be incompatible with such a right . . .

   ". . . logging in forest areas may or may not impair or interfere with an aboriginal interest. For instance, interference may occur in areas which are integral to the distinctive culture of the particular aboriginal people, e.g., an area of religious significance or where cultural pursuits are followed. In other areas there may be no interference." [20]

3. There must be a strict time limit imposed on this process in each case. Unless an incompatible aboriginal interest can be clearly

established within that time frame, the Crown lease or other tenure should be granted.

If, on the other hand, the provincial government sees the application of this policy paper as a means of establishing Utopia and serenity in an imperfect world which is always subject to competing and countervailing forces, then only grid-lock, stagnation and chaos can be expected in the future administration of the Crown lands of the Province.

Conclusion

The law in this province on the subject of aboriginal interest as determined by the Court of Appeal in *Delgamuukw* must be the guiding light to settling land claims in this province. To proceed otherwise is to ignore the rule of law and the Constitution.

It is true that negotiating settlements is better than endless litigation. But that is not the issue. There is no need for more litigation. The issue is the framework in which such negotiations should be cast. Anything less than a framework which adheres to the law as found by the Courts in this case is to invite settlements based on avarice, arbitrariness, partiality and political expediency. To do that would be to jettison the rule of law, the Constitution, and democratic principles.

Chapter 6 - Footnotes:

1. Summary of Expenditures between 1980 and March 1, 1993, obtained from DIAND to support aboriginal litigation in B.C. prepared by B.C. Fisheries Survival Coalition.

2. *Reasons for Judgment of Chief Justice Allan McEachern,* Supreme Court of British Columbia, Delgamuukw vs. A.G., March 8, 1991, 1.

3. Ibid., 191.

4. Ibid.

5. Ibid., 192.

6. Ibid., 193.

7. Ibid., 81.

8. Ibid., 225.

9. Ibid., 228.

10. Ibid., 244-45.

11. Vaughn Palmer, "Socred's advantage turns bittersweet," *Vancouver Sun,* March 11, 1991, A8.

12. Ibid.

13. Jim Hume, "Gitskan switch raises questions", *Times-Colonist,* March 7, 1992, A5.

14. Ibid.

15. Hon. Andrew Petter, "Land claims need to be negotiated, not litigated," *Times-Colonist,* April 23, 1992, A4.

16. *Reasons for Judgment of Mr. Justice Macfarlane,* Court of Appeal of British Columbia, Delgamuukw vs. A.G., June 25, 1993, 44.

17. It is important to mention that there are three fairly recent decisions of the Supreme Court of Canada dealing with aboriginal rights but they did not have to squarely face the issue of aboriginal user rights on land. They are: *Guerin vs. the Queen* (1984), *R. vs. Sioui* (1990), and *R. vs. Sparrow* (1990). *Guerin* is a case about a breach of a fiduciary duty relating to reserve lands. *Sioui* is about a treaty. *Sparrow* is about priorities in relation to fishing rights.

18. *Bear Island Foundation et al. vs. A.G. for Ontario et al.,* 83 D.L.R. (4th), 381.

19. Province of British Columbia, *Crown Land Activities and Aboriginal Rights Policy Framework,* January 25, 1995.

20. *Reasons for Judgment of Mr. Justice Macfarlane,* Ibid., 55.

The Quest for
Native Sovereignty

*"We will not allow some other society to decide what we can
do and determine the limits of our authority."*
Grand Chief Ovide Mercredi, 1993.

Patriation of the Constitution

November 5, 1981 was a momentous day in the history of
Canada's constitutional development for on that day the Prime Minister
and the requisite number of provincial premiers agreed on certain
constitutional amendments including the Canadian Charter of Rights
and Freedoms and an amending formula. In future, our Constitution
would be amendable in Canada through the federal Parliament and the
provincial legislatures. The past practice of Canada having to request
the British Parliament to amend our Constitution for us was now to be
replaced, thus ending what many considered to be the last vestige of
colonialism.

There was nothing within the amendments of November 5th, 1981,
that specifically extended aboriginal rights or interests. That was
because, in the protracted federal-provincial negotiations that had
taken place over the previous 18 months, aboriginal rights were not on
the agenda.

Aboriginal rights were however, very much on the agenda of a
parallel process that was being conducted simultaneously by a Special
Joint Committee of Members of Parliament. The native leadership
made extensive submissions to this Committee and, as a result, the
Committee recommended a clause that would read: "The aboriginal
and treaty rights of the aboriginal peoples of Canada are hereby
recognized and affirmed."

Because this clause was not contained in the federal-provincial
package agreed to by the Prime Minister and the nine Premiers,
intensive last-minute lobbying by the native leadership resulted in the

matter being reopened. As a result, the above clause, with one significant addition—the word "existing" so as to qualify "aboriginal and treaty rights"—was added. The word "existing" was meant to ensure that aboriginal rights which may have been extinguished in the past could not be said to have been revived by this provision.

These words became section 35 of the *Constitution Act, 1982,* which goes on to define the "aboriginal peoples of Canada" as including "the Indian, Inuit and Metis peoples of Canada." This provision makes no attempt to give **content** to the term "aboriginal rights." That was to be negotiated later in a series of constitutional conferences in which the native leadership would play a major part. Four such conferences took place between 1983 and 1987.

The Aboriginal Conferences (1983-1987)

At the first such Conference in March 1983, agreement was reached to amend the meaning of "treaty rights" in section 35 to include rights contained in existing or future negotiated land claim agreements. This was an amendment which, in the context of current land claim settlements, is of enormous importance. The amendment nullified half of the meaning of the word "existing" for the clause would now relate to all **future** treaties and land claim agreements as well as those existing in 1982. It is not certain that the Premiers of the day fully understood what the implications of the amendment might be. They may well have considered it highly technical and had their attention diverted to the more politically catchy agreement made at the same Conference guaranteeing aboriginal and treaty rights equally to male and female persons.

This amendment to "constitutionally protect" the rights contained in present and future land claim agreements is of enormous importance because it raises land claim agreements to the level of constitutional status. Ten comprehensive land claim agreements have been concluded since the federal land claims policy was established in 1973; ten more are expected in the Yukon; more in Quebec, and perhaps as many as fifty or more in B.C. If the agreements concluded thus far give any indication, these agreements will contain hundreds of pages of provisions covering the subjects listed in Figure 7 in Chapter 4. Scores of "rights" are extended in these kind of agreements. Thanks to section 35 of the *Constitution Act, 1982* all of these are "recognized and affirmed" or what has been dubbed, in common parlance, "constitutionalized."

In legal terms, what is the effect of the Constitution "recognizing and affirming" rights? In dealing with that question, it is necessary to first consider what the status of Indian treaties or land claim agreements were prior to the enactment of section 35. Did treaties override federal and provincial laws if there was a conflict between their provisions and those laws or, were they subservient to federal and provincial laws?

On the basis of the case law, the answer is pretty clear. Where **provincial** laws conflicted with treaty provisions, the terms of the treaty prevailed.[1] In the case of conflict between **federal** legislation and an Indian treaty, the law before section 35 was that the federal law overrode the treaty.[2] This meant that treaty Indians were subject to such statutes as the *Federal Fisheries Act* and the *Migratory Birds Protection Act.* [3]

Putting treaties above the law

All this has now changed. By virtue of section 35, aboriginal and treaty rights have been elevated above federal or provincial law to a new kind of law having constitutional status. This is buttressed by section 52(1) of the *Constitution Act, 1982* which declares that the Constitution of Canada "is the supreme law of Canada and any law that is inconsistent with the provisions of the Constitution is, to the extent of the inconsistency, of no force or effect."

The best opinion is that Indian treaties and land claim agreements will override federal as well as provincial laws.[4] Even aboriginal rights, which by their nature are more nebulous and less definitive than either treaty or land claim agreement rights, have been found by the Supreme Court of Canada, since the enactment of section 35, to override federal legislation unless the Court is convinced that such legislation is "justified."[5] The Court sets out a rigorous test to determine "justification" including requiring that the aboriginal group affected by any proposed legislation be consulted.

If treaties and land claim agreements have a standing which is above ordinary laws and into the realm of "new constitutional law," how then can those treaties and agreements ever be amended? Douglas Sanders, a leading authority on native rights says, and I agree with him, that they can only be amended by constitutional amendment or by the consent of the Indians who are a party to such agreements.[6]

But neither prospect is likely. A constitutional amendment to remove or diminish a right extended to Indians under a treaty or land claim agreement would likely never be obtained, no matter how essential such an amendment might be in the public interest. It is not altogether clear which part of the amending formula would be applicable but it might well be the provision that requires seven province approval plus the federal government. The four Atlantic provinces have exceedingly small native populations. Why should they stick their necks out in support of some other province seeking such an amendment and thereby run the risk of having visited upon them the wrath of perhaps the most powerful lobby in the country. Other provinces similarly not directly affected are likely to feel the same way.

As for natives who are a party to a treaty or land claim agreement being willing to forego any of their rights, one should perhaps not prejudge but based on the approach being taken to extract every jot and tittle from existing treaties and to pursue hundred-year-old grievances, the prospects look dim indeed.

Such is the box that Canadians have been placed in through the acquiescence of their political leadership, first by agreeing in 1981 to section 35 and then again in 1983 to what was sold to them as a mere housekeeping amendment. Sad to say, the full import of what they were agreeing to was not even understood much less discussed. I know, I was there. Others support that view. Looking back after the passage of several years, one astute observer who interviewed Premiers, Ministers and officials engaged in these Conferences said this:

> "Many respondents felt that those sections of the amendment package relating to aboriginal peoples were not well understood by governments, nor perhaps by aboriginal peoples. (The package was agreed to at the last minute by First Ministers after a very short discussion of its merits.) Elements of the package were not thoroughly discussed, there were few preliminary meetings, and there was little agreement on what the terms of the amendment meant. Many governments considered the commitment to be narrow in scope, while others interpreted it more widely.
>
> "Interviewees from both governments and aboriginal peoples' organizations spoke of governments being 'backed into' this

commitment, with the result that the commitment was not strong, and the understanding not deep."[7]

What was made abundantly clear by the March 1983 Conference was that defining aboriginal rights in a manner that would be acceptable to the federal and provincial governments and to representatives of the aboriginal peoples would be a difficult task. Accordingly, it was agreed that three more First Minister's Constitutional Conferences on Aboriginal Constitutional Matters would be held—in 1984, 1985 and 1987.

Pressing for the inherent right

At the three subsequent Conferences, the native leadership pushed hard for an amendment that would give constitutional recognition to the aboriginal right to self-government. In March, 1984, Prime Minister Trudeau advanced a constitutional proposal that would have committed governments to permit the establishment of aboriginal self-government institutions, provided they were constituted in accordance with federal and provincial legislation. Under this proposal, aboriginal governments would have exercised powers delegated to them by the senior governments. The four national associations representing aboriginal people at the Conference flatly rejected the proposal.

Figure 11 - Prime Minister Trudeau recognizing the author's long service, 1984.   *Courtesy: CICS, Ottawa.*

At the 1985 First Ministers Conference, Prime Minister Mulroney tabled what became known as the "contingent right" proposal. Under it, a general right of aboriginal peoples to self-government would be added to the Constitution on the condition that the contents of the right be worked out in negotiated agreements. The self-government rights contained in those future agreements would be approved by Parliament and the relevant provincial legislatures and would be given constitutional protection under section 35. Seven provinces representing more than 50% of the Canadian population agreed to the proposal which was a sufficient measure of agreement to see it through. For reasons best known to itself, the Assembly of First Nations would not support the proposal even though there was a non-derogation clause to ensure that whatever other rights to self-government they might have had would not be jeopardized by them agreeing to this proposal.

At the last conference in 1987, the federal government moved still further towards meeting the demands of the aboriginal leadership by proposing the recognition of what came to be known as the "explicit right." This would have specifically recognized the right to self-government, but would have required that the actual powers of aboriginal governments be the subject of negotiated agreements. Again, aboriginal leaders took the position that the right of self-government must be free-standing and independent from a requirement for negotiated agreements: in short, the inherent right to self-government. In the end the Conference failed to arrive at a mutually acceptable amendment.

So ended the formal effort to place into the Constitution the inherent right to self-government. Over 30 federal-provincial-aboriginal meetings of officials, Ministers and Premiers over the five year period could not agree on what self-government was to mean and how it would work.

The inherent right to self-government: What does it mean?

Briefly stated, the concept of the inherent right to self-government, as enunciated by the native leadership, means the right of aboriginal peoples to govern themselves by laws passed by their own institutions to the exclusion of laws passed by other governments in Canada. This assertion of exclusive authority to make laws affecting Indian peoples includes the right to determine their own citizenship and the right to apply their laws to their own people wherever they are located. It is true that the native leadership who advocate this concept foresee some laws of other governments applying to them but, in their view, which other laws apply is a matter for they themselves to decide. Grand Chief Ovide Mercredi puts it this way: "We will not allow some other society to decide what we can do and determine the limits of our authority."[8]

When the term, "the inherent right to self-government" is used, the uninitiated may mistakenly believe that it has something to do with Indians managing their reserves. It is much more than that. In concept it includes being exclusively governed by their own laws in what they claim as their "traditional territories" and even beyond that, for it is said to attach to the aboriginal person wherever he may live. It is therefore a concept which is different from a land claim. It is one involving **governance** or the power to make laws. It is not contingent on having a land base but, more often than not, it is put forward in that context. In short, it is a claim to sovereignty and not a claim to land ownership.

The consequence of accepting the concept is, as Kenneth J. Tyler points out,

> "From these propositions it logically follows that the Indian nations retain their sovereignty to this day, and all of the statutes and other legal instruments by which the British and Canadian authorities have purported to regulate the lives and lands of Aboriginal people were, and remain, illegitimate. Indeed, it is suggested that Canada itself is illegitimate as a nation because it was formed and exercises authority without Aboriginal consent."[9]

What are its origins?

If the right to self-government is "inherent," which the common dictionary definition means "not derived from any other authority," how did this right come into being? From the time the concept was first advanced until now, native spokesmen claim that it was given to them by the Creator.

The proposition was well put by Nisga'a Chief James Gosnell at the 1983 First Ministers' Conference:

> "It has always been our belief, Mr. Chairman, that when God created this whole world he gave pieces of land to all races of people throughout this world, the Chinese people, Germans and you name them, including Indians. So at one time our land

was this whole continent right from the tip of South America to the North Pole . . . It has always been our belief that God gave us the land . . . and we say that no one can take our title away except He who gave it to us to begin with." [10]

To which Prime Minister Trudeau responded:

"Going back to the Creator doesn't really help very much. So He gave you title, but you know, did He draw on the land where your mountains stopped and somebody else's began . . .? God never said that the frontier of France runs along the Rhine or somewhere west of Alsace-Lorraine where the German-speaking people of France live . . . I don't know any part of the world where history isn't constantly rewritten by migrations and immigrants and fights between countries changing frontiers and I don't think you can expect North America or the whole of the Western Hemisphere to settle things differently than they have been settled everywhere else, hopefully peacefully here." [11]

The claim to the Creator's assistance was more formally expressed in a declaration adopted by the Assembly of First Nations in December, 1980. It stated that it is the laws of the Creator that "define our rights and responsibilities" and that it is the Creator that "has given us the right to govern ourselves and the right to self-determination" which "cannot be altered or taken away by any other Nation."[12]

More recent pronouncements are inclined to move away from references to the Creator but the import is the same. In his co-authored book, Mercredi put it this way:

"We can never be truly self-governing under a form of government delegated by Parliament. The inherent right to govern means that we do not need Parliament's permission to run our own affairs, although we have a political relationship with the Crown through our governments. It means that our rights come from our own people, our own past; they cannot be delegated from the federal or provincial governments as some kind of handout." [13]

However, the right "to run our own affairs" does not apparently include the cost of doing so. Native governments' "inherent right" apparently must be matched by the "inherent responsibility" of the Canadian taxpayer to forever foot the bill.

Constitutional or legal validity

Is there any support, either in our Constitution or in judicial authority, for the concept of native sovereignty which is implicit in the inherent self-government concept? That is, sovereignty is in the Crown for non-Indians but sovereignty for natives is resident in their own institutions?

Again, aboriginal advocates point to the Royal Proclamation of 1763 which specifically referred to "Indian tribes or **nations**" and called for entering into "Treaties" as evidence that the treaties were made between sovereigns. No mention is ever made of the fact that, both the Royal Proclamation and the treaties which followed, refer to the Indians as being the King's loyal "**subjects**." Added to this, aboriginal advocates seek to invoke the principles of modern international law applicable to former colonies in Asia and Africa which have struggled to achieve independence in recent years, as showing they are entitled to all the rights of self-determination in the international sense. Having asserted such a right, most aboriginal leaders pull back from advocating its full exercise, which would mean separating from Canada. However, recent pronouncements, such as the following by Grand Chief Mercredi, advance even that as a legitimate option.

> *"So our struggle is not only to rebuild our societies, which is very important, but to re-structure Canada, to alter the fundamental thinking of the legal and the political systems of this country. If we fail to accomplish that task, we will have two alternatives. One is to choose to be subjected to the supremacy and dominance of another society. The other is to seek what some people in Quebec are seeking, and that is an independent path."* [14]

Incredibly, the present federal Minister of DIAND supports the inherent right to self-government to the full extent of giving the native people this right to self determination. Speaking to reporters outside a closed-door meeting of natives in Quebec, Mr. Irwin declared that aboriginal people living in Quebec had the right to self determination. [15] It can be readily seen that ill-thought through expressions such as these and talk about negotiating with natives on a "government to government basis" and "bringing first nations into Canada" through land claim agreements only buttresses the native claim to sovereignty and falsely raise expectations.

Is there any support in law for such an idea? It has long been trite law in this country, based on the highest judicial authority, that sovereignty in all its fullness is, by our Constitution, divided between the Parliament of Canada and the legislatures of the provinces. Which of the two levels of government has which sovereign powers is determined by the division of legislative powers and proprietary rights contained in the Constitution. There is no room remaining, under existing constitutional arrangements, for a third level of government—be it aboriginally based or otherwise—to lay claim to a third order of government.

A long line of cases going back as far as 1887[16] and up to the present day constitute an unbroken line of authority on the point. We have seen that the courts in the *Delgamuukw* case faced the issue head on. Both the B.C. Supreme Court and the Court of Appeal turned the proposition down flat. Similarly in December 1994 in Ontario, when a native band sought to justify operating a casino on reserve lands based on their so-called inherent right to do so, the Ontario Court of Appeal rejected the argument.[17]

Persistence with the politicians

Unsuccessful in attempts to entrench the concept in the Constitution, the native leadership was to find that the NDP government in Ontario provided the fertile ground in which the seed of the concept of the inherent right to self-government would take root.

On June 6, 1991, the Minister Responsible for Native Affairs in Ontario rose in the Ontario Legislature to announce that he was extremely pleased to advise that the government and the "First Nations" of Ontario had reached an historic accord on aboriginal self-government. He characterized the event as "the most important development to date in Ontario's relationship with the First Nations."

In a Statement of Political Relationship, the government formally recognized the inherent right of the "First Nations" in Canada to be self-governing. It vowed in future to deal with them on a "government-to-government" basis. The Ontario Minister said this: "We agree with the First Nations that their inherent right to self-government flows from the Creator and from their occupation of the land for many centuries before non-Aboriginal people arrived in what is now Canada."[18] The Minister went on to say: "We also agree that, under the Constitution of Canada, the First Nations have an inherent right to self-government within the Canadian constitutional framework."[19]

The fuzzy thinking that went into the whole affair is evidenced by a further clause in the Statement of Political Relationship which reads: "Nothing in this statement of political relationship shall be construed as determining Ontario's jurisdiction or as diminishing Canada's responsibilities towards first nations." Nobody apparently thought to ask how it could be that the "First Nations" of Ontario would have, on the one hand, an inherent right to self-government and yet, on the other hand, be subject to the jurisdiction of Ontario and the Government of Canada. The two concepts are clearly in conflict.

The agreement was formally signed by Premier Rae and his Minister Responsible for Native Affairs and twelve Indian chiefs at a ceremony at Mount McKay on the Fort William First Nation Reserve near Thunder Bay on August 6, 1991.

This was pretty heady stuff for the recently elected government of Ontario and for the native leadership throughout Canada. In an address to the annual meeting of James Bay Cree chiefs, one day later on August 8, 1991, Ovide Mercredi, the leader of the Assembly of First Nations, stated that "Indians should give Canada one more chance," and that the native people would be satisfied with nothing less than "a dramatically reformed nation-state."[20]

What a difference a lunch makes

That year, the Annual Premiers' Conference took place at Whistler, B.C., on August 26-27 with Premier Rita Johnston of B.C. in the chair. Ontario officials, flush from their newly-signed agreement with the "First Nations", spoke in advance to reporters on condition that they not be identified, outlining Premier Rae's wish-list for the conference. At the top of a three point list was his effort to have Premiers nation-wide recognize the natives' right to self-government.[21] At Whistler the Ontario government tabled a paper outlining its achievements on the native front since taking office in 1990.

Ovide Mercredi and other native leaders, were invited to make presentations to the premiers assembled at Whistler. In his hard hitting statement, Mercredi underlined the view that "this land you call Canada was given to us by the Creator" and that the treaty relationship indicated that the relationship between the natives and the Crown was one of equals. It, of course, did no such thing.

He went on to state, apparently unchallenged: "no oppressive regime continues for ever, and we will fight to end it in this country."[22] He then pressed for the recognition of the inherent right as also including the right of self determination for "First Nations."

The premiers agreed to discuss the matter privately over lunch. Past practice has shown that discussing these issues in private over lunch can lead to disastrous results. It was at a private lunch at the Annual Premiers' Conference in Edmonton in 1986 that the abortive Meech Lake process was spawned. Near the conclusion of a sumptuous repast with much bonhomie among the premiers, a short two paragraph draft, hatched up privately between Quebec and Alberta, was sprung on the other premiers by Quebec Premier Robert Bourassa. It lamented the fact that patriation of the Constitution had taken place in 1981 without Quebec's approval and that therefore the Meech Lake round should only deal with Quebec issues. At this lunch the premiers compliantly agreed. After all, nobody wants to be accused of being objectionable at what is basically a social lunch.

It appears a similar fate befell the premiers at their private luncheon at Whistler on the issue of recognizing the aboriginal right to self-government. Premier Johnston emerged from the luncheon to advise that all Premiers present signalled support for the inherent right to native self-government which had been so recently formally accepted in the province of Ontario. Media reports indicate that one prominent B.C. native leader present at Whistler almost fell down "in surprise when Johnston indicated the premiers had given their consent to the idea after discussing it at a lunch meeting."[23] The surprise was that the premiers acquiesced in the concept so readily.

It was this agreement that paved the way for the future NDP government of B.C. to enter into a formal protocol, similar to Ontario's. In the first Throne Speech of the Harcourt government on March 17, 1992, the following statement appears: "We recognize aboriginal title and the inherent rights of aboriginal peoples to self-government."

One analyst said this about the Throne Speech provision:
"The historical significance of this statement in the history of British Columbia land claims is profound. It is laudable to work towards a resolution of historic injustices. But the Harcourt government was elected to act in the interests of British Columbians. . . . The position of the government is somewhat equivalent to 'recognizing' after 120 years, that your

neighbours have title to your house and then entering into negotiations with them to resolve their claims." [24]

The Charlottetown Accord

The Charlottetown Accord process commenced on September 24, 1991, when the Government of Canada tabled in Parliament a set of proposals for the renewal of the Canadian Federation entitled "Shaping Canada's Future Together." These proposals were referred to a Special Joint Committee of the House of Commons and the Senate which travelled across Canada seeking the public's views. The federal-provincial-aboriginal negotiation process leading to the Charlottetown Accord began with an initial meeting in Ottawa on March 12, 1992, and continued until agreement was reached between the Prime Minister and the ten premiers at Charlottetown on August 27 and 28, 1992.

At the beginning the native leadership threatened to boycott attendance.[25] Talks bogged down on what would be the nature and scope of aboriginal governments if the inherent right to self-government was added to the Constitution. Speaking to reporters at the conclusion of constitutional talks in Vancouver on May 14, 1992, Chief Mercredi was quoted as saying:

"In Halifax we made a very good start on the inherent right to self-government and at that time all the governments were very supportive in principle. Since that time the debate has focused on more practical matters, and as you know, when you deal in practical matters, many issues get raised." [26]

Whether he knew it or not, Mercredi put his finger on one of the real problems with constitutionalizing the inherent right to self-government. It is all very well to talk about it in conceptual terms but how would it work in practice?

Would it mean that aboriginal institutions could legislate for their people on any subject including the criminal law, marriage and family law, and property laws and thereby override federal and provincial laws on these subjects? Would it allow the establishment of separate court systems and police forces? What would be the territorial reach of such laws? They would certainly be considered by the aboriginal leadership to go beyond mere Indian reserves to what they call their traditional territories, which, in B.C.'s case, is **claimed** to be 111% of the province. Presumably, the inherent right of self-government would carry with it the right to levy taxes. How would these mesh with the existing tax base? What about urban Indians? How would they share in this new-found right to self-government?

Until these kinds of questions are answered, it would be nothing short of foolhardy to put a freestanding inherent right to self-government into the Canadian Constitution and yet that is essentially what governments and the aboriginal leadership agreed to do in the Charlottetown Accord. Only the good sense of a majority of the Canadian people in the Referendum ultimately stood in the way.

Massive concessions

The Charlottetown Accord agreed to on August 28, 1992, would have given Canada's "aboriginal peoples" not only the right to determine who constitutes an aboriginal person, but having done that extend to them an enormous array of special rights, including:

- specific mention of aboriginal peoples in the Canada Clause, with the right to promote their languages, cultures and traditions;
- a provision that would make aboriginal governments one of three orders of government in Canada;
- a provision to permit "aboriginal, treaty or any other aboriginal rights" to override the Canadian Charter of Rights and Freedoms;
- special seats in the Senate for aboriginal peoples: the number to be negotiated;
- the role of the aboriginal people in relation to the Supreme Court would be negotiated, including having a Council of Aboriginal Elders that could make submissions to the Court. In the meantime, aboriginal groups would be constitutionally entitled to submit lists of candidates to fill Supreme Court vacancies;
- special aboriginal representation in the House of Commons would be considered;
- a general non-derogation clause to ensure that changes to the division of powers between senior governments would not affect aboriginal peoples and their governments;
- an amendment to recognize that aboriginal peoples "have an inherent right of self-government in Canada;"
- the exercise of this right of self-government would include the right of the aboriginal peoples' own legislative bodies to pass laws to safeguard their languages, culture, economies, identities, traditions; and to develop, maintain and strengthen their relationships with their lands, waters and environment;

- governments would be committed to undertake negotiations with the aboriginal peoples to implement self-government, including issues of jurisdiction, lands and resources, and economic and fiscal arrangements;
- although aboriginal peoples would be precluded from enforcing their "inherent right" of self-government in the courts for a period of five years, no restriction prevented aboriginal legislatures from commencing to legislate forthwith;
- the federal and provincial governments were committed to providing "the governments of aboriginal peoples with fiscal or other resources, such as land to assist those governments to govern their own affairs;"
- B.C. agreed to negotiate self-government, including land and resources to "the Metis Nation within the province" despite the fact that Statistics Canada show the total Metis population in this province is less than 4,000;
- governments agreed not to reduce their present spending levels on aboriginal peoples as a result of this Accord.

This is only an abbreviated list of provisions in the Accord that would have conferred special constitutional rights on the aboriginal people, who comprise less than 3% of the population of Canada. Never would so much have been given by so many to so few.

I wrote at the time:

"It appears that in the Charlottetown Accord the aboriginal leadership has negotiated for itself tremendous gains on a broad front. Anything that was sought by them was apparently conceded. Time and again they pushed on the open door only to discover there was no resistance. Not one political leader was apparently prepared to question where all this was leading, and what it all meant. Take the inherent right to self-government, for example. To the unsuspecting and naive, two misconceptions abound. First, that aboriginal self-government is limited to the native people running their reserves and second, that if we only put these general words in the Constitution now, governments can negotiate later what powers aboriginal self-governments will exercise.

"If "inherent self-government" goes into the Constitution now you don't have to be a constitutional lawyer to figure out what will happen. In fact it is a decided advantage if you are not.

Ordinary Canadians know what "inherent" means. It means "not derived from any other source or authority; intrinsic." Add to that the ordinary meaning of "self-government," which means the right to pass laws, set up courts, impose taxes, and decide whether the people governed are entitled or not entitled to individual rights and freedoms. These powers will be able to be exercised without agreement from other governments because they are "inherent." Once the words are in, we can expect the aboriginal leadership of this new brand of government to begin to legislate to the fullest extent. One can add to this the fact that the aboriginal lobby claims the right to exercise this kind of government over their "traditional territories"—meaning, in B.C.'s case, virtually the whole of the province.

"Top it all off with the unresolved question of how aboriginal peoples living in an urban setting, surrounded by non-aboriginals, could possibly exercise their new-found governmental power and you have something of an idea of what aboriginal self-government would be all about if it finds its way into the Constitution. If you were a Martian who had just landed, you would puzzlingly inquire how it is that grown men who occupy leadership in this country would knowingly and willingly embrace this contraption of government that would make Rube Goldberg green with envy."

One columnist close to the scene stated that the aboriginal issue will not fade out of sight—quite the reverse:

"The framework that is being hammered into place now is very likely to dominate the Canadian political agenda for 10 or 20 years. Native groups have made tremendous political gains in the past few months, succeeding well beyond most of their leaders' initial expectations." [27]

During the height of the referendum campaign, S. Brad Armstrong, a Vancouver lawyer published a paper entitled "Who Will Govern British Columbia?" in which he brilliantly analyzed the effect the self-government provisions in the Constitution would have and went on to castigate the failure of Premier Harcourt and the provincial government to uphold the interests of the province. He shared my view that the so-called "inherent" right of self-government meant that native peoples could establish their own native governments not dependent in any way in obtaining any consent from, or agreement with, the federal government, the provincial government, or the courts. Nothing could be plainer than sections 41 and 46 of the Charlottetown Accord.

Armstrong went on to state that the effect of these sections and the recognition that the right to self-government is "inherent" means that native governments may assert their authority and begin to enact laws which "displace" general federal and provincial laws, even where no self-government agreement has been reached with either the federal or the provincial government.[28] In my view, his analysis of the effect of those provisions is incontrovertible.

Gordon Gibson, former leader of the B.C. Liberal Party, in an article at the time summed it up best:

"The simple, unvarnished fact is that we are proposing to add to our Constitution more discrimination on the basis of race. We are proposing to treat natives—a term not completely defined at the moment as a race, and differently from other races. The noun for that kind of behaviour is 'racism,' the adjective is 'racist,' and it is always and everywhere wrong."[29]

Mercifully the Charlottetown Accord was defeated by the good sense of the majority of the people of Canada in the referendum of October 26, 1992.

It is no accident that natives cast the largest "No" vote of any definable group against the Accord. "Ordinary" natives feared the enormous concentration of power that would result in the hands of their ambitious "leaders." This was especially true of native women.

No answers in high places

Was there some all-knowing genius behind the scenes in government somewhere who had a clear idea how the inherent right of self-government in the Constitution would actually work and that we Canadians were simply not being told about it? Surely somewhere in the ivory towers of Ottawa there must have been a group of highly paid bureaucrats, with intellectual attainments higher than those to which the rest of us humble folk could ever aspire, that would have the answers. Not so, for just ten days after the referendum was defeated the Canadian Press obtained a paper prepared by the Privy Council office in Ottawa in which federal officials had many questions but very few answers about what aboriginal self-government would have entailed if the Charlottetown Accord had been accepted.[30]

"The number, scale and scope of groups coming forward to negotiate are uncertain" said the paper, prepared in October after the constitutional accord had been negotiated but before it was defeated. The paper goes on to state that it appears that federal and likely provincial government expectations were that self-government would be implemented at a minimal cost to governments, whereas aboriginal expectations were substantially higher particularly in the area of government funding. The document, labelled a "draft," said that as few as 20 to 30 native groups or as many as several hundred might have come forward to claim their entitlement to the inherent right to self-government.

Even the Ontario government which was so quick to buy into the concept of the "inherent right," has begun to realize that "turning this concept into reality will be a challenge." Especially since only about 60,000 of the estimated 200,000 aboriginal people in Ontario live on reserves.[31] Challenge indeed!

Acting on the premise

For those Canadians who breathed a sigh of relief over the defeat of the Charlottetown Accord and thought that its provisions would be laid aside, there is disquieting news. The famous "Red Book" of the federal Liberal party used in the October 1993 federal election campaign seems to be the government's Holy Grail. The "Red Book" has a section on aboriginal rights which includes the following statement: "A Liberal government will act on the premise that the inherent right of self-government is an existing aboriginal and treaty right."[32]

DIAND Minister Ron Irwin confirmed, shortly after the election that the government was "working steadily towards the implementation of the 'inherent right of self-government' as the cornerstone of a new partnership with aboriginal people."[33]

A day or two later Mr. Irwin was quoted as saying: "We are not going back to constitutional discussions; we are acting on the premise that it's there. Until some Court says that it's not, that's the premise that we are working on."[34]

The comment calls for two points in response. First, if the right is already in the Constitution, why did federal, provincial and aboriginal leadership negotiate for a five year period from 1983 to 1987 attempting to arrive at a suitable agreement to put the words into the

Constitution, which as is pointed out above, did not succeed? And, following that, why was it necessary to devote so much time and energy during the Charlottetown Accord negotiations to come up with a suitable constitutional formulation on the subject?

Secondly, Mr. Irwin says that he will work on the premise that it is contained in the Constitution unless some court says that it is not. Over and over again the highest courts in this country have categorically rejected any attempt to find within the Constitution a third order of government in this country. Courts have made it abundantly clear that total sovereignty is divided between the Parliament of Canada and the legislatures of the provinces. The *Delgamuukw* case in B.C. at both the Trial and Court of Appeal level said this. So did the recent decision of the Ontario Court of Appeal rejecting the inherent right argument as being the basis for natives to conduct gambling on reserves.[35] Mr. Irwin, wake up and smell the coffee, the courts have said "no" over and over again.

Justice Minister Rock suggests as well that there may have to be a separate justice system for natives "as part of the inherent right of self-government . . . Rock says the idea poses many questions: will the criminal code apply; what court will try the offences; will sentences be different?"[36] May God deliver us from such folly!

The Royal Commission weighs in

Not to be outdone, the Royal Commission on Aboriginal Peoples issued a report in late 1993 entitled "Partners in Confederation" announcing that the inherent right to self-government is already in the Constitution. This goes a step further than Mr. Irwin and the federal government. Irwin is proceeding as though the provision is "in" even though he knows it isn't. The Royal Commission would have us believe that the provision is indeed "in" the Constitution.

In the preface to the Report, the co-chairmen—one of them a Quebec Appeal Court Judge—make the astounding proposition that not only must we look to the Constitution of Canada to determine whether there is an aboriginal right of self-government, but that other possible sources for the right exist "such as international law, natural law, treaties, and the laws, constitutions, and spiritual beliefs of aboriginal peoples." This is an astounding proposition. Even a first-year constitutional law student knows that the Constitution of Canada is the supreme law of the land and all other laws, customs, constitutions, treaties, and spiritual beliefs are subservient to it. There is no other basis on which to derive an inherent right to self-government than through the Canadian Constitution. The courts have told us over and over again that it is simply not there.

Sowing the wind and reaping the whirlwind

What are the practical consequences of governments assuring native peoples that they have the inherent right to self-government and in entering into formal protocols with them to this effect? Surely it is to invite the native leadership to begin to legislate on their own without the concurrence of any other government. This is precisely what is shaping up as the following examples show:

1. After a two-day meeting of regional leaders of the Assembly of First Nations held in Ottawa within one month of the defeat of the Charlottetown Accord, Ovide Mercredi outlined native strategy. Native leaders will "proceed with their own laws in areas such as child welfare, education, and economic-development schemes such as gambling parlours. This will bolster their chances of success if they are confronted by legal action by provincial governments."[37] Mercredi is quoted as saying, "If you go to the Court with a full hand, the concern is less. The strategy is to fill the hand, to make sure the aboriginal made [sic] laws are there so that when people are challenged the law is in place."[38]

2. In a recent book which he co-authored, Mr. Mercredi says "If there is no way to negotiate self-government, we will just do it." He goes on to say that bands will assert their rights "without discussion and they will not wait for permission from the federal or provincial governments."[39]

3. On July 30, 1994, Manitoba's top native leader was charged with illegally operating a bingo game without a provincial licence. He responded that, under inherent native rights to self-government, Indian bands across Canada can set up casinos and run gaming activities without provincial permission.[40]

4. In B.C. the Alexis Creek band near Williams Lake is building a trailer park on Crown land without first seeking any governmental approval and indicates it has plans to erect permanent homes on the site. Band chief Irvine Charleyboy has few doubts about his authority to build. He states "I'm going to do my own thing in my own territory regardless of what the law says. I will log and build

houses where I want and when I want." To this blatant breach of the law David Zirnhelt, NDP MLA for Cariboo South and Minister of Agriculture and Fisheries states: "The worst thing we want is to provoke a reaction."[41]

The band's other preoccupation these days is, along with six other bands, to seek to "reclaim ownership and control" of the vast area known as the Chilcotin.[42]

5. In 1992, the Haida National Council of the Queen Charlotte Islands declared themselves to be a sovereign nation and even issued their own passports.[43]

6. A strategy paper prepared for the Assembly of First Nations entitled "Seizing the Agenda" obtained by the *Ottawa Citizen* in early May 1994 recommended that native bands should start behaving like independent governments within Canada because any other kind of self-government negotiations are fruitless. Native leaders gave approval in principle to the position paper at that time. The news report goes on to suggest that if the strategy is followed by native governments, jurisdiction over such issues as gaming, justice, education, and child care would be claimed without talks.[44]

Chapter 7 - Footnotes:

1. *R. vs. White and Bob*, 52 DLR (2d) 481 (S.C.C.)
2. *R. vs. George*, [1966] S.C.R. 267.
3. *Sikyea vs. The Queen*, [1964] S.C.R. 642.
4. Kenneth Lysyk, "The Rights and Freedoms of the Aboriginal Peoples of Canada," (Sections 25, 35 & 37), *The Canadian Charter of Rights and Freedoms* (Carswell, 1982), 467.
5. *Regina vs. Sparrow*, 1990 1.S.C.R. 1075.
6. Douglas Sanders, "Pre-Existing Rights: The Aboriginal Peoples of Canada." *The Canadian Charter of Rights and Freedoms,* Second Edition (Carswell, 1989), 730.
7. David C. Hawkes, *Aboriginal Peoples and Constitutional Reform: What Have We Learned?* (Queen's University, 1989), 9-10.
8. Ovide Mercredi and Mary Ellen Turpel, *In the Rapids: Navigating the Future of First Nations* (Viking, 1993), 95.
9. Kenneth J. Tyler, *Another Opinion: A Critique of the Paper Prepared by the Royal Commission on Aboriginal Peoples Entitled: Partners in Confederation* (Winnipeg), 6.
10. First Ministers' Conference on Aboriginal Constitutional Matters, Unofficial Verbatim Transcript, March 15, 1983.
11. Ibid., 31.
12. See Assembly of First Nations, "A Declaration of the First Nations", December 1980, reprinted in Ian A.L. Getty and Antoine S. Lussier, *As Long as the Sun Shines and Water Flow: A reader in Canadian Native Studies* (Vancouver: University of British Columbia Press, 1983), 337.
13. Mercredi and Turpel, 95.
14. Ibid., 130.
15. Ottawa Citizen, *Natives Free to Split from Quebec,"* May 18, 1994, 1.
16. *Bank of Canada vs. Lambe* (1887) 12 App. Cases 575 at 587.
17. *The Queen vs. Pamajewon and Jones et al.,* Court of Appeal for Ontario, December 21, 1994.
18. Statement to the Legislature by Hon. C.J. (Bud) Wildman, Minister Responsible for Native Affairs, Government of Ontario, June 6, 1991.
19. Ibid.
20. "Mercredi calls for dramatic reform," *Globe and Mail,* August 9, 1991.
21. "Natives seek equality with Quebec," *Globe and Mail,* August 20, 1991, A5.
22. Statement of National Chief Ovide Mercredi, Premiers Conference, Whistler, 1991.
23. "Premier's accept self-government concept after presentations by aboriginal leaders." *Vancouver Sun,* August 27, 1991, A8.
24. S. Brad Armstrong, *Who Will Govern British Columbia?* (Vancouver: September 16, 1992).

25. "Indians threaten boycott of talks," *Globe and Mail,* August 19, 1991, A1.

26. "Mercredi reports setback at talks," *Vancouver Sun,* May 14, 1992.

27. Robert Sheppard, "It may dominate the agenda for 20 years," *Globe and Mail,* June 1, 1992, A19.

28. S. Brad Armstrong, Ibid.

29. Gordon Gibson, "Let's not use racism to tackle native needs", *Globe and Mail,* June 1, 1992.

30. "Officials vague over 'aboriginal self-government'," *Times Colonist,* November 5, 1992, A10.

31. "Self-rule for natives tall order, panel told," *Globe and Mail,* July 30, 1991, A5.

32. *Creating Opportunity The Liberal Plan for Canada,* Ottawa, September 1993, 98.

33. Government of Canada News Release, *Federal Government begins discussion on Aboriginal Self-Government,* January 19, 1994.

34. "Handling of self-government issue queried," *Times Colonist,* January 22, 1994, A8.

35. *The Queen vs. Pamajewon and Jones et al.,* Ibid.

36. "Separate Indian law system wanted to ease cultural gap," *Vancouver Sun,* July 15, 1994.

37. Geoffrey York, "Natives set to move ahead with own laws," *Globe and Mail,* November 20, 1992, A5.

38. Ibid.

39. Ovide Mercredi and Mary Ellen Turpel, Ibid.

40. "Native leader charged with bingo calling," *Globe and Mail,* July 30, 1994, A7.

41. "You can't argue with an anarchist," *British Columbia Report,* December 5, 1994, 6.

42. "Government treads carefully in land dispute," *The Province,* November 16, 1994, A17.

43. "Haida encouraged by constitutional talks," *The Vancouver Sun,* May 13, 1992, B11.

44. "Tough Native Agenda pushed," *The Calgary Sun,* May 17, 1994.

The Royal Commission on Aboriginal Peoples

"With its price tag to date of $58 million, this is 'the most expensive inquiry in Canadian history.'"
Ottawa Citizen, October 21, 1994.

Its origins

The idea of a Royal Commission to thoroughly review the relationship of Aboriginal peoples with other elements of Canadian society had its origins in a desperate attempt by the Mulroney government to prevent the Meech Lake Accord from going down to destruction.

In June 1987 Prime Minister Mulroney and the ten Premiers unanimously agreed on a package of constitutional amendments ostensibly to bring Quebec "into the constitutional family." Formal approval of Parliament and the ten legislatures within three years would be necessary before the amendments could come into force and effect. As the three-year deadline approached, only Newfoundland and Manitoba had yet to pass the appropriate resolutions. Under the rules of the Manitoba legislature the resolution could be delayed by the refusal of one or more members to give consent to the abbreviation of the normal time periods for introducing and passing such resolutions through the House. The lone native member of the Manitoba legislature, Elijah Harper, made it plain that he was about to throw procedural roadblocks into the path in an effort to prevent the Meech Lake Accord from passing within the time period because the Accord failed to address native concerns.

Panic broke out in Ottawa. Every effort was made to win over Mr. Harper and the native people for whom he spoke. A key element of the federal effort was a promise to establish a Royal Commission to examine Aboriginal issues in a comprehensive way. The effort failed to budge Mr. Harper and as was anticipated, his procedural moves prevented the Meech Lake Accord from passing the Manitoba legislature within the requisite time. That, together with its non-passage in the Newfoundland legislature, spelled the death knell to the Accord in June of 1990.

Nothing more was heard of the proposal to establish a Royal Commission on Aboriginal issues until a speech by Prime Minister Mulroney in Victoria on April 22nd, 1991. The Prime Minister was about to launch another effort at constitutional reform, which later ended up in the ill-fated Charlottetown Accord. But before doing so, he wished very much to get the native people on side. He saw a Royal Commission as a parallel process which would, in a sense, keep the native issues separate and apart from other constitutional reform issues.

In announcing the Royal Commission,[1] Mr. Mulroney stated that it would deal with the "social, economic and cultural questions" facing aboriginal people.[2]

Georges Erasmus, then National Chief of the Assembly of First Nations, did not think much of the idea of a Royal Commission and is quoted as saying:

"He is talking about a commission [sic] to examine the economic, social-cultural situation. It sounds to me that he is talking about a report on our situation, and we don't need yet another report that talks about the amount of unemployment and early deaths and so forth."[3]

The rest of the national native leadership also viewed the Commission with a fair degree of scepticism. After a three-day conference of 150 chiefs at Toronto's Royal York Hotel a week after Mulroney's announcement, Mr. Erasmus described it as "a desperate attempt" by the federal government "to buy some votes." As for himself, Mr. Erasmus said he was not interested in a job with the Commission.[4] Ovide Mercredi, then a vice-president of the Assembly of First Nations, echoed Erasmus's views when he said "we don't want to be studied any more."[5]

The next move by the Government on this front was the Speech from the Throne to open the 34th Parliament on May 13, 1991, in which it was announced that the Right Honourable Brian Dickson, former Chief Justice of the Supreme Court of Canada, would be appointed to serve as a special representative of the Prime Minister in order to consult widely on the terms of reference and the make up of the membership of the Royal Commission.

Former Chief Justice Dickson conducted a consultation process over a two month period in which he held meetings with 57 native groups or individuals, experts, federal cabinet ministers, all seven native parliamentarians, senior public servants and other Canadians. He sent out 1,682 letters to natives and received 165 replies. He placed an advertisement in the newspaper and received 207 submissions in response.[6] Apparently almost 480 people were recommended to Dickson as potential commissioners.

The Commission's appointees

In the end, Chief Justice Dickson recommended a seven member Royal Commission comprised of the following people:- Allan Blakeney, former Premier of Saskatchewan; René Dussault, Justice of the Quebec Court of Appeal; Paul Chartrand, Head of the Department of Native Studies, University of Manitoba; Georges Erasmus, former National Chief of the Assembly of First Nations; Viola Robinson, former President of the Native Council of Canada; Mary Sillett, former President of the Inuit Womens Association of Canada and former Vice President of the Inuit Tapirisat of Canada; and Bertha Wilson, former Justice of the Supreme Court of Canada. His recommendations were accepted and the appointments made.

Although it is not popular to do so, one has to question the wisdom of drawing four of the seven commissioners from the aboriginal community. Without question natives should be entitled to representation on such a body, but with 3% of the nation's population—even calculated generously—one has to question whether a body of this make up can reasonably be expected to bring to its deliberations the impartial judgment expected of a Royal Commission. Indicating how far the federal government is prepared to go in accommodating native interests, one columnist put it this way:

"Could anyone imagine these days a Royal Commission into, say, the status of French speaking Canadians outside Quebec dominated by French speakers themselves? The Commission would be laughed out of court as utterly predictable special pleading. Or a Royal Commission into defence, with a majority of commissioners wearing stripes? Moreover, two of the non-native Commissioners—former Supreme Court Judge Bertha

Wilson and former Saskatchewan Premier Allan Blakeney—are deeply sympathetic to native perspectives." [7]

The terms of reference, also set by the former Chief Justice, are elaborate and extensive in scope. In abbreviated form, the Commission was instructed to examine all issues which it deemed relevant and, in particular, make concrete recommendations on all aspects of aboriginal life.

Notwithstanding his earlier expressed dissatisfaction with a Commission that would lead to "yet another report" and his avowed disinterest in being involved, Mr. Erasmus was appointed as Co-Chairman, embraced the Terms of Reference of the Commission with enthusiasm, and with his colleagues embarked upon a protracted public hearing process.

The Commission's work

The public hearing process commenced in April 1992 and concluded in December 1993.

"Over those twenty months, the Commission visited 96 communities across the country, heard more than 2,000 intervenors, sat for a total of 172 hearing days, and travelled hundreds of thousands of kilometres during four rounds of hearings. We went from the Atlantic to the Pacific and from the Canada-U.S. border to as far north as Cambridge Bay in the Northwest Territories." [8]

Initially, the Commission was expected to deliberate for over a year before making its final comprehensive report. It now appears that the report will not be ready until the fall of 1995 and with delays for translation and printing perhaps not until early 1996. [9]

Over the four rounds of hearings, the Commission heard a total of 1,623 Aboriginal intervenors, among them 1,032 Aboriginal groups, organizations or governments, and 591 individuals. There were also 444 non-Aboriginal intervenors, 361 of which were groups, organizations or governments and 83 of which were individuals.

The Commission has issued certain discussion papers and reports as it has gone along. The first such paper entitled *"Framing the Issues"* summarized the issues identified during round one and asked a series of questions. The second discussion paper *"Focusing the Dialogue"* proposed a framework for considering issues. This was in the form of basic themes that seemed to encompass the concerns raised at the first two rounds of hearings.

The release of the second report prompted the Commission's most distinguished member, Allan Blakeney, to resign. The former Saskatchewan Premier said he was unhappy with the way the seven member Commission was pursuing its mandate. In his view, the Commission should shift its emphasis from listening, to finding a way to tackle problems.[10] Georges Erasmus and Justice René Dussault, co-chairmen of the Commission, defended the report telling a news conference they wanted to put together the "big picture" of native issues before making recommendations. J. Peter Meekison, Academic Vice-President of the University of Alberta and a former Deputy Minister with the Alberta Government, was appointed Commissioner in the place of Mr. Blakeney.

The Commission issued its third discussion paper in November 1993 following its third round of public hearings. It deals with the subjects of healing, self determination, self sufficiency and relationships. It essentially reiterates the testimony given in the third round and makes no recommendations.

The fourth discussion paper, dated April 1994, entitled *"Toward Reconciliation"* deals with the national aboriginal organizations, and healing, self determination and self sufficiency—themes that had been earlier identified in paper number two.

In addition, the Commission has published two more definitive papers on two specific issues. The first entitled *"Partners in Confederation"*, published in 1993 seeks to make the case for the inherent right to self-government and has been alluded to in Chapter 7.

The second definitive report deals with the Relocation between 1953-55 of sixteen families totalling 92 people from the east coast of Hudson's Bay to Ellesmere Island and Resolute Bay on Cornwallis Island, in the High Arctic.

Cost of the Commission

The cost of this Royal Commission is an enormous expense to the Canadian taxpayer. Originally reported as expected to spend $8 million it now appears that the total bill will top $50 million[11] and may come closer to $60 million[12] making it by far the most expensive Royal Commission in the history of Canada. Up to this time the most expensive Royal Commission was the MacDonald Commission on

Canada's Economic Future conducted in the mid-1980's which cost $24.4 million.[13] How has the money been spent? The extensive travel has already been alluded to. It is reported that Co-chairman Georges Erasmus is being paid between $600 and $700 a day as chairman; René Dussault receives his judge's salary while the other Commissioners are paid between $350 and $500 a day.[14] In addition, the Commission staff number 68 people but this is only a small part of it.

No less than 544 contracts for research projects have been granted by the Commission. These contracts have been entered into with lawyers, consultants, political scientists, sociologists, academic institutions, aboriginal private organizations, etc. Up to October, 1994, $8,373,359 has actually been paid on the Commission's research program with more to follow.[15]

In addition to all of this, some $8 million has been provided to aboriginal and non-aboriginal organizations to carry out their own research under the Intervenor Participation Program (IPP). This initiative resulted in 142 organizations being funded, 126 of them aboriginal. This funding permitted various researchers, including lawyers, to prepare submissions for interest groups and others to be presented to the Royal Commission at its numerous hearings. It now appears that 14 native groups who took advantage of the research funds never submitted briefs or offered incomplete and deficient work. "And many of the remainder of the 142 groups that tapped the fund filed reports that were long on grievances and short on the practical solutions the commission wanted." [16]

Even DIAND Minister Ron Irwin is putting distance between himself and the Commission. He is reported to have said, "If I'd had my druthers, I would build the 1,000 houses we could build with the $58 million." [17]

Conclusions to be drawn

Can there be any doubt that when the final reports are forthcoming from this Commission, their recommendations will be overwhelmingly in support of more programs, more dollars, more constitutional recognition, more land, more resources, etc. for native peoples? To what extent the Commission will consider whether such recommendations are compatible and affordable to the rest of Canadian society remains to be seen.

Moreover, what is even more troubling is that in spite of the fact that this Commission has such a wide mandate, why is it that the Government of Canada is continuing with new and far-reaching initiatives directed towards the native people without waiting to test them against the recommendations of the Royal Commission yet to come?

Examples include the aboriginal fisheries strategy off the coast of B.C., which has proven such a disaster (dealt with in detail in Chapter 9); the passage of federal legislation setting up self-government in the Yukon; the recently announced program by the Minister of Health to pay $243 million to natives to help with solving abuse problems and alcohol,[18] which apparently came as a surprise to the native community; and treaty land entitlements previously described. In the interests of good government, these new policy initiatives should have awaited the outcome of the Royal Commission's final report to determine whether or not they fall within the scheme of things proposed.

This much is certain. Whatever the Royal Commission proposes in its final and comprehensive reports will almost certainly be accepted by the political leadership in power and their elites as the conventional wisdom accompanied, no doubt, with a compelling urge to put as many of the recommendations into place as possible without counting the cost in dollars or in long-term implications. Hardly a murmur of opposition or questioning is likely to arise for two reasons. In our present society, **any** proposals directed towards the native community are viewed as the politically right thing to do whether or not they might be of benefit in the long run. Secondly, much of the academic community and the legal profession, who ought to be expected to raise an impartial voice, are either intimidated by the need to be politically correct or are recipients of the monetary largesse spread widely throughout Canada in furtherance of this costly enterprise.

The High Arctic Relocation 1953-55

". . . feelings are not facts, no matter how fervently held.
They should not be allowed to obscure the historical record."
Deputy Minister, DIAND, May 15, 1990

On July 13, 1994, the Royal Commission released its report on the 1953-1955 relocation of certain Inuit families from Inukjuak, also known as Port Harrison, in northern Quebec to Craig Harbour (Grise Fiord) on Ellesmere Island and Resolute Bay on Cornwallis Island both in the High Arctic.

In the first relocation in 1953, three Inukjuak families were moved to Resolute Bay and four Inukjuak families to Craig Harbour. They were joined there by five families from Pond Inlet on Baffin Island, also in the High Arctic, to bring the total number of people relocated in 1953 to 22 to Resolute Bay and 32 to Craig Harbour. The 1953 relocatees were joined in 1955 by a further six families, four from Inukjuak and two from Pond Inlet. One of the Inukjuak families went to Craig Harbour while the rest went to Resolute Bay. In all, by 1955, the total number of relocatees were seven families at Craig Harbour and nine families at Resolute Bay for a total of about 92 people. All were transported by ship during the summer months.

The cause of the relocatees has, in recent years, been taken up by the Inuit Tapirisat of Canada (ITC), the national political organization representing Inuit, and its regional affiliate in northern Quebec, Makavik Corporation. They have asserted that the High Arctic relocation was unnecessary because the life of the Inuit in Inukjuak was satisfactory; that the relocation scheme was misrepresented to the Inuit; that promises were broken; that the relocation was imposed upon them against their own wishes; and that they suffered great hardship. The ITC claim that the government sent the Inuit to the High Arctic to assert Canadian sovereignty and that the relocatees ought now to be substantially compensated. The ITC also claim that those Inuit at Pond Inlet (who were in the High Arctic already but who moved to assist the newcomers) should also be compensated for assisting in the relocation process. $10 million has been suggested as the appropriate amount of compensation.

For its part, successive federal governments have consistently taken the position that life in Inukjuak was not sustainable for the 500 or more people that were there in the light of depressed fur prices and insufficient fur bearing animals to sustain the population. Governments have maintained that, despite some misunderstandings and unforeseeable hardships in the first year, life in the High Arctic overall was satisfactory for the relocatees. They stress that only those Inuit who consented to the relocation were considered for the move.

Threshing old straw

Repeated representations have been made for "redress" but up to now they have been categorically rejected by previous Conservative and Liberal governments. The Makavik Research Department has been pressing the matter since 1977. It came to a head in 1990 when on March 19, 1990, Makavik representatives as well as Inuit relocatees appeared before the House of Commons Standing Committee on Aboriginal Affairs, tabled a Position Paper and testified on the relocation issue.

The Deputy Minister of DIAND submitted a 10-page response to the Standing Committee on May 15, 1990, providing the government's view and stating that the

> *"records indicate, quite simply, that there was no malice or wrongdoing by departmental officers in the relocation project. The basic motivation—the assurance of country food supplies and somewhat enhanced employment opportunities—was honourable, and there seems to have been some effort to anticipate and avoid the inevitable problems of relocation."* [19]

In the words of the Deputy Minister,

> *"It is 37 years since the first people moved from Inukjuak to Resolute Bay and Grise Fiord. With the passage of time, the facts surrounding the project have become altered in the memories of the people concerned. It is important to examine the beliefs of the present, which are undoubtedly sincere, in the light of observations made at the time."* [20]

The Deputy Minister went further:

> *"feelings are not facts, no matter how fervently held. They should not be allowed to obscure the historical record".* [21]

Nonetheless, in its June 19, 1990, unanimous report to the House of Commons, the Standing Committee recommends that the government:

1. acknowledge the role played by the Inuit relocated to the High Arctic in the protection of Canadian sovereignty in the North;
2. issue an apology for wrongdoings carried out against the people of Grise Fiord and Resolute Bay;
3. carry out such an apology with due solemnity and respect;
4. accompany the apology with some form of recognition of the contribution of the Inuit of Grise Fiord and Resolute Bay to Canadian sovereignty; and
5. consider compensation to the Inuit of these two communities for their service to Canada and for the wrongdoings inflicted upon them.

Following the tabling of the Standing Committee report in the House of Commons, DIAND commissioned the Hickling Corporation, an independent consultant mutually acceptable to both Makavik and DIAND, to assess the factual basis of the allegations that led to the Standing Committee's report.

The main findings and conclusions of the Hickling report were unequivocal. It found that the primary motivation for the relocation was to improve the living conditions of the Inuit; reasonable preparations were made for the relocation, including reasonable steps to explain the relocation to the Inuit, although some Inuit may not have understood what was involved; a promise was made to return the relocatees but it was not of indefinite duration; there was no wilful wrongdoing by the government; and there was no reason for the government to apologize.[22]

Makavik persisted in its efforts taking the matter to the Canadian Human Rights Commission. Dr. Soberman of Queens University was commissioned to look into the matter. He tabled his report in December 1991. On January 15, 1992, the Minister of DIAND commenting on Dr. Soberman's report, noted with satisfaction that the report recognized "that the primary motivations for the project were humane"[23] and that "this is the second independent study to reject the claim that the project was primarily an effort by Canada to assert sovereignty in the Arctic."[24]

The Minister also noted that Dr. Soberman pointed out hardships created by supply problems in the first winter, by the separation resulting from relocation, by difficulties of communications between Inuit and non-Inuit, and by delays in returning those who eventually wanted to go back to Inukjuak. The Minister noted that all these concerns had been acknowledged by the Government of Canada, that approximately $1 million had already been provided to return relocatees, and that the moving expenses of any other Inuit who wanted to return to Inukjuak would be paid for by the government.[25]

Not content, the Inuit pressed again the Standing Committee on Aboriginal Affairs. This time its report to the House of Commons said that "new evidence" reaffirmed and reinforced the earlier views of the Committee. In response, DIAND commissioned Professor Gunther of Trent University "to conduct further documentary research into all the allegations made concerning the relocation, including those of the Inuit witnesses appearing before the Standing Committee in 1990."[26]

On November 20th, 1992, the Minister of DIAND (Siddon) in the light of the Hickling Report, the Soberman Report and the findings made by Professor Gunther then in hand, responded as follows:

1. The Inuit relocation was to assist them to continue their traditional way of life based on hunting and trapping. The relocation was not made to affirm or protect Canadian sovereignty in the High Arctic.

2. The relocation was motivated by humane intentions and based upon the consent of those moved. No apology, therefore, was appropriate.

3. The government acknowledged that there were deficiencies in the manner in which the relocation was prepared and implemented and that some Inuit suffered emotional stress, particularly in the first year.

4. The government acknowledged that it behaved inappropriately in initially refusing to honour the promise made to the Inuit at the time of the relocation to return them to Inukjuak if they were not happy in the High Arctic. Government had since agreed to return any relocatees or families to Inukjuak, provide them with housing as well as fund regular visits to families remaining in Grise Fiord and Resolute Bay.

5. The government was prepared to recognize in an official way the contribution of the relocated Inuit to the building of Canada's presence in the far north.

6. The government indicated that it was not prepared to pay additional compensation.[27]

One would have hoped that this fair degree of *mea culpa* on the part of government over events which transpired 40 years ago would have brought this much studied event to a close. Instead, on November 26, 1992, the ITC on behalf of the Inuit relocatees labelled both the government response and the Gunther report "an insult." They had other fish to fry. Two weeks later they formally referred the matter to the Royal Commission who gladly took the matter in hand. It mattered not to the Commission that it had been studied to death. The Commission clearly wanted to have its hand at historical revisionism.

The Commission's hearings

The Royal Commission convened special public hearings in Ottawa on this issue between April 5th and 8th, 1993, and again between June 28th to June 30th, and on July 5th, 1993. Thirty three Inuit were brought in as witnesses for the April hearings.

At the second round of hearings in late June and early July, 1993, the Commission heard from former officials of the Department of Resources and Development, as it was then called, former members of the RCMP who had been directly involved in the relocation, former members of the RCAF stationed at Resolute Bay, several academics who had been involved in previous inquiries into the subject, and a private citizen named Gerard Kenney who has studied the relocations extensively. The testimony given during the second round was buttressed by a great deal of documentary evidence dating back to the time of the relocations which included: voluminous government documents; letters of Inuit relocated; magazine articles; testimonials of many involved directly in the relocations; and the statements of impartial observers.

All the facts cited in the balance of this chapter are contained in the evidence and supporting documents which were before the Royal Commission in its consideration of this matter. What really did happen in 1953 and 1955? You be the judge.

Background

These relocations were not something that were hastily conceived and executed, but rather were grounded in the changing economic prospects of the Inuit people of the day. Consistently from 1949 onward, government records show that the depressed state of the long-haired fur trade and the shortage of furs put the Inuit economy in north western Quebec in jeopardy.[28] Inukjuak specifically was singled out as a place hard hit.[29] One James Cantley, an experienced Arctic trader, commissioned by the NWT Council, reported that the solution was to relocate voluntarily a portion of the Inuit population of northwestern Quebec where a better living could be obtained.[30] Similar views were expressed by those engaged in the annual Arctic patrols[31] and by other governmental officials.[32] Craig Harbour and Resolute, both in the High Arctic, were identified as potentially suitable locations to establish small Inuit settlements.

The relocation plan was considered at length with some of Canada's most knowledgeable experts in the field including the RCMP, Government officials, famous explorers, scientists, Northern Administration interpreters, Department of National Defence officials, anthropologists, Superintendent Henry Larsen, the Anglican Bishop of the Arctic, and many others. Accordingly, the relocation of 92 Inuit in the summers of 1953 and 1955 to the High Arctic, as described more fully in the testimony to follow, took place.

There was concern that the move from Inukjuak to the High Arctic would mean the people would have to contend with the very long nights at certain parts of the year which they were not familiar with. For that reason, it was proposed that some Inuit from Pond Inlet, which is located also in the High Arctic, should accompany the relocatees to Ellesmere Island. That was done.[33]

The evidence of the relocatees

In April 1993 the Royal Commission brought 33 Inuit to Ottawa from the High Arctic and Inukjuak in northern Quebec to testify on the relocations. They were dubbed "the relocatees" although it is significant to observe that of the 33 witnesses, only 14 were adults, 4 were teenagers, 13 were small children and 2 were yet to be born at the date of the relocations. Two of those addressing the Commission had remained in Port Harrison and had not been relocated, and two had been born in Resolute Bay, one remaining there and the other moving to Inukjuak. No indication is given as to how these witnesses were chosen or whether they were truly representative of those who best knew and experienced first-hand the circumstances of the relocation.

In short, all of the relocatees who gave evidence claimed a deep sense of hurt and loss as a result of the relocation. Those who came from Inukjuak did not consider themselves to be poor or in need while they were there; some said there was plenty of food for them at Inukjuak and "they had no worries or cares."[34] Others said they were "completely satisfied with their lives at Inukjuak and had all the equipment necessary to make a good living."[35] Some spoke of the distress they experienced and the lack of support they received from the government and the inadequacy of the trading store at their new location. Some complained that the RCMP members at Resolute Bay did not treat the Inukjuak Inuit with courtesy and scolded the poorer hunters and treated well the good hunters. One or two said that there was no choice but to relocate because that is what the government wanted. Several said that the promise to return was not kept by the government. Depression and despondency resulted in some families and family relationships were disrupted in various ways. An unusually large number of these witnesses used similar terminology such as they didn't have "a care in the world" at Inukjuak; that the place where they moved to was "desolate"; that they were promised the "promised land." One said their new-found home was the poorest place in all the world for food.[36]

Many relocatees called for compensation from government for this ill treatment. One of them testified that "the price the High Arctic exiles have paid and continue to pay cannot be measured in dollars" and that she could not understand why the relocatees who had some years ago asked for $10 million did not deserve recognition so that they could start the healing process and rebuild their lives. She then alluded to the money given to deal with violence against women as a result of the fourteen women killed in Montreal and the compensation given to the Japanese. She concluded by saying that the Inuit are Canadians who suffered for Canadian sovereignty and deserve the same recognition.[37]

I could go on. Suffice it to say that the 33 Inuit witnesses flown to Ottawa to give testimony spoke in unison about the alleged deprivation and shortcomings of everything to do with the relocations. There seemed to be not one redeeming feature for the move in all of their testimony.

The voices of former government officials and others

At the June, 1993 hearings the first witness was one of Canada's most distinguished former public servants, Gordon Robertson, who has the uncommon distinction for a bureaucrat of having been elevated to the Privy Council for his work and therefore is known as "Honourable." Mr. Robertson served in the Department of External Affairs from the time he joined the public service in 1941 until 1945 when he served in the office of Prime Minister Mackenzie King. Between 1949 to 1953 he was with the Privy Council office in Ottawa, and in November of 1953 was appointed Deputy Minister of the Department of Resources and Development, and also Commissioner of the North West Territories—positions he held until 1963. Subsequently, he became Secretary to the Cabinet for many years, and then later Secretary to the Cabinet for Federal/Provincial relations.

Mr. Robertson effectively debunked the proposition that the move had anything to do with sovereignty in the north. He testified that he attended every meeting of the Cabinet during 1949 to 1953 including the January 1953 meeting in which the then Secretary of State for External Affairs, Lester B. Pearson, brought the sovereignty concern to Cabinet. Mr. Robertson testified that the Canadian government was not worried about the United States challenging Canadian title to the Arctic islands. Canada had no doubt about its title to the Arctic islands and no fear of being challenged by any other country to its title over them. He pointed out that the situation with respect to the water between the Arctic islands was a different matter. The water between the islands is still regarded by the United States and by some other countries as being international waters. The Canadian position is that the waters within the Arctic islands are the inland waters of Canada. Mr. Robertson stated that the Inuit settlements in the High Arctic could not be a demonstration of sovereignty by the Government of Canada in any event. He testified further that the relocation in 1953 was never discussed by the Cabinet and, as far as the government was concerned, it had no relation to sovereignty.

Mr. Robertson testified that in April 1954, one winter after the first relocation, he visited Resolute and saw first-hand how the people were living. He visited many of the snow houses (igloos) himself, acknowledging that the initial period was harsh but that the way of life at Resolute was no different from the way of life across the Arctic. Mr. Robertson's 1954 perceptions were that both children and adults relocated were healthy and that the hunting had been quite good.

Mr. Robertson stated that in his view 95% of the department's motivation was an honest desire to reduce the over-population in relation to resources in northern Quebec and to put people in places where they would have a better chance to have a successful life on the land. He considered that senior government officials of whom Bent Sivertz was one had a "deep profound interest in the welfare of the Inuit people"[38] and that in his view it was a travesty of justice to now, so many years later, have their motives misinterpreted.

On being questioned about the sharply different perceptions of what took place between the Inuit relocatee witnesses and the testimony of government officials, Mr. Robertson, always the diplomat, said it was quite possible there was a major misunderstanding due to linguistic and cultural differences. He considered that those who were children at the time and heard their parents talk about hardships may have come to believe that that was the totality of the situation and that the hardship of the initial period may have been generalised and exaggerated.

The next witness was Mr. Bent Sivertz.[39] Mr. Sivertz joined the Department of External Affairs in 1946 after wartime service and in 1949 moved to the Department of Mines and Resources to serve as Executive Assistant to the Deputy Minister Dr. Keenleyside. Mr. Sivertz was appointed Chief of the Arctic Division in March 1954 and subsequently became Commissioner of the North West Territories. Mr. Sivertz, who is now retired in Victoria, testified that reports from the Port Harrison area at the time showed that the people were destitute. Having thoroughly satisfied himself that relocation was the best course of action, department officials consulted with the Inuit families who might wish to move North. Mr. Sivertz stressed that the Inuit decision to go was their own. No one was urged to relocate.

Mr. Sivertz testified that the department sought out those among the Inuit who were thought to be leaders, recognizing that among the Inuit decisions were not made by open vote but by consensus. The conditions the Inuit should expect to find in the High Arctic were explained to them in detail. After three consultations, separated by six month periods to allow for due consideration, several Inuit leaders stated that they and their families desired to make the move to the High Arctic. Space was then arranged in the ship for the relocatees, their sled dogs, household items, and hunting equipment. Two departmental employees supervised and assisted with the move.

RCMP Constable Ross Gibson accompanied the relocatees on their sea voyage on the vessel "C. D. Howe" and, together with the two Inuit RCMP Special Constables already stationed at Craig Harbour, supervised the relocatees' arrival. Constable Gibson, greatly admired and respected by Inuit and non-Inuit alike, remained four years in this northern posting adjacent to the Inuit community at Resolute, operating the government store, along with his regular duties.

Mr. Sivertz testified that the reports on the state of the new communities at the time indicated that the project was a success. There was plenty of game of much greater variety than they had ever seen before and help from the RCMP, health-providers when summoned, government administrators, Hudson Bay Company staff, and others, was readily available. The people were well fed and happy and appeared satisfied. Photographs show lively, healthy, smiling, happy-looking people. Living in igloos was not a hardship, it was their way of life.

Mr. Sivertz testified that Superintendent Henry Larsen of the RCMP in 1956 reported that the people at Grise Fiord had prospered and it was hard for him to realize that they were the same people that he had seen landed there in 1953 all in rags and with little or no equipment. The teacher at Inukjuak in 1953, Margery Hinds, visited Resolute in 1958 and made a similar report to Mr. Sivertz of amazing betterment on every front. In April 1954, a writer and photographer for the *National Geographic* visited the Inuit settlement at Resolute Bay. The words and pictures describe and show in detail a thriving, very happy, healthy community.

In support of the Inuit relocation, Mr. Sivertz refers to an in-depth interview given by Saluvinik, the elected leader of the Inuit relocatees at Resolute Bay for 15 to 20 years, to the Inuit newspaper, Nunatsiaq News of Iqaliut on May 25th, 1977, 24 years after the relocation. Saluvinik describes in graphic detail conditions at Port Harrison in Northern Quebec where he was born and grew up. He further states he will never forget the times his people were very hungry and food consisted of lemmings and even dogs when they were desperate. He says:

> "In 1953, I moved to Resolute Bay. An RCMP came to me and told me I could move to Resolute Bay if I wanted to. He told me there were a lot more animals up there. So I wanted to move. Since I moved to Resolute (1953), I have never wanted to return to Port Harrison. If I wanted to go back I think the Government would help us. But I would rather stay here."[40]

Figure 12 - Photos of Inuit Relocatees at Resolute Bay, 1954
courtesy of Mrs. Ross Gibson

A report tendered as evidence made by Donald B. Marsh, Anglican Bishop to the Arctic, following his personal visits to Grise Fiord and Resolute Bay in 1956, describes the conditions he found on his trip.[41] The relocatees at Resolute had clean and orderly campsites with plenty of essentials and piles of skins for clothing and good fresh meat. In addition to these findings, he also considered that the women and children were, in his words, the picture of health. The little ones, chubby-cheeked, rosy and bright eyed, were very happy and contented. This was three years after the relocation in 1956. At this time the whole settlement went on board the annual supply ship for their medical tests. The Doctor examined each resident and pronounced all to be in good health.

Mr. Sivertz also referred to the Inuit translator, Annie Padlo, who worked for DIAND for ten years during the 1950s and 1960s. She was on board the ship when the Inukjuak Inuit were taken north to their new High Arctic location. She also visited those relocated every summer over the next three years. She said:

"When we picked up the Port Harrison Inuit, they were starving and very skinny. Many were sick and had lots of head lice. One man told me how he had been living on nothing but lemmings. No one was forced to go. The two men from DIAND, Leo Manning and Walter Rudnicki, asked who wanted to move and only took those who actually volunteered."[42]

During her many visits to the settlements she said she never heard anything concerning sexual abuse and slave labour as alleged to the Royal Commission. If anyone should have knowledge of cruelty, inhumane treatment or any of the other allegations, surely the interpreter would be the first to know?

A freelance photographer, Wilfred Doucette, wrote a letter to the Editor of the Toronto Star dated August 5, 1991 in which he describes his experiences with the Eastern Arctic patrols of the years 1951 through to 1956. Mr. Doucette observed that the new community was thriving, healthy, and happy when he visited it in 1954/55. In his letter, Mr. Doucette states that the claims by some natives who moved north in the early 1950s for compensation from the Canadian Government are simply without foundation.

Margery Hinds, wrote a book entitled *"High Arctic Venture"* about her many years teaching school in Inuit communities. She had helped put together the group from Inukjuak for the relocation. She followed up by going to the High Arctic herself a year or two later to teach and observe and help her long-time friends adjust and learn. She states in her book:

> "While in Resolute Bay, the Eskimos came on board the ship from time to time, among them people I had known at Port Harrison. It was very difficult to recognize many of them. All were well dressed. Younger ones had grown tall, and older ones fat, so that even before they said that life was good at Resolute Bay, it was very obvious they were no longer destitute and starving as they had been prior to the relocation."[43]

Mr. Sivertz stated that the first time he heard any stories of unhappiness concerning the relocatees was about 1975 or 1976. He testified that if the group had been unhappy, he would have taken them back and called the whole thing off. There were no risks of extreme hardship. The RCMP posts had radio facilities able to call for help if necessary. He testified that there was no suffering. Year after year his officers asked if the people wished to return to Inukjuak and the people said no. Individual Inuit among the relocatees came forward from time to time with problems of health, family catastrophe, and old age loneliness and requested a temporary return to Inukjuak. Usually a place in a plane was found courtesy of the RCMP or RCAF. Mr. Sivertz recalls 10 to 20 such cases and thought there may have been more.

Of the former government officials who testified, perhaps the most outspoken was Dr. Graham Rowley, an archaeologist and anthropologist, whose work and interests over almost sixty years have been centred in the Arctic.[44] In 1958 he was Secretary and Coordinator of the Advisory Committee on Northern Development. He was in full agreement with the move, after having discussed it with Mr. Sivertz and RCMP Superintendent Larsen. In his view, the only reason for the move was to benefit the Inuit and without any question the move was voluntary. He testified of the hardship and starvation that had plagued Northern Quebec Inuit in the past. For example, in the winter of 1942-43 over a hundred Inuit and Indians starved to death near Fort Chimo in Northern Quebec.

He bluntly maintained that the complaint about the relocation had been fabricated and that the witnesses who gave evidence before the Commission in April were selected by an organization (ITC) that had already stated its position on the issue and that the "witnesses who did come were instructed to say nothing positive about their lives in the north."[45]

Gerard Kenney was also called as a witness.[46] His evidence was compelling. Kenney worked in the Arctic in the 1960s and 70s as a telecommunication engineer. He became interested in the north and its people and particularly in the media stories about the relocation. He began archival research to look for the official documents which would establish whether sovereignty concerns were really the motive for the relocation. His research turned up no documents which remotely tied the relocation to national security concerns even though all of those documents have now been made public on the basis of the 30 year rule.[47]

His research uncovered a massive amount of documentary evidence pointing to another reason for the relocation, namely a sincere concern on the part of the government for the welfare of the Inuit living on the "hungry coast" on the eastern side of Hudsons Bay. He approached his subject convinced by media coverage that the move was motivated by sovereignty concerns but at the end of his research concluded the very opposite. He testified that he began his research in the fall of 1991 in the National Archives in Ottawa and has pored over thousands of pages of official government documents, many marked 'Secret' or 'Top Secret' but now declassified. He says: "In fact, I turned up not one pertinent document that remotely tied the 1950's relocations to national security concerns for protecting the Arctic against claims of foreign powers."[48]

In referring to the earlier testimony given by the Inuit relocatees, he said:

> "Where the Inuit have said that they went hungry and underwent terrible sufferings in their new High Arctic homes after the relocations, I found absolutely no documentary evidence of this. What I did find, though, was plenty of hard documentation showing that the Inuit were far better off in their new homes than they had ever been in Inukjuak, that they had more food and fur resources, that they were the healthiest communities of Inuit in all the Arctic, and that their communities were financially prospering, especially Resolute Bay. Much of this documentation to which I refer is in the form of letters written by the relocated Inuit themselves living in Resolute Bay."[49]

He goes on:

> *"It has been said that the Inuit were promised they could return to their old homes within two years if they were not happy. This contention is, in fact, supported by documentary evidence. What is not supported, though, is that they asked to go back. Instead there is documentary evidence to the effect that they were so satisfied with their new homes that they did not want to go back . . . Where requests to go back were expressed in the Inuit letters, they were almost invariably for temporary visits to see relatives or to take care of aging parents."* [50]

He went on:

> *"If the evidence appears to be heavily one-sided, that is because the documented evidence is one-sided. There is virtually no documentary evidence supporting the Inuit allegations relating to hardship, suffering, and wrong-doing in connection with the relocations. In fact, the evidence is much to the contrary."* [51]

Mr. Kenney referred to the testimony of two of the relocatee witnesses in April which completely contradicted statements that the same persons had made previously. In the first case, the witness before the Commission had bitterly complained about the trip by ship to the High Arctic: high winds, darkness, poor food, no tea, forced to eat the same old food every day. This same witness was on a CBC television program in Grise Fiord in 1986 in which she said: "The trip here was OK. It was pleasant enough. I didn't mind that boat trip at all."

Another witness testified at the April hearing: "I don't remember being hungry at all in Inukjuak . . . I remember we never went hungry in Inukjuak." The same witness in an interview reported in the Inuktitut Magazine for December, 1981, said: "We used to be very hungry in Inukjuak."

Mr. Kenney then produced twenty letters written in the 1950s, 1960s and 1970s by relocated Inuit. With one or two exceptions the original letters were written in syllabics and translated by Inuit translators in the Canadian government. Words of contentment, satisfaction, and an unwillingness to leave their new locale is a theme that runs through them all. Many of them request relatives to be brought north to join them. After reading in the twenty letters, Mr. Kenney in his testimony came to the nub of the issue:

"We have been told at the April hearings that Inuit oral history is very accurate and that it must not be questioned. However, there are obviously two Inuit histories: that presented at the Royal Commission hearings here last April and, on the other hand, that revealed by letters written from the High Arctic in the 1950s and 1960s by Inuit who had been relocated, by an article written by a relocated Inuit, and by magazine and TV interviews of a relocated Inuit. Which of the Inuit histories are we to believe? Which is the more credible, the history presented at the April hearings, which I will call history A, based on:

- *memories of events that took place forty years ago?*
- *memories which at forty years distance are surely not immune to fading and distortion due to the effects of passing time?*
- *memories of forty year old events recounted by witnesses, some of whom were three, four, five, or six years old when they took place? Surely these must be discounted as relevant testimony.*
- *memories that are subject to tremendous peer pressure? How well received by peers would have been an Inuk who had testified at the April hearings about the good parts of his or her life as a result of the relocations?*
- *memories that are subject to the obvious distorting pressures of a potential prize of ten million dollars if the Inuit are shown to have been victims? The distorting pressures of such a situation, especially when coupled with peer pressure, can be enormous.*

"Or is it more reasonable to believe in the following history, history B, based on the writings of the relocated Inuit in the 1950s and 1960s:

- *history that is based on letters spontaneously written by adult Inuit in the 1950s and 1960s in the period following the relocations;*
- *letters that had no possible hidden agenda but which are a true and innocent expression of the writer's feelings and opinions;*
- *letters that are not written to influence any potential $10 million prize. There was no prize.*

- *letters that were not subject to any peer pressure. There were individual and private initiatives. No lawyers were involved.*
- *letters which said that the Inuit were happy in their new homes where game was more plentiful than in their old homes;*
- *letters that, with few exceptions, said the writers did not want to go back home. The exceptions were requests for temporary visits or to help out aging parents;*
- *letters that several times said the white people in the RCMP helped the Inuit and were good to them and, in particular thanked Ross Gibson for the help he gave them because 'Ross is very good for the Eskimos'.*

"This then is the question that the Royal Commission must ponder and attempt to answer. Which of the two Inuit histories is to be believed—for there are two of them, diametrically opposed to each other, history A and history B."[52]

Conclusions of the Royal Commission

The Commission's report and its two supplementary volumes comprise about 600 pages of fascinating reading. The testimony itself is fascinating but, more than that, is the way in which the Commission attempts to reconcile the overwhelming documentary and oral evidence in support of the relocation versus the diametrically opposite oral evidence given by the new-found witnesses for the relocatees. The intellectual wriggling and contortions which the Commission goes through in attempting to reconcile the evidence would make a modern-day Houdini green with envy. The fact of the matter is that the two sets of evidence are clearly irreconcilable. One has to be believed and the other disbelieved to get to the truth of the matter.

In the face of the testimony briefly summarized above, the findings of the Royal Commission and its recommendations were:

Findings

1. The relocation was **not** aimed at relieving population pressure on limited game resources, but was to do with the ability of the fur trade to sustain the income levels of Inukjuak Inuit.[53]
2. The goal of the relocation was to restore the Inuit to what was considered to be their proper state. It was a rehabilitation project.[54]
3. Relocation to the uninhabited High Arctic islands was reinforced in a material way by concern for Canada's sovereignty.

4. The Department proceeded with the High Arctic relocation without proper authority.
5. The relocation was not voluntary. It proceeded without free and informed consent.
6. Many Inuit were kept in the High Arctic for many years against their will and the government refused to respond to their requests to return.
7. The government was negligent in its planning and implementation of the relocation.
8. The relocation was an ill-conceived solution that was inhumane in its design and in its effects.
9. Great wrongs have been done to the relocatees and it is incumbent on the government to accept the fundamental merit of the relocatees complaints.
10. An acknowledgement of the wrongs suffered by the relocatees and their families as well as their communities coupled with an apology is warranted.
11. An acknowledgement of the special contribution of the relocatees to the maintenance of Canadian sovereignty in the High Arctic is appropriate.
12. Compensation in an adequate amount and form is warranted, taking account of the specific and general effects of the relocation.

Recommendations
1. The government should acknowledge the wrongs done to the Inuit and apologise to the relocatees.
2. The government should acknowledge the special contribution of the relocatees to the maintenance of Canadian sovereignty in the High Arctic.
3. The government should meet with representatives of the relocatees to settle all aspects of compensation.
4. The process of negotiation should be agreed to by the representatives of the relocatees.
5. Compensation should be in the amount and form agreed to between the parties.
6. The costs incurred by the relocatees or their representatives (meaning lawyers, advisors, etc.) in attempting to resolve these complaints should be reimbursed.

The Government's response

Mixed signals have been forthcoming from the government in response to the report. Initially the Minister said the Department "would carefully review the findings of the Commission."[55] On September 20, 1994, the Minister was quoted as saying he wanted to wait at least until next spring, when the final report of the Royal Commission would be forthcoming.[56] However within 24 hours the Minister appeared to do a flip-flop, acknowledged "wrong doing" on the part of government in relocating the 92 Inuit and stating that he "will meet with Inuit leaders soon to discuss taking the matter to Cabinet.[57]

Media reaction to the report

What has been the media's reaction to the Commission's report on the High Arctic relocations? Mixed. Several of the main line newspapers wrote editorials demanding that the government immediately apologise and pay compensation to the relocatees or their survivors. Obviously the editorial writers of those newspapers did little more than read the introduction to the Report and the Report's findings and recommendations. Had they read the testimony of the witnesses and the documentation they would have not been so quick to jump to such a conclusion.

Some editorial writers and columnists took a different view. William Johnson of the *Montreal Gazette* says that the High Arctic move should be seen in the context of the times[58]; Douglas Fisher of the Ottawa Sun gives a sympathetic word to Dr. Marguerite Ritchie, QC,[59] President of the Human Rights Institute of Canada, who has written to DIAND Minister Irwin, asking him to withhold any decision on the report claiming that the Commission did not deal fairly with the evidence and acted in a biased manner.

In an editorial, the *Globe and Mail* state that to give an apology and compensation in this case would amount to "applying a retroactive morality, satisfying a need to assert the contemporary cant of political correctness."[60]

In his column appearing in the *Toronto Star* entitled "What's the real truth about the Inuit relocation?" Pierre Berton supports the view of history put forward by Gerard Kenney and the former government officials. He points out that the commissioners appeared to have made up their minds before all the evidence was heard. He cites that back in June 1992 at the time the Commission decided to hold hearings on this subject, co-chair René Dussault called the relocation a "human catastrophe". After the Ottawa hearings in April 1993, but before the former government witnesses had testified, Bertha Wilson talked about a "cruel and inhumane government policy". This premature pronouncement of judgment caused Berton to support Kenney's call for a judicial inquiry.[61]

A new meaning for "Reconciliation"

Throughout its reports and pronouncements, the Royal Commission asserts that the conflicting testimony has been reconciled. Early in its report, this statement appears:

"The challenge in understanding this relocation is to open one's mind to the oral history and to read the documentary record in an enquiring spirit, ever mindful of the people who were relocated. The object is not to seek validation of the oral history in the written record."[62]

Another choice quote, which must be the ultimate in doublespeak, reads:

"The government position rests on a large volume of documentary material, with the result that much time and effort have been spent on understanding the written record. With the benefit of the new information in the relocatees oral testimony, it has been possible to reconcile apparent conflicts in the evidence. This reconciliation of the evidence makes it possible for those who hold conflicting views about the relocation to reconcile their differences."[63]

Again, in the Preamble to its Recommendations is says this:

"The Commission's process has allowed new light to be shed on the relocation. The apparent conflicts in the evidence have been reconciled."[64]

In the press release accompanying the Commission's report on July 13, 1994, this continued reference to reconciling the evidence is referred to. Commission Co-chair Georges Erasmus is quoted as saying:

"We feel it is a major accomplishment that we were able to reconcile the various strands of testimony and in so doing, weave together an accurate picture of the relocation."

Differences in the testimony reconciled? Nothing could be further from the truth.

The fact is that on the one side stands the overwhelming documentary evidence accompanied by the testimony of some of Canada's most distinguished former public servants as well as the testimony of many of the Inuit involved who freely expressed themselves in years gone by. On the other, stands a group of witnesses, many of whom were young children at the time, transported to Ottawa, hotelled and fed, to testify in furtherance of the prospect of an award of $10 million.

You be the judge.

Chapter 8 - Footnotes:

1. "Aboriginal affairs commission planned," *Globe and Mail,* April 24, 1991, A1.

2. At this Victoria announcement, Prime Minister Mulroney also announced that funding for native students at universities would be increased by $320 million over 5 years. He also promised an infusion of resources that would clean up outstanding land claims within the next 9 years.

3. "Aboriginal affairs commission planned," Ibid., A2.

4. "Native leaders wary of federal proposal," *Globe and Mail,* April 29, 1991.

5. "Aboriginal affairs commission planned, Ibid., A1.

6. Opening Statement by the Rt. Hon. Brian Dickson on the occasion of the launch of the Public Hearings of the Royal Commission on Aboriginal Peoples, Winnipeg, Manitoba, April 21, 1992.

7. Jeffrey Simpson, "The telling nature of the new Royal Commission on Aboriginal Affairs," *Globe and Mail,* August 30, 1991, A14.

8. Royal Commission on Aboriginal Peoples, *Toward Reconciliation, Overview of the Fourth Round,* April, 1994, Preface vii.

9. "Native commission's big bill irks Irwin," *Times-Colonist,* October 22, 1994, F8.

10. "Blakeney quits aboriginal enquiry," *Times-Colonist,* April 3, 1993, A12.

11. "Native study to cost $50 million," *Toronto Star,* July 14, 1993, A10.

12. "Native commission's big bill irks Irwin," *Times-Colonist,* October 22, 1994, F8.

13. "Native study to cost $50 million", *Toronto Star,* July 14, 1993, A10.

14. "Native commission's big bill irks Irwin, Ibid.

15. News Release, "Indian Industry at Work," John Duncan, MP, March 24, 1995.

16. "Native commission's big bill irks Irwin," Ibid.

17. Ibid.

18. "Ottawa tags $243m for 5 years to help natives conquer abuse," *Times-Colonist,* September 28, 1994, B7.

19. Royal Commission on Aboriginal Peoples, *Report on the High Arctic Relocation 1953-55,* Ottawa, 1994, Appendix 5, 180.

20. Ibid.

21. Ibid.

22. Ibid., 181.

23. Ibid.

24. Ibid.

25. Ibid., 182-83.

26. Ibid.

27. Ibid., 184-85.

28. Royal Commission on Aboriginal Peoples, *Report on the High Arctic Relocation 1953-55,* Ottawa, 1994, Summary of Supporting Information, Volume II, 291.
29. Ibid., 311.
30. Ibid., 294.
31. Ibid., 314, 317, 341.
32. Ibid., 308.
33. Ibid., 341.
34. Ibid., Vol I, 29.
35. Ibid., 30.
36. Ibid., 46.
37. Ibid., 78.
38. Ibid., 130.
39. Ibid., 134-143.
40. *Nunatsiaq News*, May 25, 1977.
41. *The Arctic News*, Anglican Church Periodical, October 1956, 6.
42. Matthew Spence, "Interpreter says exiles don't deserve compensation," *Nunatsiaq News,* November 30, 1990.
43. Margery Hinds, *High Arctic Venture* (1956), 11.
44. Royal Commission on Aboriginal Peoples, *Report on the High Arctic Relocation 1953-55,* Summary of Supporting Information, Volume I, 143-157.
45. Ibid., 155-56.
46. Ibid., 199-223.
47. Mr. Kenny has recently written and published a book on the High Arctic Inuit relocation entitled, *"Arctic Smoke and Mirrors"* published by Voyageur Publishing, Prescott, Ontario.
48. Ibid., 199.
49. Royal Commission on Aboriginal Peoples, *Verbatim Transcript of Evidence,* June 29, 1993, 465.
50. Ibid., 465-466.
51. Ibid., 467.
52. Ibid., 494-498.
53. A distinction without a difference.
54. Is that bad?
55. *Government of Canada News Release,* Ottawa, July 13, 1994.
56. "Minister shelves apology to Inuit," *Ottawa Citizen,* September 20, 1994.
57. "Minister admits relocating Inuit was 'wrong thing'," *Ottawa Citizen,* September 21, 1994, A3.
58. William Johnson, "Move to High Arctic must be seen in context of times," *Montreal Gazette,* July 16, 1994.

59. Douglas Fisher, "Don't believe all you read," *The Ottawa Sun,* October 14, 1994, II.

60. "Relocated Inuit," *Globe and Mail,* July 15, 1994.

61. Pierre Berton, "What's the real truth about the Inuit relocation?," *Toronto Star,* April 16, 1994.

62. Royal Commission on Aboriginal Peoples, Report, Ibid., 2.

63. Ibid., 161.

64. Ibid., 3.

The Aboriginal Commercial Fishery in B.C.

"The Sparrow decision did not, despite the fact that many people have acted as if it did, ever give authority for the sale—the commercial sale—of food fish. . . .
. . . We have to say that [the AFS] *hasn't worked, but also there has to be a clear understanding that it is not the law today."* Hon. John Fraser, PC, QC, Chairman, Fraser River Sockeye Public Review Board, March 1995.

During the past fifteen years, perhaps no other industry in Canada has felt the impact of government acquiescence to the native agenda more than the commercial fishery of British Columbia. Long before other Canadians even became aware of aboriginal demands, the B.C. commercial fishery was suffering financial losses as the federal Department of Fisheries and Oceans (DFO) transferred fish allocations from the racially-blind commercial fleet to native-only fisheries.

The industry was forced to defend its interests against the federal government, especially DIAND, which desperately wanted to create some type of increased resource base for B.C. natives at its expense. Being the only natural resource under federal jurisdiction, it was perhaps inevitable that fish were referred to in Ottawa as "land claims dollars."

Furthermore, the powerful aboriginal lobby outflanked a fragmented and divisive fishing industry. For politicians this meant that the risk of any political backlash from the industry was minimal. With virtually every B.C. native group demanding increased allocations, the federal government quietly delivered tens of millions of dollars in fish allocations to aboriginal groups throughout the 1980's with little organized opposition from the fishing industry.

An excerpt from a 1990 discussion paper submitted to DFO's National Aboriginal Fisheries Committee illustrates one of the options the federal government was considering. It states:

> "It is estimated that the total coastal native [sic] claims allocation would be between 40-50% of the TAC [Total Allowable Catch] if we use the proposed Nisga'a allocation as the precedent. In all likelihood the amount sought in subsequent claims will be even higher than the Nisga'a allocation."[1]

Had government proposed to reallocate 50 per cent of the jobs in the mining, forest or automobile industries solely to aboriginal people, the coast to coast outcry would have been deafening.

Two critical events in 1982 and two in 1990 were used by the federal government to justify this intention to reallocate the resource in a major way. Taken together, they would prove revolutionary in their impact on what used to be a multiracial commercial fishery. Few would have guessed that these events would lead to the devastation of prized B.C. salmon runs and DFO's reputation for world-class fisheries management. Moreover, these events would lead to different standards of justice among Canadians, a federally funded misinformation campaign, and disregard for the Constitution of Canada.

Removing the basis for detection

Dr. Peter Pearse's September 1982 Royal Commission report on Pacific fisheries policy was the first event. Buried in its 300 pages was the following recommendation: "The present regulation requiring Indians to remove the dorsal fins and snouts of their fish should be rescinded."[2]

The Minister of Fisheries subsequently adopted Pearse's recommendation and thereby laid the basis for a fisheries management disaster. No longer did natives have to cut off the snouts and dorsal fins from their food fish. As a result, DFO enforcement officers could not distinguish between a salmon caught as native food fish and a salmon caught under a commercial fishing licence. The only fish that can be legally sold in Canada are those caught under a commercial fishing licence so it was necessary to distinguish between food fish and commercially caught fish.

The regulation was important because, outside of the commercial fleet, only natives were permitted to use commercial vessels, nets and other commercial fishing gear to harvest fish for food purposes. As such, natives have the ability to harvest millions of fish. Obviously some means were necessary to separate the two types of fish.

Prior to the deletion of the marking regulation, a cursory examination of any salmon would determine whether it was one which was allowed to be sold or whether it was native food fish. Salmon without snouts and dorsal fins were obviously native food fish and non-natives in possession of such fish were subject to immediate prosecution. Natives without a commercial licence, who had salmon in their possession with fin and snout intact were also subject to prosecution.

After the regulation was cancelled, no longer could enforcement officers walk into a restaurant kitchen or cold storage facility and simply by looking at the salmon determine whether it was native food fish. Instead, fishery officers had to witness the actual sales transaction.

This problem is aptly noted in a 1991 memo from the Director General of DFO's Pacific Region. He wrote:

> *"I should point out, however, the difficulty of obtaining necessary evidence to sustain charges for illegal sale of food fish. Once fish enters a commercial facility (ostensibly for storage) it is virtually impossible to control, or to obtain evidence that fish have entered commercial markets."* [3]

Collecting evidence that would withstand courtroom scrutiny suddenly became time-consuming, expensive and fraught with hazard and difficulty. As noted in a DFO discussion paper on the sale of native food fish, "the danger faced by fishery officers in enforcement is akin to the dangers to policemen investigating drug offenses . . ." [4] The major difference was that police officers could readily identify illegal drugs, but DFO bureaucrats had made it impossible for fishery officers to readily identify illegally sold fish.

Politics and enforcement

Even if the marking regulation had remained in place, however, a lack of political will to enforce laws against aboriginal fishermen was equally damaging to DFO's ability to manage the aboriginal food fishery. As a forerunner of what was to come, the second significant event of 1982 was the first public occasion when political interference resulted in the dropping of charges against poachers solely because they were aboriginal.

The fall of 1982 marked the conclusion of a six month undercover investigation into the illegal sale of Fraser River salmon. Undercover DFO officers had spent the previous summer buying salmon from various people who were selling native food fish in the lower Fraser River region. When the results of the investigation were made public, with the charging of over twenty persons, DFO was accused of engaging in a racist operation because most of the people charged were natives. Under pressure, the charges were dropped.

This event marked the beginning of significant political interference in the enforcement of aboriginal food fishing regulations. In 1991, the Deputy Minister of Fisheries instructed his senior staff, "that DFO should not spend disproportionate resources on enforcement of prohibition on sale of native [sic] food fish."[5] In another instance, in the spring of 1992, moments before an alleged illegal seller was to be arrested by undercover DFO fishery officers posing as fish buyers, the fishery officers were called off by their superiors. DFO apparently became a party to the illegal sale of native food fish when they sold $250,000 worth of chinook salmon and forwarded the proceeds to those engaged in the attempted illegal sale.

The government's reluctance to prosecute natives for fishing offences and the repeal of the marking regulation led to a dramatic increase in salmon poaching. In the lower Fraser River, annual native "food" fishery catches of the valuable sockeye salmon increased from 66,364 pieces in 1980 to 487,198 pieces in 1990 (approximate wholesale value in 1994 prices is $10 million).[6] By 1990, annual native salmon allocations for "food" in the region exceeded over 450 pounds of salmon for every native man, woman and child.[7]

The *Sparrow* Decision

The third event to further complicate DFO's deteriorating management efforts was the Supreme Court of Canada's 1990 judgment in *Regina vs. Sparrow.*[8] Perhaps no decision in the legal history of Canadian fish management has been more widely misread or been the subject of more seminars and discussions. The Court ruled that aboriginal people have a right, protected by the Constitution, **to harvest fish for food, social and ceremonial purposes**. The Court stated that, in the management of the fishery, conservation is the first priority, fish for aboriginal food, social, and ceremonial purposes is the second, and commercial and recreational fisheries is the third.

Though narrow in its legal import, this decision became a convenient excuse for eager bureaucrats and compliant politicians alike to argue that they were no longer able to regulate the native food fishery. DFO believed that negotiated agreements with native bands, and in some cases, allowing the sale of food fish and awarding multi-million dollar annual grants were the only viable means of "controlling" the native food fishery. Proceeding on this basis, it soon became apparent that DFO's management of aboriginal fisheries was in a precarious state.

DFO had crippled their enforcement officials by taking away the tools of enforcement and federal Ministers had no stomach for enforcing the law even when DFO fishery officers did gather enough evidence to lay charges. This left DFO with two alternatives: one, enforce the law prohibiting the sale of food fish and endure months of native protests, or two, take the easy way out and legalize the sale of food fish and endure one or two protests by the multiracial commercial fishery. DFO took the easy way out.

There was one more event which would provide the final impetus to the sale of native food fish and pave the way for a racially segregated commercial fishery.

The impact of Oka

That event was the Oka crisis. Senior DFO officials often stated that the AFS was in large part, due to Oka. Typical of these comments is an excerpt from the minutes of an August 23, 1990, meeting of DFO's National Aboriginal Fisheries Committee:

> "It was noted that the ADM, Indian Services, DIAND is preparing an Aboriginal Agenda for government post-OKA action. It will be comprehensive in scope and will address new approaches to specific claims, comprehensive claims (especially B.C.) Indian social justice (policing) economic development, Indian education, Self-government, etc . . . "[9]

These four events, combined with a 1993 federal election on the horizon, meant that confrontation with native groups was out of the question. So DFO hastily responded to aboriginal demands by implementing a scheme called the Aboriginal Fisheries Strategy (AFS) in June of 1992, which allowed the sale of native food fish and created a native-only commercial fishery.

A success story: The multiracial commercial fishery

Before outlining the details of the AFS, it is important to note the size and structure of B.C.'s commercial fishing industry. Commercial fisheries in British Columbia were relatively healthy until the introduction of the AFS in 1992. About 20,000 people find employment in the industry that creates annual sales of over $1 billion of which $850 million are export sales.[10]

There is no other industry in Canada where native people have over a great many years participated so successfully than the commercial fishery of British Columbia. Native people participate at a rate exceeding ten times their population. Although DFO and many aboriginal advocates choose to ignore this fact, today, natives take about 30% of the total salmon and herring catches through their participation in the B.C. commercial fishery though they comprise less than 3% of B.C.'s population.[11]

Though the early decades of the commercial fishery were marked by incidents of racism directed principally at Japanese and native people, there is no evidence that aboriginal fishermen were ever marginalized from the industry. While native participation fluctuated for various social, economic, and political reasons, it always well exceeded their proportion of the population.

In recent decades, various government actions have helped increase native participation well beyond traditional levels. One example of government action that benefited native fishermen occurred during World War II when persons of Japanese ancestry were forcibly removed from the coast to the interior of British Columbia. Their property, including hundreds of fishing vessels, was confiscated and most of them were sold to native people at a reduced cost.[12]

On other occasions, senior governments have purchased commercial fishing vessels and licences and transferred them directly to aboriginal fishermen. DFO also issued newly created licences to aboriginal people, long after ceasing to issue them to other Canadians.

The following graph demonstrates native licence holders in existing multiracial commercial fisheries in B.C.:

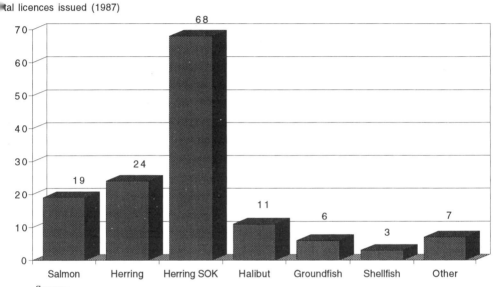

Figure 13
Native Commercial Fishing Licences

Source:
B.C. Fisheries Survival Coalition, Vancouver.

Excerpts from the *Economic Impacts of Native Participation in the British Columbia Fishing Industry* prepared by Price Waterhouse for the Native Fishing Association in July, 1989, attests to the current importance of the industry to aboriginal people:
- Aboriginal investment in vessels and licences totals over $292 million;
- 2,500 aboriginal jobs in fish harvesting;
- 1,900 aboriginal jobs in fish processing;
- 41% of the fishing industry jobs in northern B.C. are held by aboriginal people;
- Aboriginal people own 64% of the herring spawn on kelp licences. (These licences are valued at $800,000 each.)[13]

The following pie chart illustrates the percentage of the value of the landed catch paid to native fishermen in the existing multiracial commercial fishery.

Figure 14

Value of Landed Catch
($ Millions)

1990 Commercial Salmon & Herring Fisheries

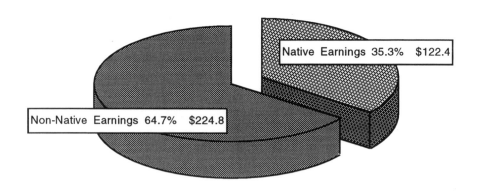

Native Earnings 35.3%　$122.4

Non-Native Earnings 64.7%　$224.8

BC POPULATION

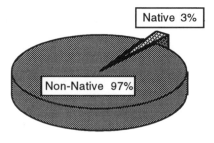

Native 3%

Non-Native 97%

Source:
B.C. Fisheries Survival Coalition, Vancouver.

In the light of these figures showing such substantial native involvement in the multiracial commercial fishery, DFO's claim in 1992 that there was justification on economic grounds for a separate native commercial fishery has a hollow ring indeed!

Ignoring native success and risking the resource

Despite native success, in the late 1980s DFO abandoned any attempt to further increase native participation in the traditional multiracial commercial fishery. DFO refused, for example, to guarantee a loan of union pension funds to the Native Fishing Association for the purchase and transfer of additional fishing vessels to native people. Instead, DFO's self-imposed paralysis of their enforcement capabilities, political acquiescence to native demands and the *Sparrow* decision provided the window of expediency for a native-only commercial fishery.

In June of 1992, only days before the start of the commercial salmon fishing season, DFO announced that it was implementing a program called the Aboriginal Fisheries Strategy (AFS) in response to the 1990 Supreme Court of Canada decision in *Sparrow*. DFO stated that the AFS formed "the basis of a new . . . social contract . . . among government, Aboriginal people and non-native fishing groups." Its purpose was "to increase economic opportunity in Canadian fisheries for Aboriginal people while achieving predictability, stability and enhanced profitability for all participants."[14]

Under the AFS, DFO negotiates agreements with each aboriginal band. The agreements set out the number of fish to be caught (i.e. an allocation) by the members of the band and which of DFO's management duties will be undertaken by the band. Instead of DFO issuing fishing licences to each band member, the band determines who can fish. Instead of DFO verifying fish catches, and closing the fishery when the allocation is reached, the native band could assume these duties. Enforcing regulations governing openings/closures, licensing, catch reporting and other regulations necessary to manage a fishery, could also be transferred to the native band. Fish enhancement activities, such as stream clearing, spawning bed counts, and hatchery management could also be assumed by native bands under AFS agreements. More than 150 agreements worth over $15 million were signed with various aboriginal organizations in 1992, the first year of the AFS. The Fraser River, the largest salmon producing river in the world, became the site for an experiment with a racially-segregated commercial fishery.

Most commercial and sport fishing groups opposed the new racially-based commercial fishery with vehemence. They warned DFO that if it was determined to proceed, responsibilities for enforcement and catch data collection must not be delegated to aboriginal or any other fishermen. These warnings reinforced earlier warnings by DFO officials such as senior enforcement officer Al Gibson who wrote:

> *"While we had no problem with the delegation of full responsibility for determination of who goes fishing and how many fish each Indian can catch within the allocation, there can be no delegation of responsibility for the collection of catch and escapement figures or for the regulation of the fishery. To provide this control would be to let the fox in the chicken house."* [15]

First year of the AFS: A disaster

Right from the start of the 1992 AFS commercial fishery there were rumours about wide-spread native poaching and 24 hour per day unregulated fishing with no DFO enforcement presence. But Deputy DFO Minister Bruce Rawson, in meetings with recreational and commercial fishing representatives, denied that there was any substance to the rumours and insisted that "things were never better."[16] By mid-August reports of severe salmon spawning shortages gave the rumours a more ominous tone.

On August 18, 1992, members of the B.C. Fisheries Commission (an umbrella group of B.C. commercial and recreational fishing organizations) demanded a meeting with senior DFO officials to review Fraser River salmon escapement. Few events better illustrate how far DFO was prepared to go to satisfy native demands than DFO's actions during this early evening meeting in Vancouver.

To the dismay of the Commission's directors, DFO opened the meeting by confirming critical salmon escapement shortfalls in virtually every river, creek, and stream affected by the AFS fishery—escapement concerns that DFO's Deputy Minister had denied just three weeks previously. Somewhere between Mission, located up-river from the mouth of the Fraser, and the spawning grounds, in waters where the native-only fisheries occurred, some 713,000[17] sockeye salmon had disappeared. This figure was in addition to the native recorded catch of some 356,000 sockeye that were allotted native bands under the AFS fishery.

The Upper Pitt River needed 25,000 spawners, but by early September only 1,282 completed the journey. The Bowron River needed 16,000, but only 2,560 were on the grounds. The Nadina River should have had 17,000 spawners, but only 3,149 survived the journey. Escapement to the hundreds of streams that make up the early miscellaneous salmon runs needed 212,000 spawners, but only 30,551 made it to the spawning grounds.[18]

With the rumours confirmed, two immediate issues remained; what was the cause or causes of the disaster, and what would DFO do to protect the remaining summer and late summer sockeye runs which were beginning their perilous Fraser River migration to the spawning grounds?

DFO explained that the escapement shortfall was likely due to fish dying from high water temperatures or an over-estimation of the number of fish entering the Fraser River. DFO made little mention of the AFS fishery. Although this was the only fishery in the region where the fish disappeared and there were numerous reports of widespread poaching, DFO discounted poaching as a possible cause.

Because DFO refused to even consider poaching as a cause of this unfolding disaster, they rebuffed demands by Commission members to close all fishing activities on the Fraser River. Arguing in favour of a ban, Mr. Mike Hunter (a Commissioner representing the Fisheries Council of B.C., an organization of major fish processing companies) argued that the only factor under DFO's control which could increase the number of fish on the spawning grounds was a ban on all Fraser River commercial, aboriginal and recreational fishing.

DFO adamantly refused to close the Fraser and asked for more time to determine the scope and causes of the escapement shortfall. Mr. Jack Nichol (a Commissioner representing the United Fishermen's and Allied Workers Union) then advised DFO that CBC Radio had asked him for an interview the following morning and he would not only release the data about the escapement shortfalls, but he was prepared to be extremely critical of DFO's refusal to close the river. For his part, Mr. Hunter added that he would seek legal advice as to whether sports and commercial organizations could obtain a court injunction to force DFO to close the river.

The next morning Mr. Nichol went public on CBC radio with news of the escapement shortfall and the Fisheries Council of B.C. initiated an injunction application destined for B.C. Supreme Court. Shortly before the application was heard, DFO announced a temporary closure of the Fraser River. The legal pressure, a dramatic public protest by 300 commercial fishing vessels, and threats by commercial fishermen to blockade Vancouver Harbour forced DFO to close the Fraser River on August 28th for the remainder of the season. This saved the remaining salmon stocks from the fate of the early season runs.

Observers outside the fishing industry were in a state of disbelief. Few believed that DFO would ignore their statutory responsibility and allow poachers to pillage sockeye runs that had been carefully nurtured to near record levels over the previous 25 years. Few could believe that DFO would squander decades of work to rebuild salmon runs like the Horsefly River sockeye run. In 1941, the Horsefly run was on the verge of extinction when only 918 salmon spawned. By 1989, after decades of careful management, almost 1.9 million Horsefly sockeye made it to the spawning grounds. But for industry insiders, DFO's refusal to close the Fraser River was simply the latest in a long series of disastrous decisions involving the mismanagement of aboriginal fisheries.

Dr. Pearse investigates

The resulting public outcry over the devastation of the stocks eventually forced Minister of Fisheries, John Crosbie, to launch an investigation into the matter. Dr. Peter Pearse, the early architect of the AFS through his 1982 Royal Commission report, was appointed to head the investigation. His report was fairly critical of the 1992 AFS. He concluded:

>*"Reports and other evidence I received of fishing from Mission to Lillooet tell the story of unprecedented intensity, management confusion, weak surveillance and enforcement, and general excess.*
>
>*"Not only were there more fishermen and nets, but fishing, which had traditionally been limited to four days per week in previous years, was almost continuous, unregulated and uncontrolled in 1992."* [19]

Perhaps his role in developing the AFS prevented Dr. Pearse from recommending its termination. Instead, he suggested a number of lesser changes such as better enforcement and stock monitoring. Dr. Pearse failed to identify who poached the fish even though he had solid evidence of at least some of the guilty parties. Even the native-run Lower Fraser Fishing Authority (LFFA), an umbrella organization which "managed" the AFS fishery on the Fraser on behalf of most of the bands, confessed to at least partial responsibility. In an internal report they wrote:

"Interview B1, a small time buyer. By his own account, he has annually been in the business for about eight years, selling 8-10,000 fish annually, for an untaxed income of about $30,000 per annum. . . .

"Interview S2, a member of the Cheam band, estimates that he sold from 150-200 sockeye daily for at least two months this past season, all but one of the buyers do not turn up on sales slip counts obtained by DFO. "I didn't keep a count," he said."[20]

Just these two buyers (the report states there were dozens of buyers like B1), described by the LFFA as "small time", moved some 20,000 sockeye. Dr. Pearse ignored this information and instead wrote, "We cannot say who took the unrecorded catch, whether they were Indians, or not . . ."[21] Thus groups like the LFFA, although they admitted partial responsibility in their unpublished internal report, were quick to claim, "Vindication. Complete vindication."[22]

Other native leaders, especially those upriver from the native-only commercial fisheries were neither vague, nor shy to point fingers at the guilty parties. Chief Nicholas Prince of the Necoslie Indian Band some 500 miles up-river wrote in a letter to the editor of the *Vancouver Sun*:

"I have told my people many times that once permission is granted to commercially net the spawners in the Fraser River, the salmon would be finished . . . We must go without our traditional foods because of the greed of the first nations of the Lower Mainland . . . The only way that thousands of fish can disappear is by overfishing and selling the fish, and to hell with everybody else . . . We all know where the blame lays and we should not point fingers at others."[23]

Second year of AFS—1993

The most significant event of the 1993 season, in addition to the record size of salmon runs in recent history, was a week long native blockade of the critical CN railway mainline serving the Port of Vancouver. The protest was organized by native leaders of the LFFA who had been allocated 630,000 sockeye under the AFS Fishery.[24] Although the natives had already caught 590,000 of their allocation (the remaining 30,000 pieces would be caught in upcoming fisheries) and received $1.9 million in government funding to manage their fisheries, when record runs appeared, they demanded a bigger share of the harvest.

Weeks prior to the blockade, in response to questions by commercial fishermen, DFO officials, such as Regional Director Pat Chamut, vehemently denied that any changes would be made to the AFS fishing agreements no matter how many fish appeared in that year.[25] DFO officials were incensed at suggestions by commercial fishermen that it would simply cave-in to native demands in the event they caught their allocation before the season was finished. Despite DFO's promises, five days after the railway blockade began, Deputy Fisheries Minister Rawson flew out from Ottawa and negotiated an end to the blockade by giving the natives additional fishing time which ensured that they would exceed their earlier allocation.[26]

For 1993, there were the usual internal DFO reports indicating widespread native poaching, financial mismanagement and unreported catches, but the poaching was masked by the largest number of salmon arriving up the Fraser River in 80 years.

Third year of the AFS—1994

After the 1992 spawning disaster, DFO promised to improve the monitoring and enforcement of AFS fishery. Although it refused to eliminate the native self-enforcement program DFO promised that: "All fish caught under Aboriginal Fishery Agreements, whether used for sale, personal consumption, ceremonial, or social purposes will be accounted for in a comprehensive catch monitoring program."[27]

In 1994, the inadequacy of DFO's efforts and the difficulty of managing the AFS native-only commercial fishery would be apparent once again. In what was expected to be another year of record runs, early in the 1994 season, as an omen of things to come, the estimated run sizes were downgraded. Reports of native poaching were widespread even before the traditional multiracial commercial salmon fishery had its first opening for Fraser River sockeye. Once again, the salmon had disappeared somewhere on the river in areas where only native people were permitted to fish with nets. The result was that the Early Stuart sockeye run was devastated. Once again, Chief Nicholas Prince and his people would have gone without their food fish except for the fact that this time DFO trucked ocean caught sockeye salmon some 1,000 kilometres inland to the people of the up-river Necoslie Indian Band.

By September 15th, the news was far worse. In a repeat of 1992, massive escapement shortfalls were evident in virtually every sockeye run that had entered the river prior to the end of August. Predictably, DFO repeated their 1992 statements blaming warm water or a malfunctioning of the fish counting mechanism. The Minister of Fisheries boldly stated, "This season's stringent catch monitoring and reporting measures indicate that the in-river [aboriginal] sockeye harvest is not the source of discrepancies in sockeye counts."[28]

Eighteen-year veteran Fraser River fishery officer Scotty Roxborough knew differently. He wrote to the Minister:

"For a desk pushing biologist to stand up and say that 1.3 million salmon died in the river before reaching the spawning grounds is laughable . . . . the salmon were caught by legal and illegal means."[29]

Immediately following DFO's less than honest announcement, dozens of leaked documents began pouring out of DFO that contradicted their official position. The *Globe and Mail* published excerpts from the first leaked document just days after DFO told Canadians about their "stringent monitoring." It reported that "Despite promises to improve the policing of British Columbia's lucrative salmon fishery, the federal government left some gaping holes in its system to stop illegal fishing . . . . fisheries officers lacked staff and budget at a crucial time this summer to monitor the aboriginal fishery on the Fraser."[30]

Other leaked DFO documents detailed matters such as the illegal movement of fish caught in AFS fisheries into the United States and Alberta, heavy poaching under the AFS, increased pressure by natives not permitted to sell food fish but attempting to launder their fish through natives with AFS sales agreements and a myriad of other abuses and DFO inadequacies.[31]

To the dismay of those who care about the resource, the damage caused by the AFS was not limited to the Fraser in 1994. In the words of DFO's Enforcement Supervisors on Vancouver Island and even certain native leaders, the 1994 native fisheries under the AFS were "out of control." DFO South Coast Vancouver Island supervisors noted:

"Due to a high degree of contact between Commercial fishers and Native fishers it has become common practise to fish for food and ceremonial fish prior to or immediately after commercial fish openings providing ample opportunity to launder illegal fish into the

commercial market . . . reports of large scale laundering of AFS fish have been reported throughout this division . . . "[32]

The Fraser River Sockeye Public Review Board

In mid-September 1994, when the disappearance of 1.3 million sockeye was announced, another formal investigation was launched. The Minister of Fisheries, Brian Tobin, appointed a Public Review Board under the distinguished chairmanship of the Hon. John Fraser, a man eminently suited for the job. The Board released its findings on March 7, 1995. It found that the AFS was one of two factors that caused DFO management during the 1994 season to become dysfunctional. No clear lines of accountability existed and confusion as to who was in charge greatly weakened effective enforcement. The validity of in-river catch data was found impossible to verify.

All in all, 35 recommendations were made. Foremost among them is the need for DFO "to exercise its constitutional authority over fisheries."[33] This is a rebuke to DFO for being so mesmerized by the decision of the Supreme Court of Canada in *Regina vs. Sparrow* as to ignore its management and conservation responsibilities. More than that, it is message for DFO to enforce the law.

Commenting on DFO's statement about no evidence of poaching, the Board wrote that "evidence will not be found if no resources are assigned to look for it."[34] Although the Board recommended no expansion of the AFS, it fell short of recommending termination of the program because, "turning back could easily lead to a more contentious and corrosive situation than prevailed in 1994."[35] In other words, cancelling the native-only commercial fisheries could lead to native protests and blockades. It was apparently better to risk the future of Fraser River salmon, than risk native protests. Once again, government policy was to be shaped by intimidation.

The Board speaks of the need for "reaching social harmony and justice for First Nations and other Canadians."[36] I suggest that the industry had that very thing before the AFS was conceived in 1992. Continued policies based on race will not bring it back.

The AFS—A monumental failure

Even if one ignores two salmon spawning disasters in three years, increased poaching of major proportions, and a form of racism inherent in the program, the AFS has been a monumental failure. Its fishery self-enforcement program is but one example. In DFO's weekly enforcement report for the week ending September 4, 1994, the following is noted about the aboriginal fisheries guardians appointed to enforce the law:

> "Up to this point their participation with enforcement of the Aboriginal Fishery has been very ineffective.
> - Boat patrols are conducted with break downs almost always occurring taking them out of the fishery.
> - Very few early a.m. into evening patrols are conducted by themselves.
> - Their ability to pursue and prosecute violators within the fishery has not improved.
> - When patrols are conducted by DFO staff re: opening and closure times, violators are found when no problems are observed by Aboriginal fishery officers.
> - DFO has no idea what the Aboriginal Officers have been doing for the last three months. Needless to say there are many problems with the Aboriginal Fishery Officers programs which need to be addressed. Far too many to list here, all of which were pointed out in 1993. The same problems exist in 1994." [37]

These problems were not new. Dr. Pearse noted a number of problems with the aboriginal fisheries guardian program in his 1992 report:

> ". . . Another was that some guardians were fishermen themselves and therefore had an obvious conflict of interest. A third was that guardians were often stationed where they were expected to enforce regulations against family members and themselves." [38]

Though aboriginal fisheries guardians were heavily criticized outside the native community, their treatment by members of their own community was far worse. One DFO enforcement supervisor wrote in his evaluation of the guardians:

> "The guardian was enforcing fishing laws against some natives from other bands. The bands were in conflict over several fishing sites. The conflict caused some natives to threaten the guardian. The guardian was unable to approach the sites due to the threats; therefore, unable to gather any information from them. These sites were where most of the illegal activity was occurring." [39]

The aboriginal fisheries guardians are placed in an untenable position. The reality is that enforcement must be in the hands of officers trained by, employed by, supervised by, and responsible to, DFO. It is unrealistic to expect those who use the resource for personal gain—whatever colour their skin—to police it in the public interest.

From an economic perspective the AFS certainly has also been a failure. A review by Gardner Pinfold Consulting Economists Limited, a Nova Scotia consulting firm under DFO contract, in April 1994, concluded that revenues to aboriginal fishermen on the Fraser River totalled some $2.6 million in 1993. This compared with enforcement costs alone exceeding $2.8 million. This does not include the additional millions of dollars DFO spends on administration, travel, legal, consulting and other expenses, neither does it include the lost revenues caused by the spawning disasters. The consultant also failed to address whether the expenditures and revenues were creating economic benefits for the whole native community or just a few individual leaders.

Over $50 million dollars has been spent on the AFS since it was implemented in 1992—not a single audit had been completed until BCTV reporter Clem Chapple ran several stories about questionable financial dealings. This resulted in a single audit by KPMG Peat Marwick Thorne, Chartered Accountants, of the Sto:lo Fisheries Authority (their predecessor was the LFFA and the LFAFC). On February 28, 1995 KPMG delivered the results which indicate a series of questionable financial activities involving sums of over $400,000.[40] At the time of writing, neither the Department of Justice nor DFO has taken further action.

Adverse impacts on other DFO operations

Negative impacts of the AFS are felt in every other DFO program and operation. In a warning of what was to come during the 1994 fishing season, DFO official Ben Covey risked his career to warn the public about a coming disaster. In an article by Quentin Dodd of the *Campbell River Courier* on April 13, 1994:

"Covey said the district has orders to cut another 25 per cent out of its operating budget within the next four years . . . As a result enforcement and other personnel are being severely cut back.

"Covey also attributed a sizable amount of cutbacks to the AFS, however, he said huge quantities of money have been put into that, taking way from the rest of the Department of Fisheries and Oceans. "There's only one pot (of money). A very large amount of money has gone into AFS and it's come out of our budget . . ."

Typical of the reports of unprecedented illegal fishing by natives and many non-natives throughout the B.C. coast, is a report by DFO enforcement supervisor, Ron Kehl, in a leaked secret memorandum to his superior:

"In the short time I have been in Port Alberni, Fishery Officers including myself have attempted unsuccessfully to follow three separate loads of salmon that apparently have been harvested at night from the head of Uchucklesit Inlet by the Uchucklesit Band . . .

"Due to deplorable staff shortages in this Field District, there has been no apprehensions to date. Where in 1989 there were nine full time fishery officers and two term guardians working in Port Alberni there are now only two full time fishery officers and two term guardians . . . Local fishery officers are extremely frustrated and demoralized with their inability to work effectively due to severe manpower shortages . . . The Fishery Officers now, given the limited capabilities of addressing serious conservation issues, are being reduced to "meter maid" enforcement with a "band-aid" approach."[41]

Large budget and staffing cuts were being made to DFO's Pacific Region operations at the same time the multi-million dollar AFS was being introduced. DFO's Pacific Region budget dropped from $172 million in 1991 to $148 million in 1993.[42] Grants to aboriginal groups under the AFS totalled over $15 million annually during the same period. This does not include DFO's substantial administrative costs of delivering the AFS. A leaked memo by Mr. Don Lawseth, Acting Chief of the Salmon Enhancement Program, to his community advisors indicates the extent to which the AFS affected other DFO programs:

"We have been instructed in no uncertain terms that the No. 1 priority of DFO is the AFS . . . It is expected that your No. 1 priority will be to satisfy the needs of the AFS This means explicitly, when called, you drop everything else to respond."
[43]

Aboriginal fishing rights and the law

The last issue that must be discussed in any review of the native-only commercial fishery is its constitutional validity. As noted above, the Supreme Court of Canada decision in *Sparrow* did not find that there was an aboriginal right to fish commercially. The Court stated:

> "We . . . confine our reasons to the meaning of the constitutional recognition and affirmation of the existing right to fish for food and social and ceremonial purposes."[44]

DFO blatantly misinterpreted the clear decision in *Sparrow* to justify the establishment of the AFS. When questioned about native-only commercial fisheries or a lack of enforcement of native fisheries they simply replied that the *Sparrow* case justified their action or inaction. For example, DFO's *Impact Statement of the Aboriginal Communal Fishing Licences Regulations* which was printed in the Canada Gazette May 1, 1993, states: "These regulations will better enable the federal government to implement its Aboriginal Fisheries Strategy, which is consistent with the principles set out by the Supreme Court of Canada in the *Sparrow* decision . . ."

DFO also spent hundreds of thousands of dollars on a misinformation campaign to convince Canadians that the AFS co-management program was made necessary by *Sparrow*. In wording taken from full-page advertisements that DFO ran in most B.C. newspapers and magazines in February and March 1993, DFO stated: "The Aboriginal Fisheries Strategy (AFS) is a strategy designed to implement the 1990 Supreme Court of Canada decision in *Sparrow* . . ."

Internal DFO documents tell a different story. In a secret September 14, 1992, memo to Prime Minister Mulroney, the Clerk of the Privy Council writes: "The strategy not only responds to, but goes beyond the direction outlined in the 1990 Supreme Court *Sparrow* decision . . ." Also, in a June 20, 1990, analysis of the *Sparrow* decision, DFO advisor Obert Sweitzer notes that co-management is, "not a requirement of the *Sparrow* decision . . ."

It was only after these types of documents leaked out of various government offices that DFO finally admitted that *Sparrow* had little to do with the AFS. On May 6, 1993, John Crosbie, Minister of Fisheries, told the Parliamentary Standing Committee on Fisheries and Forestry that:

"We are not saying we have to do this because of Sparrow. We're doing this because we think it's the best public policy, because we've known for years and years in British Columbia and elsewhere there's been poaching of fish. We call it poaching. The aboriginals say they have a right to do it. The aboriginals have been taking fish and selling the fish illegally in great quantities."[45]

Subsequently, senior DFO officials began to argue that a Supreme Court of Canada ruling creating an aboriginal commercial right was inevitable. John Fraser, when he released his Board's report into the 1994 AFS disaster set the matter straight in a few words when he said:

"The Sparrow decision did not, despite the fact that many people have acted as if it did, ever give authority for the sale - the commercial sale - of food fish. We know that some people in DFO and perhaps in other places in the government of Canada took the view that when one considered what might happen in the Supreme Court of Canada and what might happen in land claims settlements then they may as well move a bit ahead of the law and the settlement and establish a regime which would go part way to meeting what they anticipated what would happen.

"Now it wasn't our mandate to say whether that policy [the AFS] *was right or wrong, but what we have to say is that it hasn't worked, but also there has to be a clear understanding that it is not the law today."*[46]

The B.C. Court of Appeal ruled on whether aboriginal fishing rights included a commercial right to fish in five judgments delivered in late June, 1993. These decisions were anxiously awaited by all interested parties while an expanded panel of five judges deliberated for over two years.

The stakes riding on these decisions was made clear by a leaked June 16, 1993, DFO document titled *Contingency Plan for Protest Fishery*. It dealt specifically with the impending B.C. Court of Appeal decisions and noted that, if the aboriginal litigants were successful, DFO would immediately implement a native-only commercial fishery throughout British Columbia operated under the same principles as the loosely regulated native food fishery. Presumably this would have meant that just as there is no catch limit to the native food fishery, because it is an aboriginal right, there would likewise be no catch limit, save the limits of conservation, on a native-only commercial fishery.

Other Canadian fishermen—commercial or recreational—would be entitled to "the fragments that remain." In essence, a win for the native litigants meant little less than the complete decimation of B.C.'s recreational and multiracial commercial fisheries.

The B.C. Court of Appeal rejected the claim to a native-only commercial fishery. Writing for the majority in the precedent setting case, *Regina vs. Van der Peet,* Mr. Justice Macfarlane of the Court of Appeal stated:

> '[This case] *raises the issue not decided in Sparrow.*
>
> *"While I would not give effect to the defense that Mrs. Van Der Peet was exercising an aboriginal right when she sold the fish, that is not to say persons of aboriginal ancestry are precluded from taking part, with other Canadians, in the commercial fishery. But they must be subject to the same rules as other Canadians who seek a livelihood from that resource."* [47]
>
> (emphasis added)

Fishing industry leaders applauded, describing the cases as a "major win for the principle of equality of rights in the commercial fishing industry . . . The government will now have to face the reality that it is not applying the law in the AFS, it is changing it."[48] Don Ryan, leader of the Gitskan Wet'suwet'en natives in northern B.C. said, "We got hammered. This has pushed us back to the high water mark."[49]

Though supposedly governed by the rule of law and the Canadian Constitution, DFO ignored the decisions, even though their own document, discussed above, indicated that if the aboriginal litigants were successful, the Court of Appeal decisions would be implemented immediately. Instead, in a typical response the Minister of Fisheries stated, "The Supreme Court of Canada has granted leave to appeal in those cases. Therefore, the question of an aboriginal right is still unanswered."[50] The appeals are expected to be heard by the Supreme Court of Canada late in 1995.

The AFS and Treaty Negotiations

Though DFO initially denied that the AFS had anything to do with treaty negotiations, it is now recognized that the AFS is inexorably tangled up in the costly complex process of B.C. treaty negotiations.

Despite the damage caused by the AFS and the almost universal acknowledgement of its failure, provincial and federal negotiators in the Nisga'a land claim negotiations, unlawfully in my view, have offered the

Nisga'a a treaty right to a commercial fishery complete with fish allocations, management and enforcement rights. Like all treaty rights, Nisga'a fisheries would be constitutionally entrenched and therefore almost impossible to change in the future. It would pave the way for a similar provision in the more than 40 additional upcoming treaty negotiations in other parts of B.C.

Third party interests are outraged. Nine members of the Treaty Negotiations Advisory Committee (TNAC), including fishing, forestry, mining, wildlife, and ranching interests, and the B.C. Business Council fired off a letter, dated January 4, 1995, to Fisheries Minister Brian Tobin:

"We are dismayed at the position being advanced by federal negotiators . . .

"The federal position ignores years of input from "third party" advisors, and exhibits either a lack of understanding of this input or deliberately ignores this advice or both . . . The proposal that the Nisga'a be allowed to sell their "food fish", **a provision that would see constitutional protection of a commercial activity for the first time in Canada,** *is neither equitable nor advisable from a resource management perspective . . .*

"We are anxious to discuss these matters with you. In the meantime, in our capacity as members of the Treaty Negotiations Advisory Committee (TNAC), we have made clear our view that we have no confidence in the negotiators nor in the process. We have advised officials at TNAC that the negotiators should seek a new mandate from Cabinet . . ."

In the midst of all this turmoil, a breath of sanity is heard in the words of Ms. Debbie Logan[51], an aboriginal woman belonging to the same Sto:lo tribe that advocates the continuance of the native-only commercial fisheries on the Fraser River. She wrote to the Prime Minister thus:

". . . I and my family regard the special treatment and privileges accorded Indians as a tacit way of indicating the government's conviction that Indians are less intelligent and less capable than average Canadians. This is insulting and demeaning and we want no part of it . . .

"My husband and I have been involved in the commercial fishing industry many years without the benefit of such a

program as the AFS, and are appalled at the deliberate actions of your Fisheries Ministry with respect to the treatment of Indians. Due to their misinterpretation of a single Supreme Court decision (Sparrow) initially, a rift has been created along racial lines, in an industry heretofore noted for its colour-blindedness. . . .

"Based on my own experience, and that of other Indians, I believe that given the generally favourable, evenly applied opportunities and benefits of the average Canadian, any Indian can succeed at whatever he or she undertakes.

"We, the productive tax-paying Canadians whose ancestry is Indian ask that you set aside your politically correct program for Indians, and acknowledge us as average Canadians. If our culture is valuable, it will be retained, as is true of any ethnic group, without government's overflowing cornucopia of grants and programs. It may be a long difficult road, considering the damage already done, but in the end, we will not disappoint ourselves, or you."

Chapter 9 - Footnotes:

1. DFO Discussion Paper, National Aboriginal Fisheries Committee Meeting, Vancouver, December 10-11, 1990, Annex G.

2. Commission on Pacific Fisheries Policy, *Turning The Tide: A New Policy for Canada's Pacific Fisheries,* Minister of Supply and Services, 1982, 184.

3. DFO, Memo from Pat Chamut, Director General, Pacific Region to J. E. Hache, Assistant Deputy Minister, Fisheries Operations, dated October 21, 1991.

4. DFO Discussion Paper considered by the National Aboriginal Fisheries Committee Meeting, Ottawa, September 13, 1990, 3.

5. DFO, "Main Points of National Aboriginal Fisheries Committee Meeting," January 15, 1991, 1.

6. A. L. MacDonald, *The Indian Food Fishery of the Fraser River: 1991 Summary,* (Department of Fisheries and Oceans, May, 1992), 23.

7. DIAND, Schedule of Indian Bands, Reserves and Settlements, December, 1990.

8. *Regina vs Sparrow* [1990] 4.W.W.R. 410 (S.C.R).

9. DFO, Condensed Minutes of National Aboriginal Fisheries Committee Meeting, August 23, 1990, 3.

10. Statistics of Fisheries Council of British Columbia.

11. B.C. Fisheries Survival Coalition, Submission to Parliamentary Standing Committee on Fisheries, March 30, 1994.

12. H. Hawthorne, C. Belshaw and S. Jamieson, *The Indians of British Columbia* (Toronto: University of Toronto Press, 1958), 113.

13. CFV Sales, Licence Evaluation Estimate, December, 1994.

14. DFO, "Backgrounder," B-HQ-92-24.

15. DFO, Memo from A. Gibson to G. E. Jones, Director, Field Services Branch, March 24, 1966.

16. Meeting between DM Bruce Rawson and the B.C. Fisheries Commission, Vancouver, July 28, 1992.

17. Pacific Salmon Commission, preliminary estimates of fishery catches and total run of Fraser River sockeye salmon during the 1992 fishing season, by country and area.

18. DFO, 1992 Fraser River Sockeye Salmon Preliminary Escapement Status Report, September 3, 1992.

19. Dr. Peter Pearse, *Managing Salmon in the Fraser,* Report to the Minister of Fisheries and Oceans on the Fraser River Salmon Investigation, (Department of Fisheries and Oceans, November 1992).

20. Report into 1992 Fraser River AFS Fishery, Lower Fraser Fishing Authority, November 17, 1992, 7.

21. Dr. Peter Pearse, Ibid., 28.

22. "Native leaders delighted with report on sockeye," *Vancouver Sun,* Dec 8, 1992.

23. *Vancouver Sun,* September, 1992.

24. "Cheam natives put chokehold on CN," *Vancouver Sun,* August 30, 1993.

25. Notes of Phil Eidsvik, Executive Director, B.C. Fisheries Survival Coalition, of Meeting at DFO headquarters, Vancouver.

26. "Natives wanted more, but 'compromised,'" *Province,* September 5, 1993, and "Blockade's end sparks charge of blackmail," *Vancouver Sun,* September 4, 1993.

27. DFO News Release, "Catch Monitoring and Enforcement Practises Intensified," March 26, 1993.

28. DFO News Release - September 15, 1994.

29. Letter to the Minister of Fisheries and Oceans from Fishery Officer Scotty Roxborough, October 19, 1994.

30. *Globe and Mail,* September 20, 1994, 1.

31. B.C. Fisheries Survival Coalition, *The 1994 B.C. Salmon Fishery: A Collection of Internal and Protected Department of Fisheries Documents Obtained Through Leaks and the Access to Information Act,* March 2, 1995.

32. Ibid., 80.

33. Report of the Fraser River Sockeye Public Review Board, *Fraser River sockeye 1994: problems and discrepancies,* Public Works and Government Services Canada, 1995, 45.

34. Ibid., 21.

35. Ibid., 65.

36. Ibid.

37. Conservation and Protection, Fraser River Division Weekly Narrative Summary Report. Area:Fraser Valley East, week ending: September 4, 1994, 1-2.

38. Dr. Peter Pearse, Ibid., 36.

39. DFO Memorandum from R. Nelson to R. Martinolich, File 8270-7, February 24, 1994.

40. Audit of the Sto:lo Fisheries Authority, for the Department of Justice completed by KPMG Peat Marwick Thorne, Chartered Accountants, February 28, 1995.

41. Memorandum from Ron Kehl, Field Supervisor C7P to Norm Lemmen, Area Chief, C&P, South Coast Division, September 2, 1994.

42. J. Ronald MacLeod, *DFO's Capability to Protect Salmon Stocks in 1994,* June, 1994.

43. DFO memorandum, Don Lawseth, Acting Chief of Salmon Enhancement Program, to his Community advisors, January 7, 1993.

44. Comments of Hon. John Fraser at a Press Conference at the time of releasing report of Fraser River Sockeye Public Review Board, March 7, 1995.

45. Transcript of the hearings held by the Parliamentary Standing Committee on Fisheries, May 6, 1994, Ottawa, 20:15.

46. Honourable John Fraser, comments at the new conference held for the release of the Fraser River Sockeye Public Review Board Report on March 7, 1995, Vancouver.

47. Reasons for Judgment of Mr. Justice Macfarlane in *Regina vs. Van-Der Peet,* Court of Appeal of B.C., June 23, 1993, 92.

48. B.C. Fisheries Survival Coalition News Release, June 25, 1993.

49. *Vancouver Sun,* June 26, 1993.

50. Letter from the Minister of Fisheries to the B.C. Fisheries Survival Coalition, June 13, 1994.

51. Debbie Logan, Letter to Prime Minister Jean Chrétien, March 11, 1994.

Chapter 10

Fiscal Folly

"In the last decade, more and more Indians living on reserves have become beneficiaries of social assistance funded by the federal government. For many of them, federal social assistance is equivalent to a means of survival."

1994 Report of the Auditor General of Canada

Whatever the government's motivation—paternalism, ideology, imagined or real treaty obligations, or a sense of guilt—Canada spends billions of dollars in special programs for status Indians and Inuit each year. In 1994-95, DIAND was budgeted to spend over $5 billion, an 8% increase from the previous year compared to a 2.1% spending increase for the federal government budget overall. Most of this goes to aboriginal programs—$4.23 billion. The remainder goes to northern governments for "development." In 1975-76, the amount of DIAND's budget spent on Indians and Inuit was $587 million so that, in 20 years, DIAND's budget has gone up 721%.

Figure 15 - DIAND Spending

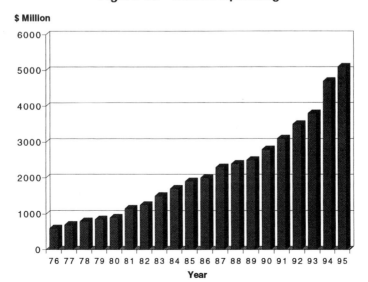

$ Million

Year

But DIAND's expenditures are only part of the picture. The Department of Health alone spent $896 million on status Indians and Inuit in 1994-95. On top of this is spending by Forestry Canada, Industry Canada, the Department of Justice, the Canada Mortgage and Housing Corporation, the Department of Employment and Immigration, the Department of Canadian Heritage, the Solicitor-General, the Department of Fisheries and Oceans, the Public Service Commission, and the Department of National Defense. Taken together, total federal government expenditure on Canada's status Indians and Inuit, to say nothing of payments to northern governments, will in 1994-95 approach $6 billion.

Figure 16 - Federal Programs for status Indians and Inuit 1994/95 Main Estimates[1]	
Department	**$ Millions**
Indian Affairs and Northern Development	4,231.8
Health Canada	895.9
Human Resources Development	200.0
Canada Mortgage and Housing Corporation	293.9
Industry Canada	75.0
Canadian Heritage	38.6
Public Security	50.3
Fisheries and Oceans	23.2
Privy Council Office	22.3
Justice Canada	11.5
Natural Resources	7.8
Public Service Commission	4.0
National Defence	5.3
Total:	**$5,859.6**

In addition, status Indians are eligible to receive all universal social programs: Unemployment Insurance, Social Assistance, and Old Age Security. As Indians, they live a relatively tax-free life: they do not pay income tax, provincial sales tax, property tax or GST for transactions which take place on their reserves. And they receive free medical benefits not covered by provincial medical insurance such as dental care, subsidized housing on reserves, post-secondary education subsidies, and immunity from seizure of real or personal property on reserves.

Indian programs are budgetary volcanoes rising in a sea of public debt. Whereas other government departments have come under pressure to slash their budgets and most discretionary spending has actually declined in the face of the country's debt crisis, federal spending on natives has gone unchecked. In fact, it has grown twice as fast as overall federal spending.

The spiral of spending continues. In Finance Minister Martin's 1995-96 budget, DIAND is the only government department to be given a spending increase—a hefty 6% with 3% promised for each of the following two years. This increase does not include payments owing under recent land claim settlements which so far are modestly calculated at about $8 billion.[2]

Poverty, misery and despair

And yet, the economic situation of Canada's Indians remains one of poverty, misery and despair. There are few economic opportunities for Indians and even fewer chances for one to make an independent living while remaining on a reserve. The employment rate of on-reserve Indians is half that of the Canadian employment rate.[3] Spending on social assistance to Indians is growing faster than the rates of inflation and population growth of on-reserve Indians combined.[4] Social assistance dependency rates are high and on the rise: in 1992, 43% of Canada's on-reserve Indians were on welfare.[5]

Social conditions on reserves are described by a 1993 government report as abysmal: a suicide rate twice that of the overall population; the percentage of dwellings without central heating double that of the Canadian rate; the percentage of dwellings that are defined as crowded is 16 times that of the Canadian rate; the percentage of Indians with less than a grade nine education is double the Canadian rate[6]; and, as of 1992, the largest cause of death among Indians was injury and poisoning.[7]

Nevertheless, Indians remain on reserves because they are heavily subsidised to do so. The government provides housing, policing, and schools. No matter how uneconomic the communities, the federal government has seen it as a duty to sustain them.

Although welfare didn't cause these social and economic problems, it has perpetuated them. Indeed, the failure of Canadian Indian policy to lift natives out of their plight illustrates the paradox of the welfare state: welfare creates disincentives to work, erects barriers to achieving self-sufficiency, and breeds an attitude of entitlement that erodes a willingness to seek economic advancement.

Even the federal government itself is beginning to recognize the failure of central planning to lift Indians out of their economic pit. A 1985 Task Force examining the efficiency of all government programs, chaired by Deputy Prime Minister Erik Nielsen, concluded:

"Despite the best efforts of governments, the relative deprivation of most native communities continues to be a persistent feature of Canadian life. The net impact of government stewardship over the social and economic development of native people has been frustratingly marginal. In the face of negative social and economic indicators that seem set in concrete, federal intervenors have evidently left few ideas untried." [8]

How Canada's Indians got into this state could be the subject of another entire book. Certainly, government intervention and central planning is more likely the cause of Indian economic hardship than the solution. As one author put it:

"Why are Indians today in a state of dependence? . . . Successive Canadian governments brought about this result by interfering with the normal evolution of the Indian economy. If the Indian economy had been allowed to follow the normal course of economies, the decline of their traditional means of subsistence would have been compensated for with other forms of self-sufficiency. In a land of opportunity alternative forms of subsistence, such as farming, ranching, industry, would gradually have supplanted traditional Indian means of hunting, fishing, and gathering. But the Canadian government erected barriers to such an evolutionary process. Specifically, Indians were prohibited from engaging in a variety of commercial activities, such as selling agricultural products off reserve. In effect, they were denied the opportunity to participate in the Canadian market economy. [9]

The reserve economy

The reality of Indian reserve economies is that most of them face substantial structural weaknesses: remote location, poor infrastructure, little access to capital and markets, and an unskilled labour force. [10]

"There is no ready solution to meeting the challenge," concluded the Auditor-General in his 1994 report, "and it is unlikely that the Department [DIAND], by itself, can effectively reduce the increasing demand for social assistance on reserves."[11]

These kind of structural weaknesses are precisely those that were the subject of the much discussed remarks in the House of Commons of Herb Grubel, Reform MP (Capilano-Howe Sound) on June 9, 1994, during debate on the *Yukon Self-Government Act*. Grubel was vilified for likening many reserves to "south sea islands," which his critics incorrectly assumed he meant to be idyllic paradises. Actually he was saying the very opposite: that, in economic terms, remote south sea islands are like the native communities in northern Canada—far removed from markets and unable to sustain or produce sufficient wealth to offer residents a high standard of living.

Based on sociological studies, Grubel considered the traditional state of northern native communities to be, like the societies of south sea islands, relatively content with their own traditions and way of life. But attempts to transform them into communities able to sustain a standard of living similar to mainstream Canada was simply not viable and government economic initiatives to do so were ill-founded.[12]

Still, the spending goes on.

DIAND

DIAND is the primary agent of federal spending on Indians. It provides a range of services to status Indians and Inuit. DIAND provided the following description of its spending in 1993-94:

- **Indian Government Support:** Expenditures totalled $271.0 million to support the operation of bands and tribal councils and enable them to hire general administrative staff and, in the case of tribal councils, provide advisory services to member bands. Funds are used for salaries, travel, office expenses, audit fees, contributions toward pension plans and administrative expenses.
- **Education:** The cost of elementary and secondary education, including teaching, transporting and supporting approximately 101,000 students was $695.5 million. In addition, $212.2 million was spent on post-secondary education to support approximately 22,000 students.
- **Social support services:** Expenditures totalled $267.3 million, of which $184.9 million was for child and family services such as

providing institutional care, selecting families for foster care, selecting group homes and payment of maintenance. Approximately 4,900 children were in care.

- **Social maintenance:** Expenditures on social assistance were $557.9 million. An average of approximately 145,000 on-reserve people per month received social assistance.
- **Construction and maintenance of houses, schools, roads, bridges, sewers and other community facilities:** Expenditures on housing were approximately $132.8 million. Total capital and maintenance expenditures (excluding expenditures on housing) was $566.2 million. Almost 4,365 new housing units were built and 3,916 were renovated in 1993-1994.
- **Management of trust funds:** At the end of the fiscal year there was almost $1.1 billion in some 16,000 accounts including capital funds of $774 million; $94 million in revenues and $191 million of individual money.
- **Management of lands:** DIAND spent $28.6 million on the management of 6.8 million acres or 2.8 million hectares of reserve land, $41.0 million on environmental protection, and $12.9 million on the registration of individual Indians, administration of revenues and band governance.
- **Oil and gas management and development:** DIAND collected $37.7 million on behalf of bands for royalties and return on investments, and supervised the drilling of 35 wells.
- **Resources development:** This program provides services to Indian, Inuit and Innu communities including maintenance of basic on-reserve resource inventories as well as financial assistance to negotiate access to resource development opportunities. Expenditures in the area are also used to attract investment in community-owned resources and to establish economic benefits from large-scale projects.
- **Commercial development:** Forty loan guarantees valued at $1.8 million were approved in 1993-1994. Loan portfolio sales totalled approximately $8.5 million by the end of the fiscal year. Industry Canada's Aboriginal Economic Programs has lead responsibility for financing Native businesses, and over $68 million was provided for this purpose.
- **Community economic development:** The Community Economic Development Program (CEDP) is DIAND's major economic

development program. $46.3 million was provided to nearly 379 community economic development organizations; $3.8 million for the Regional Opportunities Program. The CEDP program emphasis is on providing communities with the means to have qualified staff live and work in the community and provide a full range of programs and advisory services to their constituents.

• **Indian taxation services:** The Indian Taxation Advisory Board, created in 1989, advises band governments and the Minister of DIAND on the establishment of Indian real property taxation systems on-reserves. The Board is appointed by the Minister and comprises ten members, seven of whom are Indian leaders.[13]

The department historically has acted as a sort of benevolent dictatorship over Indian reserves—maintaining their welfare, managing their property, dispensing allowances and writing laws. Until the late 1950s, the federal government's paternalism was all-encompassing—it funded, delivered and administered all aboriginal programs and services.

After this period, especially through the 1970s, department philosophy shifted toward turning over administration to tribal councils and band governments. DIAND's role, in turn, evolved into a traditional bureaucracy enforcing a set of regulations governing the conduct of band affairs and allocating government funding.

By the late 1980s some native bands had attained considerable administrative autonomy. Many could now deliver federally-funded services without government oversight or audit. And in March 1994, the federal government announced that it intended to go the next step: Minister Ron Irwin stated that DIAND would eventually be "dismantled."[14] In December 1994, this promise began to take tangible form with the signing of a framework agreement to eventually hand over DIAND functions to 60 Manitoba Indian bands. The weakness in the proposal is that the federal government will continue to fund all Indian programs—only the bureaucracy will change.[15]

Social Assistance

The relationship between Canada's governments and the nation's Indians has evolved into one of welfare financier and welfare client. DIAND offers social maintenance such as money for food, clothing, shelter and a child allowance; social support services such as institutional care for children, counselling, emergency shelters in cases of family violence; and services to Indians in the transition to living off-reserve.

According to the Auditor-General, for many natives, "federal social assistance is equivalent to a means of survival." Consequently, the overall costs have grown enormously. Spending on social assistance in 1994-95 grew 12% from the previous year. Social assistance rates on reserve averaged 38% between 1981 and 1992 compared to 7% for Canada as a whole, excluding on-reserve Indians.[16] As the Auditor-General says, "the situation in many first nations communities has been serious for years and has shown no sign of improvement."[17]

This rise has come in spite of years of government spending to ease the economic plight. Among the programs are the Work Opportunity Program, Band Work Process, New Employment Expansion Development Program, and the Indian Community Human Resources Development Strategies. While the federal government has remained the financier, the administration of programs has been shifted and many native bands are finding that they are unprepared for the responsibility, especially in the areas of economic development and social assistance.

On the other hand, DIAND itself appears incapable of managing the task of delivering social assistance to natives. The provision of social assistance by DIAND has been the subject of a number of critical reports from Canada's Auditor-General in recent years. According to his scathing 1994 investigation on the department's management of social assistance, DIAND has no legislative authority to deliver social assistance, its administration is "complex, cumbersome and difficult to manage," and it does not monitor its own efforts.[18]

Economic development

The latest government initiative to try making natives economically self-reliant is the Canadian Aboriginal Economic Development Strategy (CAEDS), launched in 1989 as a joint initiative of DIAND, the Department of Industry, Science and Technology, and the Department of Employment and Immigration (now, Human Resources Development Canada), intending to "promote Aboriginal economic self-reliance through greater Aboriginal participation in Canada's national economy.[19]

The strategy includes DIAND's Community Economic Development Program and Resource Development Program which funds native organizations to prepare community economic strategies, initiate projects with seed money, take equity positions in enterprises, and support job training and employment programs. These are supplemented with a Commercial Development Program, a Resource Access Negotiations Program, and a Regional Opportunities Program. It also administers a research and advocacy program in conjunction with the other two departments.[20]

Human Resources Development Canada is responsible for skills development and urban employment programs, primarily through the Pathways to Success strategy. This was implemented by creating 86 local aboriginal management boards which define training and employment priorities in conjunction with Canada Employment Centres.[21]

The Aboriginal Business Development and Joint Ventures program is the flagship of Industry Canada's CAEDS efforts and the largest of the CAEDS programs in terms of funding. It puts up 30-40% of financing for the establishment, expansion, acquisition or modernization of a commercial business and for the production of products; up to 60% for the costs of marketing; up to 75% for the costs of developing business plans, studies, business follow-up assistance and training; and up to 90% of developmental pilot project costs.[22] Applications are approved in conjunction with aboriginal economic development boards.

The financial arm of the plan are the Aboriginal Capital Corporations which make commercial loans to native businesses. As of 1993 there were 33 corporations with a capital base of $200 million but an examination of 11 of these showed that seven had 25% or more of their loans in arrears, and two of the corporations had even eroded part of their capital base.[23] Four of these 11 had federal funding approved without assurance they were in compliance with the terms and conditions of the program.

Is CAEDS working? The evidence suggests not. A 1993 Auditor-General report said that CAEDS has been a financial black hole into which the Canadian government has poured over $1 billion since 1989. According to his report, the departments implementing CAEDS have little concern for the viability of proposed economic projects, target money at the Indian elite with college educations, and monitor few of the projects for their success.

Health Canada

Much of the Department of Health's Indian programs are targeted to public health problems endemic in some native communities: drug and alcohol abuse, child mortality, family violence and diseases associated with poor living conditions such as tuberculosis. Indian and Northern Health Services is the focal point for the delivery of public health in these communities, amounting to $896 million in 1994-95, 11% of Health Canada's entire budget.[24]

Federal spending covers non-insured health benefits such as dental costs, vision care, drugs and medical transportation ($508 million); public health services ($224 million); and the native component of the Department of Health's Child Development Initiative which focuses on mental health, solvent abuse, child development and parenting skills. Environmental health and surveillance monitors native communities for contaminants in their environment. And the government operates six general hospitals, numerous clinics and provides medical staff for all the facilities.

Twenty-seven Health Transfer Agreements have now been signed with 82 bands allowing them to exercise control over the delivery of their own health services. $27.5 million is transferred annually. Another 77 transfers are in the planning stages involving 213 bands.[25]

In his 1993 Report, the Auditor General notes that the Department of Health's Indian program has no statutory basis; the mandate is unclear; expenditure control processes are deficient, and that the cost of the entire program is buried because "there is no 'distinct expenditure component.'"[26] In short, the program is an unauthorized shambles.

Indian culture and identity

The federal government has taken on the responsibility of protecting Indian heritage and identity. The Department of Canadian Heritage is the leading agency in this mission. It will spend $38.6 million in 1994-95 to "define and participate in the resolution of the social, cultural, political and economic issues affecting their lives in Canadian society."[27]

What this means is explained in the Canadian Identity Program, which, for example, offers an Aboriginal Friendship Centre Program to "improve the quality of life for Aboriginal peoples residing in or travelling through urban communities."[28] These centres, located in urban areas to reach off-reserve natives, offers referral services and support programs and employ 1,800 people. Cost: $18.1 million.[29]

The Northern Native Broadcast Access Program funds a regional network of production facilities, radio and television programs to 400 native communities in their own languages—a native CBC. This provides a "source of cultural wealth, . . . alternative information, and a symbol of legitimacy of Native languages."[30] Cost: $10.1 million in 1994-95.

The Aboriginal Representative Organizations Programs funds native advocacy groups that "enable Aboriginal peoples to participate in the political, social and economic life of Canada." Cost: $5.8 million.

The Aboriginal Constitutional Review Program funds groups pressing for constitutional recognition of self-government during the constitutional talks that concluded with the Charlottetown Accord in 1992. Groups that have received money include the National Indian Brotherhood, Native Council of Canada, Metis National Council, and the Inuit Tapirisat of Canada. Cost: $27.6 million over two years ending in 1993.

The Aboriginal Womens' Program "encourages Aboriginal women to initiate or influence public policies and decision-making. . . ."[31] The rationale for this program is that it "enables Aboriginal Women to advance their interests through the initiation of activities and projects that improve the depressed socio-economic conditions of their home communities while maintaining cultural distinctiveness and preserving cultural identity."[32] The program has included funding for the Family Violence Initiative which promoted "networking, the building of coalitions, and the empowerment of decision-making at the community level."[33] Cost: $2.3 million in 1994-95.

The Native Social and Cultural Development Program is focused on individual natives cultivating talent in cultural fields. Money goes to native arts groups, language revitalization, cultural festivals and conferences. Cost: $900,000.

The federal government has also signed Aboriginal Languages Agreements with natives in the Territories in order to provide government services in a variety of native languages as well as provide educational material.

And the federal government has moved to recognize native heritage through a few small programs in Parks Canada, such as native participation in visitor interpretation centres and the Aboriginal

History Northern Sites Initiatives to commemorate sites of importance to northern natives.

Native policing

Although most policing on native reserves is still conducted by the RCMP with DIAND funding, a growing favourite of native governments is the creation of an independent police force. The First Nations Policing Program is operated by the Solicitor-General's Aboriginal Policing Directorate at a cost of $48 million per year.

To provide counselling for Indians in trouble with the law, the Department of Justice funds the Native Courtworker Program. This program also "assists the criminal courts to better take into account the culture, values and traditions of native people, as well as their socio-economic backgrounds."[34] Cost: $4.2 million in 1994-95.

The Department of Justice is also funding an Aboriginal Justice Initiative Fund ($2 million), Legal Studies for Aboriginal Peoples Program ($492,000), and aboriginal legal research ($238,000).

Accountability and waste

The lack of accountability identified by the Auditor General in the economic development programs also plagues other spending on Indian programs.

In 1992, the Auditor-General told a House of Commons committee that there was no accountability for $2 billion in taxpayers' money transferred to Indian bands and tribal councils through Alternative Funding Arrangements, Flexible Transfer Payments, contributions and grants. "I am particularly concerned," he stated, "that there is no formal redress at the Band level for Band members. There is no way for them to appeal when they believe they are being treated unfairly or are not receiving what they are entitled to receive."[35] The fact is that in many cases much of the funds do not trickle down to the band members who most need them.

According to one source, a 1985 study found that in regard to one program for every $20 of spending by DIAND only $1 found its way to the aboriginal peoples targeted for help.[36] Many native programs are multi-departmental in nature. Reading between the lines of several Auditor General Reports, it appears that no Minister or Deputy is in overall charge, with the result that no one can be held responsible for managing the monitoring of expenditures and accountability generally.

Many dissident groups have sprung up because of this unaccountability. One report written by a native women's group in Norway House detailed the potential for abuse: "Because all monies remain at the Chief and Council level, most often this centralized system can contribute to misappropriation or mismanagement. The Band members are participating in a system that may be working against them, and most of the time they are unaware of how this money is spent, or how and where it is transferred."[37]

And even though federal agreements with Indian bands mandate accountability measures for band members, "where and when there is a breach of an Agreement, the Department of Indian Affairs makes no effort to rectify the problem, and usually do not acknowledge any written complaints they receive from Band members."[38]

DIAND itself has probed welfare spending by Saskatchewan Indian bands. The federal government transfers funds to individual bands who administer social assistance programs themselves. Native residents are then subject to the distribution of the band's welfare money by their leadership. In a study of five bands, DIAND found that four had "deficiencies" in how they administered the program. Application forms went uncompleted, assistance was given to off-reserve Indians, some recipients of utility supplements were not on band housing lists, people with independent incomes were receiving assistance, and there were numerous instances of fraud where individuals were collecting band welfare from different bands.[39]

Another form of abuse relates to misappropriated or misused funds. A March 1993 audit of business start-up loans to Indians in Manitoba, the Atlantic provinces and the Yukon, reported that $3.3 million out of $4 million in loans examined are uncollectible or doubtful.[40]

The latest word is from an audit done by DIAND and released on January 23, 1995, reviewing the fiscal health of Canada's 522 Indian bands. The report shows that between 1988 to 1993 one-third of the country's bands are in the hole to the tune of $537 million. The Manitoba bands were deepest in the hole having tripled their debt over the period to $54 million.[41] These are the ones that DIAND Minister Irwin is in the process of handing over programs to administer themselves under his much ballyhooed DIAND dismantling project.

Wholesale transfer of money and authority

Will the wholesale transfer of government programs—with all the cash and bureaucracy that it entails—be sufficient to lift Canada's natives from the economic depths? Almost certainly not. Central planning and dependence upon government have never boosted a "disadvantaged" group into prosperity, let alone dignity. So why, then, have successive Canadian governments carried on the welfare philosophy that drives Indian policy? The usual bureaucratic answer is that much of the spending is mandated by treaty obligations that the Government of Canada must fulfil. This is not true. According to the 1985 Nielsen Task Force:

> *"The large proportion* [of Indian spending] *devoted to status Indians and Inuit is commonly attributed to federal obligations under the treaties or the Indian Act. In fact, only 25 per cent of these expenditures can be directly attributed to these obligations. The remainder go largely to services of a provincial and municipal nature and stem from decades of policy decisions designed to fill this void which have, by convention, come to be considered as though they were rights."*[42]

The report concludes that when one takes account of provincial obligations, 37% of federal spending on Indians fall into the category of "discretionary."[43]

The Nielsen report identifies three elements to the DIAND ideology: adherence to "universality" in which services are considered a "right"; an effort to recreate modern urban suburbs in remote areas with "no consideration of the communities' long-term economic capacity to pay for the maintenance and replacement of this level of service"; and the goal of developing a system of local native government based on the federal government model instead of more suitable rural government units.[44]

The report says this has spawned an "artificial world on Indian reserves where reliance on government is almost total."[45]

> *"In effect, the government has created communities in which housing and other services are often far better than those in surrounding communities. . . . In so doing it has also unwittingly created a disincentive to move to areas of economic opportunity.*
>
> *"This has only been accomplished at great cost to the federal government. As notable, however, is the incalculable human*

cost in lost pride, purpose, independence and self-motivation." [46]

Chapter 12 suggests alternatives to this debilitating cycle of dependency.

Native Indians and Taxation in Canada

"In this world nothing is certain except death and taxes."
Benjamin Franklin, 1789.

Although he lived to the ripe old age of 84, Ben Franklin could not avoid the inevitable call of the Grim Reaper, but if he had lived a hundred years or so later and looked northward to Canada, his adage about taxes would have been proved wrong for native Canadians living under the jurisdiction of the *Indian Act.* Despite enjoying the rights and benefits afforded to every Canadian, some 565,000 status Indians in this country have been given the enormous advantage of virtual immunity from all taxes, federal, provincial and municipal.

Immunity and exemption from taxation

Tax freedom for Indians does not spring from some ancient inherent native right or rite or even from treaties but from section 87 of the *Indian Act* enacted many years ago by Parliament. The incredible benefits this section provides include the following:

Sales taxes and GST

First, status Indians are immune from provincial sales, gasoline, alcohol and tobacco taxes, and the federal Goods and Services Tax for anything purchased on their reserve. Thus, if a Squamish Band member shops on the South Side of Park Royal Shopping Centre in West Vancouver (located on the Reserve), he avoids taxes on everything he buys but if he crosses Marine Drive to the North Side (off the Reserve) his immunity doesn't apply. Elsewhere, ingenious techniques are used to arrange sales transactions "on reserves."

Not all the ingenious techniques are devised by the natives. Revenue Canada has ruled that even though goods may actually be purchased **off** the reserve, they will not be subject to GST if they are delivered to the reserve by the seller. Common carriers and the postal service are considered "agents of the seller" for this purpose.

What surely must take the cake, is that status Indians, although not subject to the GST in the above circumstances, are nonetheless eligible for the GST **rebate** credit, paid quarterly by government to modest-income Canadians.[47]

Real property taxes

Secondly, status Indians living on reserves are placed beyond the reach of provincial and municipal real property, school and hospital taxes. Although they enjoy the benefits of local police and fire protection, connection to municipal water and sewer services, roads, and access to schools and medical facilities, bands cannot be **compelled** to pay taxes to local governments or even to share taxes collected by the bands on reserve lands.

Income tax

Thirdly, status Indians pay no taxes on incomes earned on the reserve. Recently the Supreme Court of Canada held that an Indian who lived on a reserve but worked for and received his pay from a company based off the reserve was not exempted from paying income taxes. In the face of that decision, Revenue Canada issued most modest guidelines, which provide that a mere 3,000 Indians who fall into this category will, as of January 1, 1994, have to pay income tax.

As a result, all hell broke loose within the native community. Native protesters occupied Revenue Canada's downtown Toronto offices for weeks while government officials watched and wrung their hands. Expensive full-page newspaper ads alleged unfair treatment of Indians. One spokesman is reported to have told a protest rally, "They're screwing us." Another declared that Indians were considering quitting their off-reserve jobs because, "It's just not worth it."

The whole thing is farcical. Whether they realize it or not the native protesters have focused public attention on the broader issue of tax exemption for Indians. As all other Canadians feel the breath of the tax collector bearing down ever more closely, it's time for a major overhaul of tax policy as it relates to Indians. The exemptions were provided to prevent Indians from losing their reserves through the imposition of liens and other levies upon their lands. I doubt that they were ever designed to provide exemption from consumer taxes or income tax. In fact the *Indian Act* predates the imposition of income tax in 1917.

No wonder Mr. Justice Muldoon of the Federal Court has recently declared the *Indian Act* a "racist" document that favours aboriginal people over the rest of society. "It makes financial dependents of those who pay no taxes as an eternal charge on those who are taxed to meet the expense of such dependency," the judge said. Along with treaties, he declared that the *Indian Act* fosters the establishment of apartheid in Canada.[48]

Chief Ovide Mercredi weighed in to declaim that forcing equality of tax responsibility onto Indians was a blatant violation of treaty rights despite the Court's finding to the contrary. Mercredi wants a court case on the issue. "That's the democratic way to resolve the issue," Mercredi says. But on being asked what would happen if his side lost the lawsuit, Mercredi is reported to have said that aboriginals simply won't pay the tax.[49] He didn't explain how they could avoid compulsory tax deductions at source by employers. In any case, treaty rights have nothing to do with it. The exemption is contained in the *Indian Act* which can and should be changed.

Taxation by Indians

By contrast, the Indians are far from lenient when they themselves are the tax collectors. In 1985, the *Indian Act* was amended to permit bands to impose "taxation for local purposes of land, or interests in land, in the reserve, including rights to occupy, possess or use land in the reserve."

The consequences of this amendment have been devastating to many municipalities. Central Saanich has lost about $240,000 of its annual tax revenue (4.8% of its tax base) since the Tsawout Indian Band started collecting property tax on its non-native occupiers in 1994. DIAND approved the band taxation by-law without giving the municipality time to negotiate a comprehensive servicing agreement with the band. The municipality provides fire protection, sewer, water, street lighting, roads, parks and recreation, and will no longer receive any revenue to recover the cost of providing these services unless it is able to enter into a satisfactory agreement with the band. It is reported that the band has been dragging its feet on entering into a servicing agreement. Negotiations are currently underway. In late January, 1995, it was reported that the band had offered a meagre $31,000.[50] Meanwhile its own taxation efforts are in high gear.

Similar events have transpired in the West Vancouver Municipality. In a 1993 note to residents, the Municipality pointed out that it would lose 4% of its $58.3 million tax revenue ($2.3 million) to the Squamish Band and spoke wistfully of "band cooperation" in returning $950,000: "The municipality has absorbed the difference at this time pending finalization of an agreement and a review of the service implications."

In the fall of 1994, the City of Cranbrook learned to its dismay that it had to pay $300,000 taxes to the St. Mary's Indian Band for its airport land which it leased from the Crown in the belief it was no longer part of the reserve.[51]

Secrecy of band by-laws

Virtually always, when Acts authorize statutory bodies (such as labour relations boards, transport commissions, etc.) to make rules or regulations, such "subordinate legislation" must be sanctioned by Cabinet approval. In that way there is always assurance that elected representatives have an opportunity to review this material before it becomes law. Section 83 avoids this salutary practice by requiring that band by-laws be approved only by the Minister of Indian Affairs. This usually means the Deputy Minister who never has to account to the voters.

Another usual safeguard against government secrecy is a requirement that all rules and regulations be printed in the Gazette which can be searched out and read in Courthouses and libraries around the country. Indian taxation by-laws are exempted from this requirement. Even a reserve taxpayer has no right to see what are his rights and obligations under by-laws that can be very costly to him.

Self-exemption of Indians

While the 1985 amendment opened the door for the potential of taxation of Indians by Indians (although some Indians dispute this), band by-laws are careful expressly to exempt Indians, bands and band-owned corporations from paying any taxes on land and improvements occupied by them on the reserves. The result is that while Indians enjoy the benefits of streets and sidewalks, fire and police protection, water, sewers, lighting and other municipal services on reserves, only the non-Indian residents pay for them. This cannot be easily remedied because the *Indian Act* prohibits non-Indian residents on reserves from voting. A contemporary of Old Ben Franklin, William Otis, coined the battle cry of the American Revolution, "No taxation without representation," but Canadian legislators seem to have forgotten that grim precursor to civil war when they created this provocative and racist distinction between neighbours on reserves.

Band use of tax revenues for personal benefit?

Because the 1985 amendment says the taxation must be for "local purposes", it would be reasonable to assume that the monies would be spent on normal municipal services and developments. Perhaps not. In affidavits filed in recent litigation it is alleged that a major use for these tax monies was for other purposes unrelated to municipal services.[52] The affidavits speak of building restaurants and service stations on the highway and developing ginseng farms in the interior to provide employment and income for bands and their members.

"Star Chamber" tax assessments

Under provincial law, an independent body, the B.C. Assessment Authority, employs trained appraisers to determine taxable land and improvement values in all parts of the province. If a taxpayer considers the valuation of his property to be unreasonable, he can appeal to the Court of Revision. If dissatisfied with its decision, he may go further to another province-wide authority, the Assessment Appeal Board. All members of these bodies are appointed by Cabinet and paid by the province. The municipal or other taxing bodies have no control over them and often appear before them to oppose taxpayer appeals. This reasonable and democratic process is not available to non-native lessees on reserves.

Under band by-laws, assessors chosen and paid by the bands do the initial appraisals and, often, represent the bands on assessment appeals. The appeals go before tribunals again chosen and paid for by the bands. By-laws often provide that a member of the band may be a member of the appeal body. No tenure of service is fixed so that board members who decide against the wishes of a band may never get to sit on another appeal. Fortunately, the Supreme Court of Canada has recently held that these biased boards are invalid[53] and many bands are having to amend their tax and assessment by-laws to correct these offending provisions.

Protection from payment of debts

The *Indian Act* provides another nasty little surprise: protection of native property and assets located on reserves from any process of garnishee, execution or attachment for debts, damages and other obligations, including taxes, however justly due and owing.

In 1990, a chartered accountant who had negotiated a refund of almost $1 million for a group of Indian bands from Manitoba Hydro for "illegally" imposed provincial sales taxes on power sold on reserves, found to his shock that he could not collect his fees the band owed him by garnisheeing Hydro before they paid the monies to the Indians. It went to court and the Supreme Court of Canada held that Section 89 barred recovery of the bill and, adding to the accountant's misery, ordered him to pay the costs of the litigation. Even though the money was not located on the reserves, the Court held that:

> ". . .the protection against attachment ensures that the enforcement of civil judgments by non-natives will not be allowed to hinder Indians in the untrammelled enjoyment of such advantages as they had retained or might acquire pursuant to the fulfilment by the Crown of its treaty obligations. In effect, these sections shield Indians from the imposition of the civil liabilities that could lead, albeit through an indirect route, to the alienation of the Indian land base through the medium of foreclosure sales and the like."[54]

The exemption has nothing to do with "treaty obligations." It has everything to do with Section 89 of the *Indian Act* that only awaits a courageous federal government to bring about its repeal.

Who would not like to live his life free from the fear that his civil iniquities would be threatened by recovery by persons legitimately aggrieved?

Chapter 10 - Footnotes:

1. Indian and Northern Affairs Canada, *DIAND Programs and Services for Indians and Inuit,* Information Sheet No.15, November 1994, 5.

2. "8 billion owed in unsettled land claims," *Ottawa Citizen,* October 21, 1994.

3. Indian and Northern Affairs Canada, *Growth in Federal Expenditures on Aboriginal Peoples,* (Ottawa: 1993), iv.

4. Auditor General of Canada, *1994 Report of the Auditor General of Canada,* vol.23, 5.

5. Ibid.

6. *Growth in Federal Expenditures on Aboriginal Peoples,* iv.

7. DIAND, *Basic Departmental Data,* 1992, 28.

8. Task Force on Program Review (Nielsen Task Force), *Improved Program Delivery: Indians and Natives* (Ottawa: Government of Canada, 1985), 21.

9. Menno Boldt, *Surviving as Indians* (University of Toronto Press, 1993), 225.

10. Auditor General 1994, 23-12.

11. Ibid., 23-12.

12. Hansard, *Commons Debates,* June 9, 1994, 5071-73.

13. Indian and Northern Affairs Canada, *DIAND Programs and Services for Indians and Inuit,* Information Sheet No.15, November 1994, 3-4.

14. "Ottawa launches program to let Indians run own affairs," *Vancouver Sun,* March 10, 1994, A5.

15. Michael Jenkinson, "Made-in-Manitoba apartheid," *British Columbia Report,* December 26, 1994, 10.

16. Ibid., 23-9.

17. Ibid., 23-10.

18. Auditor General, 1994, 23-5.

19. Government of Canada, *Department of Industry, Science and Technology, 1994-95 Estimates,* 1994, 3-20.

20. Auditor General of Canada, 1993, 284.

21. Ibid., 285.

22. *Federal-Provincial Programs and Activities: A Descriptive Inventory, 1992-93* (Ottawa: Government of Canada, 1993.

23. Auditor General of Canada 1993, 292.

24. Government of Canada, *Health Canada Estimates, 1994-95,* 1994, 2-71.

25. Ibid., 2-7.

26. Auditor General of Canada 1993.

27. Government of Canada, *Heritage Canada Estimates, 1994-95,* 1994, 3-29.

28. Ibid.

29. Ibid., 3-30.

30. Ibid., 3-31.

31. Ibid., 3-31.

32. Ibid., 3-32.
33. Ibid.
34. *Federal-Provincial Programs*, 18-2.
35. House of Commons, *Minutes of the Proceedings and Evidence of the Standing Committee on Public Accounts*, Issue No. 36, December 3, 1992.
36. Library of Parliament, "A proposed reform to the system of payments to Aboriginal peoples," May 3, 1994.
37. Norway House, Native Women's Group, *"Decentralization of Funding for Native People"* (Norway House First Nation, Manitoba, undated), 1.
38. Ibid.
39. "Indian bands under federal audit," *The Taxpayer*, Vol.6, No.5, 11.
40. "Millions lost in loans to Indians, audit says," *Montreal Gazette*, May 30, 1994.
41. "Indian Bands fall into debt, audit says," *Globe and Mail*, January 24, 1995, A2.
42. Ibid.
43. Ibid.
44. Ibid.
45. *Task Force on Program Review*, Ibid., 22.
46. Ibid., 23.
47. "Goods and Services Tax," *The Complete Guide*, (Third Edition), Volume 1, Commentary and Analysis, Ernst and Young.
48. "Indian Act 'racist,' judge says," *Globe and Mail*, January 6, 1995, A3.
49. "Mercredi plans court appeal," *Times-Colonist*, December 21, 1994, A3.
50. "Tsawout Band's taxation issue appears headed for courtroom," *Times-Colonist*, January 23, 1995, C9.
51. *St. Mary's Indian Band vs. Cranbrook*, Supreme Court of B.C. (Unreported), May 20, 1994.
52. The affidavits are filed in *Matsqui and other Indian Bands vs. Canadian Pacific*, January 26, 1995 (Unreported), SCC file #23643.
53. Ibid.
54. *Mitchell vs. Peguis Indian Band* [1990] 2 S.C.R.85.

Considering the Reasons for Failure

*"Whenever you **give** an individual or group their basic needs they will lose their desire to fight for these things and therefore lose their self-respect, pride and self-reliance."*
Dr. Keith Martin, MP (Esquimalt-Juan de Fuca), June 9, 1994.

Reviewing the present

A Liberal government recognized in 1969 the failure of discriminatory policies leading to dependence and paternalism, and set out a new direction to revolutionize Canada's native policies. Tragically, it retreated from principle in the face of short-sighted opposition.

Instead, against all liberal-democratic principles it and successive governments have continued in the old direction which fosters more dependence and paternalism and entrenches further division based on race and ethnicity. The policies and programs of governments directed towards native people over the past 22 years, but particularly in the past 5 years, reviewed in this book, can only be described as "bizarre." Major reform is called for.

The motivation for such bizarre policies

What has motivated law-makers and those in authority to act, by any reasonable assessment, in such an irrational way? The criticism is not just that this largesse is extended only to a segment of Canada's population, which generously calculated is about 3%, but the fact that these policies are based on race. Canadians rightfully abhor racism and are always in the forefront of efforts to stamp it out at home and abroad. And yet these policies and programs are based entirely on race and ethnic origin. Does our national vision suffer from the malady of the man in the parable who could see the sliver in his neighbour's eye but could not see, or was unwilling to do anything about, the log in his own?

How is it that we as a nation can proudly point to our efforts in opposition to apartheid in South Africa when we are well on the way to establishing that system in Canada through native self-governments based on the ill-found concept of the inherent right? Racism anywhere and everywhere and under all circumstances is wrong. It is anathema to all democratic principles that we as a nation hold dear.

Some readers may think my views are rather quaint and outmoded. Others may accuse me of being some right-wing extremist. To those, all I can say is that there are certain fundamental principles that do not become dated with the passage of time—unless, of course, we are prepared to sacrifice what we have stood for as a nation.

Two spokesmen on this issue who could never be accused of falling into that category are Gordon Gibson, former leader of the Liberal Party of B.C., and Sid Green, a cabinet minister in a former NDP government of Manitoba.

Mr. Gibson says this:

"South Africa has taken the definitive steps to shutting down its massive, evil and failed system of apartheid. Now maybe we in Canada should stop expanding our own smaller, but equally failed apartheid system relating to natives. We still assign political rights on the basis of race where it affects Indians. . . . The South Africans have ended "homelands," where blacks were hived off into a kind of "third order of government," as we say in Canada. We are not just continuing our homeland (Reserve) system, we are expanding it—perhaps mightily so in British Columbia, where the details of land negotiations remain secret." [1]

In an article entitled "Separate status should be opposed"[2] Mr. Green points out that 25 years ago it was generally the view of "'progressive minded people' that our Indian fellow citizen had been done a great injustice by being specially designated in the Constitution and relegated to living on reserves."

Mr. Green goes on:

"The desire of progressive-minded people to seek common brotherhood with the Indian citizen has in the past few years given way to ethnic nationalism as expressed by recognized Indian spokesmen and all major political parties. The notion of Indian sovereignty is being pursued despite the fact that most of these politicians admit that they do not know what they are talking about.

*"The Indian spokesmen know full well what they are aiming at.
They talk about national status, meeting with governments on a
nation to nation basis, territory, resources, sovereignty and a seat
at the United Nations. In fact, they are talking about a country
based on Indian ethnic origin carved out of land within the
boundaries of Canada. Those non-Indians who support this notion
are, in fact, supporting the kind of apartheid that they condemn in
South Africa."*

He goes on to quote from the biography of T. C. Douglas, first leader
of the NDP, written by Doris Shackleton. In it the concerns of Mr.
Douglas toward the native people are detailed. She writes:

*"The practical, obvious 'solution' to Douglas . . . was to do away
with the reserves and the degradation that went with 'wardship'
and integrate the Indians with all speed into Canadian
society. . . ."*[3]

Collective guilt

So, what have been the motivating factors pressing upon
governments that have caused them to produce such bizarre policies
and programs? I can think of some.

First and foremost, Canadians have allowed themselves to be
overwhelmed with a collective sense of guilt over alleged past dealings
with native peoples. We should not have allowed ourselves to be thus
overwhelmed. The fact is that we can be proud that those who
emigrated to this country—and we are all immigrants, even the native
peoples—brought with them all that was best of their respective
civilizations to establish a society in this country noted for its honest
dealings, its even-handedness, its compassion, its tolerance and its
diligence. The native peoples share in these bounties, except to the
extent that by unwisely singling them out in our 1867 Constitution, we
relegated them to reserves and began to see and treat them differently.

When I think of our country's early development, I think of the men
and women who devoted a life-time of service to improving the
conditions of those with whom they came in contact.[4] I think of Dr.
Wilfred Grenfell who for 40 years provided desperately needed medical
care to white settlers and natives alike on the barren coasts of
Labrador. His legacy in rescuing hundreds of families from disease and
despair lives on in the hospitals and institutions dedicated to his
memory. I think of Jacques Cartier, the famed French explorer, who

first reached the New Brunswick Coast in 1534 and established a mission work among the Indians on the Bay of Chaleur.

Likewise the Father of New France, Samuel de Champlain, who brought his fervour and faith to bear on the early expeditions and settlements of what is now Quebec, showed throughout his life an abiding empathy for the native people. I think of Jean de Brebeuf who committed his life to working among the Hurons studying their language, compiling a Huron dictionary and grammar, and translating the Catechism, and who was ultimately burned at the stake during inter-tribal warfare. I think of Joseph Norbert Provencher of St. Boniface who, in the mid-1800s, was vitally involved in founding and directing schools in the west. He worked with white settlers, Metis and Indians alike and through innovative agricultural techniques did much to ease the transition of the latter from a nomadic lifestyle, made difficult by the disappearance of the buffalo.

I think of Methodist missionary, James Evans of Manitoba who in the 1830s developed a phonetic Cree language system which dramatically enhanced written and oral communication with native people all across Canada. I think of Robert Rundle, sent by the Methodists to Fort Edmonton in 1840, who founded some of the first schools in Alberta open to white settlers and Indians alike. I think too of the Oblate Fathers, invited by Chief Snat of the Squamish Band, to work among his people. I think of Father Pandosy who first planted apples in the Okanagan valley in 1859 and who at age 76 died from exposure in the arms of a close Indian friend. And I think of William Henry Collison, first missionary to the Haida of the Queen Charlotte Islands and the first Englishman to work at the headwaters of the Skeena as well as the founder of the first mission at Hazelton. From a deeply engrained honesty that saw men as equals, it could be written of him after 40 years of labour: "Chiefs and slaves, shamans and renegade whites, all knew Collison as their friend. . . . his name remains a synonym for courage and honesty in British Columbia's Pacific Northwest."[5] To this day, many Haida have taken his name.

Were there exceptions to these admittedly rather glowing accounts? Were there abuses and deprivations imposed upon the natives? Of course there were: sometimes tricks were played, promises were broken, and abuses endured.

Without question evil men in the past took the grossest advantage of native children enrolled in the Indian residential school system established by the federal government. Such evil men are rightfully being punished even until today. But for every scoundrel, how many dedicated and upright teachers and school administrators devoted their lives in the good cause of education for native children within these schools?

These kind of shameful events were not confined to the native peoples. Ask any early-century homesteader on the Canadian prairie about promises made to induce settlers to Canada. Little or no government help was forthcoming to them. They soon found that it would be self-reliance, sheer grit and hard work that would be necessary to succeed in carving out a home from the wilderness or the dust blown prairie.

No, the greatest disservice done to our native people was that done by the Fathers of Confederation in singling out Indians in the Constitution to be dealt with differently. If this book carries any message, it is that this approach has not worked and yet those in authority over us by their present and proposed actions would confirm the distinction forever into the future. It's a mistake. As one wise Canadian observer said: "The greatest gift in our grant is to make someone an ordinary Canadian. Why should natives deserve any less?"[6]

Reinforcing collective guilt

This underlying sense of collective guilt visited upon non-native Canadians is reinforced at every opportunity by the national native leadership. It was a refrain drummed into federal and provincial delegates at virtually every meeting during the five years of constitutional conferences held with the native leadership between 1983 and 1987. Those native leaders who castigated governments at these conferences for the abysmal conditions on their reserves often flew back home first class, while Ministers of the Crown and their Deputies travelled economy.

Nisga'a land claim negotiators recently revealed some startling land claim strategies that relate to this issue. According to *B.C. Report* newsmagazine, in a transcript produced by one of the bands attending a negotiating seminar hosted on May 21, 1994, by the Squamish band, Nisga'a Tribal Council president Joe Gosnell is quoted as saying "make use of 'past insults' to win concessions." He goes on:

"Don't play it down and don't ever forgive. Use these issues to the hilt in your negotiations, add them to your arsenal of information.

. . . Take the circumstance, i.e. natives not allowed to get an education; then measure what might have been possible against the status quo. Research carefully, then demand fair and just compensation. Past wrongs are debts that must be paid." [7]

Reform MP Mike Scott (Skeena) put his finger on the issue in the same article:

"They're using these issues as a means to enhance the guilt factor. We have this collective guilt about what happened in the past. They're saying 'we have to keep the guilt at the fore when we're negotiating.' That's not a bad strategy."

Ministerial ignorance

Besides a sense of collective guilt there are other factors that have resulted in the bizarre native policies and programs of governments over the past 20 years.

One is the "revolving-door" nature of the incumbent who at any given time occupies the position of Minister of Indian Affairs. Over the past few years, DIAND probably has had more ministers than any other federal department and therefore those who occupy the position do so, on average, for a shorter period than other ministries. The consequence of this is first, the Minister, probably unknowledgeable on the subject when he takes the job is only marginally more knowledgeable when he vacates it. He is a captive of his Deputy Minister and senior bureaucrats. The issues are complex, the Deputy and the senior bureaucrats are supposed to know them, so, in effect, they call the shots. The second consequence of a short-term in the job is the Minister's desire to show that he has achieved results—that he has **done** something. It matters not a great deal that what he "does" may be a land claim agreement with long-time adverse consequences. He won't be in the job that long and therefore won't be around to face the consequences anyway. The important thing to the Minister is to be seen to be doing something—anything. After all, to be a "successful" Minister of Indian Affairs is often a stepping stone to a larger and more prestigious portfolio.

Role of the bureaucracy

Another factor is the role of the bureaucracy. Senior bureaucrats in most departments of government measure their success by the amount of money they spend and the number of people over whom they exercise control. In DIAND major land claim agreements "successfully" negotiated are a decided plus. Little regard seems to be given to the public interest in all of this. Referring again to the native negotiating seminar above discussed, a Nisga'a spokesman is reported to have said:

"There is a fundamental difference in the responsibility of the federal and provincial negotiators and us. We are answerable directly to our people and they are not. It's just a job to them. The worse that can happen to them if they screw up is to get fired, while we would have to live with our mistake for the rest of our lives."[8]

Appeasement

The final factor that accounts for bizarre government policies and programs in this subject area is called appeasement. Give in to virtually every native demand, no matter how ill-founded, and attempt to meet the insatiable demand for more government money for every and all unrequited "needs," lest the native leadership call for reprisals such as road blocks, sit-ins, or even more serious illegal activities.

Last spring when Nisga'a negotiations reached an impasse, Nisga'a Tribal Council president Joe Gosnell is reported to have said: "If serious negotiations do not begin right away, we will begin planning a comprehensive program of civil disobedience that could lead to a total shut down of the Nass valley." The threat worked. Negotiations soon got going again. Grand Chief Mercredi uses the threat of what he calls "civil disobedience" constantly liking it to the actions of Gandhi against an undemocratic and repressive regime in India. How foolish is the analogy!

Over and over again, I have heard government spokesmen justify a weak-kneed response on the ground that they did not want another Oka. Premier Harcourt used it recently to justify the B.C. treaty-making process.[9] Federal and provincial tobacco tax policy has been bent out of shape with a massive loss of provincial and federal taxes, with presumably an increase in the number of teenage smokers, rather than come to grips with a serious smuggling problem on Indian reserves that straddle the Canada-U.S. border. Of course nobody **wants** another Oka, but should not our nation's territorial integrity and adherence to the rule of law and the Constitution be our paramount concerns?

Prime Minister Mulroney made a major speech in the House of Commons shortly after the Oka incident in which, although deploring the incident, he used it as the motivation to shower an array of further government benefits on native people, accelerated the process of comprehensive land claims, and poured hundreds of millions of dollars more into specific claims of the kind described in Chapter 5.

More recent examples are the unlawful actions of the Penticton and Upper and Lower Similkameen bands in B.C. On November 2, 1994, these bands erected blockades on Green Mountain Road—a public highway—thus preventing access to Apex ski resort. The blockade cost the resort $1 million a week in lost business. Within six weeks, the Harcourt government had signed a treaty-like agreement with these bands—dubbed the Okanagan First Nation—in which the government recognized the bands "aboriginal rights" to over 1,000 sq.kms. bounded by Hedley, Keremeos, Cawston, Olalla, Yellow Lakes, Kaleden, Penticton and Summerland. The agreement allows the bands to "co-manage" cattle grazing rights, mining claims, logging and other operations on Crown land. The ranchers, miners and loggers in the area were not consulted.

Towards anarchy?

What then should guide Canadians as they seek to develop new policy on this subject? The concept of the rule of law is absolutely fundamental to our society and is highlighted in the preamble to the Canadian Charter of Rights and Freedoms. What is the rule of law?

The great British constitutionalist, A. V. Dicey, defined "the rule of law" as it applies to governmental action as "the absolute supremacy or predominance of regular law as opposed to the influence of arbitrariness, of prerogative, or even of wide discretionary power." Far from being some theoretical concept only of interest to legal scholars, adherence to the rule of law is the warp and woof of any democratic society and is what distinguishes a democracy from a totalitarian state. Any society, on the other hand, that thrives on arbitrary governmental actions breeds tyranny and despotism.

Grand Chief Mercredi, however, condemns the concept of the rule of law and wants to get rid of it. He states:

"We also have to work hard to fight another concept, another old idea, that is part of Canadian society. We saw it during the army occupation at Oka, and it is called the rule of law. Government ministers condemned the Mohawk people, and in particular the warriors of that society, for their acts of defiance. They

condemned all Mohawks for the defence of their land. And how did they generate public support for the use of the army against the Mohawk people? They did it by rallying Canadians around the concept of the rule of law, the nation that everyone must obey their laws, even if those laws are unjust. It is a concept imposed on us to support the government's dominance. "[10]

It is understandable why the Grand Chief wants to get rid of the rule of law. For one thing, the concept of the inherent right to native self-government—having no constitutional support—cannot survive along side the rule of law.

The rule of law and the Constitution have been virtually ignored by governments' efforts of recent years to acquiesce in the furtherance of the native agenda. Consider the following examples:

1. The establishment of what amounts to a new province–Nunavut–without obtaining the approval of at least seven of the existing provinces, as is required under section 42 of the *Constitution Act, 1982.*

2. The entering into land claim agreements which extend a cornucopia of land, money, resources, and power far beyond the scope of what any court of law has found the concept of aboriginal title embraces. Consider the modest findings of the Court of Appeal of B.C. in the *Delgamuukw* case as to what constitutes the aboriginal interest. Compare that to what obliging political leaders at both levels have included and are prepared to include in land claim settlements. When, in the settlement of land claims, governments abandon the principle of legal entitlement as determined by the Courts and substitute arbitrary, ill-defined and politically expedient solutions, then the rule of law and the Constitution has been sacrificed. Moreover, after-the-fact ratification by a legislature compliant to the government's wishes will not remedy the inherent defect.

3. The wholesale giveaway of massive chunks of the NWT and Yukon can hardly be considered to be the administration of the public lands of Canada in the public interest. Such actions are about to be visited upon British Columbia.

4. So-called specific claims and treaty land entitlements that, for the most part, would be thrown out of court if ordinary legal principles (which apply to all other Canadians) were applied in these cases.

5. An aboriginal-only commercial fishery on the west coast instituted by the federal government as an aboriginal right, in the face of

numerous court decisions at a high level which have found that the aboriginal right to fish only extends to fishing for food, social, and ceremonial purposes. No claim for such a commercial fishery can reasonably be advanced on the grounds that this is affirmative action directed toward a disadvantaged group because over 30% of the ordinary commercial fishery is already in native hands. This separate fishery, arbitrarily imposed and without constitutional justification, has destabilized the whole west coast salmon fishery—both recreational and commercial—to say nothing of wreaking havoc on the spawning grounds.

6. Governments at both levels proceeding on the basis that the concept of the inherent right to self-government is a third order of senior government in Canada despite the fact that Courts at the highest level have rejected the concept.

7. The province of B.C. has engaged in land claim negotiations even though there is a distinct possibility that a Court might find that the province has discharged its obligations to the Indians by fulfilling Article 13 of the Terms of Union. If such a judicial finding were made, it would be up to the federal government alone to discharge the aboriginal interest.

Conclusions

Canada's 130 year-old social experiment with the native peoples has failed. We tried isolating them, making them completely reliant on government, cutting them off from the economic market place, putting bureaucrats in charge of their lives, creating more special government programs and new levels of government to deal with any problems that arose, and generally treating them like irresponsible children. The result—economically and socially—is like something out of the third world.

This social experiment has destroyed any sense of self-reliance among many native people. Dr. Keith Martin, MP (Esquimalt-Juan de Fuca) made the point with such poignancy, during debate on the Yukon Self-Government Bill:

"As a physician I have spent much time in northern British Columbia working with native people. The plight of these individuals breaks my heart. I have seen individuals raped, had their heads put through walls, beaten up, smashed up, shot and killed, people who have suffered the ravages of alcoholism. I have

seen them go for years, suffering these ravages only to have to pronounce them dead on the gang plank of an emergency department.

"It is intolerable for this to have occurred and it is intolerable for it to continue. Part of the blame rests on the non-native population and in particular Canadian governments that have continued to treat people in a paternalistic fashion by providing for them many of their basic needs without trying to do much to stimulate self-reliance. Whenever you give an individual or group their basic needs they will lose their desire to fight for these things and therefore lose their self-respect, pride and self-reliance.

"I also put a large part of the blame squarely on the shoulders of the native population and native leaders who in my opinion have been unwilling to take the bull by the horns and ask what they can do to pull their communities out of these tragic situations. . . .

". . . it is incumbent on the native people to ask themselves what they can do to help themselves. In my discussions with native people, it has been sorely lacking. They speak about getting back pride and self-reliance. I can tell members that the only way to get back pride and self-reliance is if you earn them yourself. You only achieve these things through your own hard work, your sweat and your desire to fight for your basic necessities and your life.

"Pride and self-respect are not things that are given to someone, paid for or bought. They are only things that come from within your heart and soul and only from your ability, as an individual or community, to fight for your own life. I do not mean this in a pugilistic sense or by taking up arms. I mean this figuratively and in a spiritual sense.

"When one works hard and fights for one's life in this world, win or lose, one develops a sense of pride, self-respect, self-reliance, self-esteem that nobody can take away. It is the only way that this will come to the native communities."[11]

To seek to generate a greater degree of self-reliance on the part of the native people themselves must be the cornerstone of a new native policy. The rest of this book suggests ways how this might be done.

Chapter 11 - Footnotes:

1. Gordon Gibson, "Time to do away with our apartheid," *Vancouver Sun,* May 3, 1994.

2. Sidney Green, "Separate status should be opposed," *Winnipeg Free Press,* May 31, 1992.

3. Ibid.

4. The historical references in this part are taken from *Canada: Sharing our Christian Heritage,* edited by Paul Knowles (Toronto: Mainroads Productions, 1982).

5. William Henry Collison, *In the Wake of the War Canoe,* edited by Charles Lillard (Victoria: Morris Printing Company Limited, (Reprinted), 1981, inside front cover.

6. Gordon Gibson, "Let's not use racism to tackle native needs," *Globe and Mail,* June 1, 1992.

7. "Throw tantrums, rant and rave," *B.C. Report,* January 16, 1995, 8.

8. Ibid.

9. "Indians don't want it all, premier says," *Vancouver Sun,* April 4, 1995, A3.

10. Ovide Mercredi and Mary Ellen Turpel, *In the Rapids: Navigating the Future of First Nations* (Viking, 1993), 129.

11. Hansard, *Commons Debates,* June 9, 1994, 5105.

New Directions

*"The greatest gift in our grant is to make someone an
ordinary Canadian. Why should natives deserve any less?"*
Gordon Gibson, June 1, 1992

One might be tempted to entitle this chapter "A New Native Policy"
but to do so would perpetuate the old, discredited, and discriminatory
mindset—one policy for non-native Canadians and another for native
peoples. Insofar as this is a new native policy, it will be the last,
because when it has been implemented over a number of years, our
native peoples will be fully Canadian like everyone else in the country.

Certainly they will still be Cree, or Naskapi, or Inuit or Sahtu **as well**
as being Canadians. Their rich cultural, social and linguistic heritages
will continue to strengthen their souls and add a unique and valued
dimension to the Canadian mosaic. Many may continue traditional
lifestyles in their communities if that proves viable. But they will be
Cree, Naskapi, Inuit or Sahtu standing proudly on their feet, free of the
bonds of dependence and paternalism.

A new policy must be built on two principles—native self-reliance;
and equality under the law. Such a policy must deal with land claims,
federal native programs, and self-government.

Self-reliance

Attempts to deal with natives differently and separately have been
a miserable failure almost 130 years, and there is little evidence to
suggest that the current misdirected policies of governments will end
this tragedy. The bold but practical answer is to foster self-reliance.
This can be achieved, or at least begun, by a new form of integration.
In the past, this word has been associated with attempts to physically
integrate, to bring natives in off the reserves to urban areas. Insofar as
native people wish to move to new environments, they should of course
be free to do so. But this form of integration is not a cornerstone of this
new policy.

What I am proposing is "jurisdictional integration" which breaks
down the thicket of laws, regulations, and procedures that separate

natives from their fellow Canadians and with it would break down stereotype attitudes and mindsets. A massive array of laws passed by native self-governments will not bring about jurisdictional integration. It would simply substitute one different and separate set of laws for another different and separate set of laws—again based on race and ethnic origin.

How can a greater degree of self-reliance be achieved? Perpetual welfare payments by government year after year will not do it. Massive land claim settlements and more government institutions and bureaucracies in remote communities would not build self-reliance but would be a boon confined to those who exercise power in such communities. Reliance on government by anyone stifles rather than enhances self-reliance. Lack of accountability, which is the by-word of most native programs, as the Auditor General has shown, does not lead to self-reliance.

Moreover, when leadership—aboriginal or non-aboriginal—makes most of the decisions for their peoples without effective input or a chance to influence the decisions of the leadership, then that leads to frustration and a lack of self-worth.

There is another dimension to this. Self-reliance is born of self-confidence. Self-confidence, in part at least, is a product of how we perceive others see us. Here non-aboriginal society is at fault. Too often we look at our native people as being different from us and therefore inferior. Little wonder, when the Fathers of Confederation singled out natives as special wards of the federal government. That mentality still exists and has to go. Natives are different because governments, and by extension the non-native population of Canada, sees them to be different. Federal government laws, programs and largesse act as a cocoon which insulates native people from the larger provincial community that surrounds them. The social interchange with this surrounding provincial community is not open to them and they are not encouraged to reach out to it.

There is no panacea that can be applied that will automatically and instantly achieve self-reliance. I have only identified a few of the steps along the way. There are others, education, technical training, small business assistance, social improvement assistance, but these must not be seen as handouts but as something earned through measurable results on an equal footing with other Canadians. That is the way to build self-reliance and a feeling of self-worth.

Equality under the law

The second principle on which a new policy must be built is the principle of law which treats all Canadians equally. It is contrary to all that Canada stands for to support a policy that extends special privileges based on race or ethnicity. This is a principle so fundamental to liberal democratic societies that it should not even be necessary to state it. And yet, this principle is ignored by governments in Canada in furtherance of the native agenda.

On the other hand, some Canadians would go so far as to call for a brand-new native policy that would wipe the slate clean by cancelling Indian reserves, dismantling native programs, discontinuing further land claim negotiations, and abrogating existing treaties and land claim agreements. By doing that, in one fell swoop, they would argue, all Canadians, regardless of race, would be equal under the law. But here the rule of law and the Constitution, discussed in the last chapter, and so despised by Grand Chief Ovide Mercredi, properly comes to the defence of lawful native interests. In short, the rule of law and the Constitution requires that a new policy must honour existing treaty rights and aboriginal interests as defined by law. Because of the rule of law and the Constitution, a new policy must also honour Indian's rights to reserves and their rights in their established native communities.

Beyond that, the rule of law extends no solace. For example, the scores of native programs and benefits extended by ordinary legislation are subject to amendment or repeal to the same extent as programs and benefits provided to other Canadians. This would include the provisions of the *Indian Act* including the tax exemption provisions. Such programs and benefits are subject to shifting government priorities and the fiscal capacity of governments to sustain them.

But the rule of law and the Constitution cuts both ways. It also protects the interests of non-native Canadians. In the area of aboriginal title, for example, the Courts have found an aboriginal interest which is cast in the narrowest of terms. To that extent, but only to that extent, the native peoples are legally entitled to have that interest recognized and discharged by government (perhaps only the federal government in B.C.'s case.) When over-zealous politicians go beyond that legal entitlement in settling land claims, in my view they offend the rule of law and the Constitution because they are conferring land and other benefits which are rightfully the entitlement of all Canadians. This is precisely what is happening in B.C. land claim negotiations. It ought not to be. I am often asked whether such government actions could be restrained through legal proceedings. I do not know the answer but it is a question that should be considered.

In sum, a new native policy must be built on the twin principles of jurisdictional integration for natives within the mainstream of Canadian society, thus enhancing a sense of self-reliance and personal achievement, and on the principle of equality under the law consistent with the rule of law and the Constitution. Moreover, such a policy must be formulated and implemented absent any sense of collective guilt over what may have happened in times past. Until now, this sense of guilt has been allowed to hang like a pall over all efforts at native policy reform.

The three major components of a new policy to be addressed in the context of these principles are: land claims, federal government programs for natives, and native self-government.

Land Claims

Recommendations:

- Obtain a judicial finding as to whether B.C. has a constitutional obligation to be involved in discharging the "aboriginal interest".
- Limit land claim agreements to the modest aboriginal interest found by the Court of Appeal in *Delgamuukw.*
- Require extinguishment of other undefined aboriginal interests as a condition of entering into land claim agreements.
- Establish a Treaty Ombudsman in whom the citizens of B.C. can have confidence.
- Recognize specific claims only on a strictly legal basis.

Comprehensive Land Claims
Should B.C. be involved at all?

In the early pages of Chapter 4, I make the point that the constitutional obligation of the Province toward the Indians was set out in Article 13 of the Terms of Union of 1871 under which British Columbia entered Confederation. That obligation was to set aside Crown land for Indian reserves. By 1924, the federal government acknowledged that B.C. had fully discharged its obligation in that regard.

Now the Court of Appeal in *Delgamuukw* has determined that there is a modest aboriginal interest that must be discharged. We must honour that finding because that is the law of the land based on the Constitution. But the Court left open the question of which order of government—federal or provincial—has the obligation to discharge it. In my view, a good case can be made that it is the federal government and it alone that has that obligation. One of the leading texts on native rights in Canada, in reviewing the subject of native rights in British Columbia concludes:

> *"Following Confederation, only the Dominion Government has jurisdictional authority to deal with Indian lands. This means that only the Federal Government has the authority to extinguish aboriginal title in British Columbia."* [1]

What has been the practice elsewhere in Canada? With the exception of Quebec, all Indian treaties entered into since 1867 have seen the federal government as the sole signatory on behalf of government. In northern Quebec the situation is different because the constitutional obligation of the government of Quebec is different. When the vast northern territories were added to Quebec by federal legislation in 1912, it was expressly conditional upon **Quebec** obtaining surrenders of aboriginal rights, "and the said province, subject to federal approval, shall bear and satisfy all charges and expenditure in connection with or arising out of such surrenders." [2] It is pursuant to that special constitutional obligation relating only to Quebec that the government of Quebec entered into modern treaties with the Cree and Inuit of northern Quebec in 1975 and the Naskapi Indians in 1978.

No similar express constitutional obligation falls on the government of British Columbia. In fact, it can be argued that the very opposite is the case because section 13 of B.C.'s Terms of Union imposes on the federal government "the charge of the Indians."

How is it then that the present government of B.C. is in the treaty-making business? Did the B.C. government conclude that because the government of Quebec entered into treaties, B.C. is obliged to do likewise? Was there a serious analysis made of the constitutional differences between Quebec and British Columbia on this issue before B.C. plunged head-long into the process?

This is not merely some kind of academic issue akin to how many angels can dance on the head of a pin. The answer to it determines whether the Canadian taxpayer at large or the B.C. taxpayer will pick up the tab for land claim settlements. More than that, the Crown land in the province is owned by the Province. If the responsibility for settling claims is the federal government's alone, then it would be required to buy from the province, presumably at fair market-value, any land or resources it wished to include in a land claim.

This might have the desirable effect of lessening the tendency of government land claim negotiators to be as generous as they seem willing to be with land and resources.

I conclude by suggesting that consideration should be given to suspending the present land claim process so as to allow the B.C. government to refer this issue to the Court of Appeal for judicial determination. The government has the power to take such a reference and a decision from the Court on this narrow but vital issue could be expected within a reasonably short time.

The modest nature of the aboriginal interest

The term "land claim" itself is a misnomer. The native interest must be recognized and discharged by government, because the Courts have said so. But, as we have seen, the entitlement is much more modest than a claim to the **ownership** of land. The Court of Appeal in the *Delgamuukw* case found that aboriginal title is:-

a) an activity;
b) that takes place on land but that is not a proprietary interest in land; and,
c) that must have been an integral part of the distinctive culture of the particular band before the arrival of the white man.

Mr. Justice Macfarlane in *Delgamuukw* elaborated on the matter when he held that the nature and content of aboriginal rights are determined by asking what the ancestors of the claimants regarded as "an integral part of their distinctive culture" at the time British sovereignty was asserted in 1846. He asserted that although this would vary from tribe to tribe, those rights might include hunting, fishing, trapping, and harvesting other fruits of the soil. The Court went on to say that commercial practices (mining, commercial fishing, commercial logging, and other European influences), which came with the arrival of the colonial authority, are not aboriginal rights because it cannot be said of them that they were integral to the distinctive culture of the aboriginal society at the time of discovery. It will be readily seen that this finding of aboriginal rights is far narrower in scope than the benefits extended in recent land claim agreements in the territories. We must not make that mistake in B.C.

Recent land claim agreements in the territories have included massive fee simple transfers of land, and a host of other benefits. Most of these agreements go far beyond what is necessary to discharge the aboriginal interest. In my view, on the basis of the application of the rule of law and the Constitution, future land claim agreements in B.C. should be limited to compensating for only those matters which the *Delgamuukw* case has found to constitute the "aboriginal interest." Nothing more, nothing less. In many cases this obligation could be discharged through cash compensation.

Conveyances of full ownership over land and extensive social and economic benefits should not be included in land claim agreements in B.C. because these are beyond the Court's definition of what constitutes the aboriginal interest.

Such agreements would be constitutionally entrenched as section 35 of the *Constitution Act, 1982*, provides.

Finality

To the fullest extent possible, land claim agreements must bring about finality. For reasons previously stated, this can best be achieved by natives who are parties to such agreements relinquishing any other aboriginal interests over land.

The need for a Treaty Ombudsman

Who can be trusted to represent the interests of ordinary Canadians in land claim negotiations? These are not matters to be horse-traded by compliant politicians or eager-to-please bureaucrats who measure their success by the number and scope of land claim agreements, without a great deal of regard for the public interest. Certainly so-called "third party" interests should be represented in such negotiations. At present these interests are "heard" at best but there is little indication that those interests weigh in the decisions reached.

But over and above third party interests, there is a "public interest" to be represented. British Columbians are showing increasing signs that they do not trust their governments' representatives to safeguard their interest.

At the federal level, DIAND has a fiduciary relationship to native peoples in certain respects. How then can DIAND represent the "public interest" through its appointed land claim negotiators? Whose interest do they represent?

A debate in the B.C. legislature at the end of the process and after land claim agreements have been signed, would be nothing more than a farcical charade. Witness the futility of such a process during the "debate" in the House of Commons on the NWT and Yukon deals discussed in Chapters 2 and 3.

A partial answer to this need may lie in the establishment of a special kind of Ombudsman to oversee land claim negotiations from the perspective of the public interest. The position would be established by provincial legislation and would require the **unanimous** approval of the legislature. He or she would be an officer of the legislature, reporting to it and therefore not accountable to the party in power. Such an Ombudsman would have security of tenure for say, a 10 year term, only removable before then by unanimous vote of the legislature or by public recall based on reasonably low thresholds.

This Ombudsman, and small staff, would have unfettered access to all land claim negotiations although not be actually engaged in negotiations. The Ombudsman would have the power to order that any or all aspects of a proposed settlement be put to the people of B.C. in a referendum if he deemed it appropriate in the public interest to do so. Moreover, he would be required to provide a formal opinion on each proposed settlement as to whether, in his view, the public interest would be served by it. If his opinion were to be negative in a particular case, then ratification of that agreement through the legislature would require a 75% affirmative vote of members.

Specific Claims

Chapter 5 sets out in detail the enormous amount of money and land that has been conveyed under this category for alleged deficiencies that occurred up to a hundred years ago but which have only been put forward within the past dozen or so years. Hundreds more await the consideration of sympathetic DIAND bureaucrats. Most of these fall outside the appropriate statute of limitations and would be caught by the doctrine of *laches*. Many of them would not be sustainable in a court of law for other reasons. Under a new policy, only those claims that would be considered to be valid in accordance with ordinary legal principles would be entertained. Savings of further hundreds of millions of dollars would result.

Native Programs

Recommendations:

- Phase out over time all native programs.
- In their place, make all existing federal and provincial programs applicable to all native people.
- During the phasing-out stage, as much as practicable, make payments direct to Indian people rather than to band leaders.

Repeal existing programs

Section 91 (24) of the Constitution gives the Parliament of Canada the constitutional authority to legislate in a special way for "Indians and Lands reserved for Indians." The *Indian Act*, the establishment of DIAND and the scores of special native programs, which now approach $7 billion a year, represent examples of the exercise of that legislative power. But there is no obligation on the Government or Parliament of Canada to continue to have these programs. To the extent that Parliament does not legislate specifically for Indians, laws of general application, both federal and provincial, apply.

The point to be made is that it is within the power of the Parliament of Canada, through the actions of the federal government, to repeal its special legislation in relation to Indians, **or** any part of it, and do what is said "vacate the field." When it does that, then the laws and programs at both the federal and provincial level, previously supplanted, begin to apply.

The answer to waste, unaccountability and a system of programs that discourages self-reliance among native peoples is not to transfer their program delivery function to the native leadership for administration, as DIAND Minister Irwin is proposing in Manitoba. The result of that is to merely substitute another category of bureaucrats for those of DIAND. The answer lies in phasing-out special programs for natives altogether.

We would do well to remember that whatever shortcomings may exist among native peoples are likewise present, to a greater or lesser degree, among non-native persons as well. Wherever these shortcomings appear, they should be dealt with by the same government programs. Alcoholism, suicide, wife-beating, and sexual abuse are not the private preserve of native peoples. All of these scourges can best be met by the full range of programs that are in place at both the federal and provincial levels. But present jurisdictional arrangements preclude this from happening for native peoples. That should not be so.

In the future, native people to the fullest extent possible, should be treated within their province as full and equal citizens entitled to share in the benefits and responsibilities of all other Canadians. It is at the provincial level where social programs are developed and administered to meet local needs. It makes no sense to exclude natives from the full operation of such programs and provide some lesser substitute as is presently the case. It is at the provincial level where complex systems integral to community life offer the best prospect. Services ought not to be provided by separate agencies to an ethnically identified clientele. To do so is to isolate, to marginalize and to exclude. Such an approach has 130 years of miserable failure to show for it.

Phasing out native programs would result in a significant shift in fiscal obligations to the provincial governments to provide services to status Indians that they have not had to provide, heretofore. To cushion that blow, the federal government should compensate each province to the same amount that the federal government would have spent in that province on native programs had the transfer of responsibility not taken place. Such compensation would extend for say a 10-year period and be phased out by the end of that period. After that, provinces would be totally financially responsible for extending their programs to natives. And why not, native peoples would by then be provincial citizens too.

Until phasing out of native programs fully occur, these programs should be redesigned to put the monies paid under them into the pockets of individual natives rather than into band coffers. Too often complaints are heard from individual Indians that they are not provided with adequate housing or other services on reserves, even though there has been money made available by DIAND. Payments direct to individual band members would alleviate, to some degree at least, this problem. However, such direct payments should carry with it a corresponding obligation on the band member to pay for the services he or she receives. Such services would no longer be free but would have to be paid for by the individuals receiving the services—to the same extent that such services are paid for by non-native Canadians.

Self-Government

Recommendations:
- Rationalize reserves.
- Transfer ownership of reserves to Indians.
- Encourage self-government along the Sechelt model, but with certain safeguards.
- Repeal the *Indian Act.*
- Finally, ring down the curtain forever on the Ministries of Indian Affairs, both in Ottawa and Victoria, and in other provinces.

Indian reserves

There are no less than 2,323 Indian reserves in Canada, 1,634 of them are located in B.C.[3] Their total land area comprises 10,021 sq. miles—one of the largest land holdings in the free world. They are as varied in size, situation and economic prospects as the snow flake. Some are postage stamp in size. Others cover thousands of acres with all sizes in between. The number of people living on them ranges from two to 12,000.[4] Of the 842 reserves that are inhabited, 375 of them have less than 500 people.[5] In total, the number of Indians living on reserves in Canada is about 305,247 or 1.2% of the population of Canada.[6] In B.C. the number living on reserves is about 49,756 or 1.6% of B.C.'s population. Some are classed as remote, others rural and still others as urban. 1,442 or 63% of all reserves are unoccupied.

The ownership of most reserves in Canada is vested in the federal government but they are held in trust for the particular band. As long as this trust relationship exists, the government as trustee must supervise the use and activities related to reserve lands. It does this through the *Indian Act.* The various provisions of the *Indian Act* have hobbled the bands who occupy them from developing them in a viable way. Consider some such inhibiting provisions:
- reserve lands cannot give a mortgagee the right to enforce his interest against the land in the event of default. This stifles efforts at economic development;
- bands can only lease reserve lands by complying with an undue amount of DIAND red tape;
- reserve lands cannot be sold even though it may be the overwhelming wish of the band members to do so.

As a stepping stone toward native self-government on reserves, two reforms should be implemented: the rationalization of Indian reserves and the transfer of outright ownership of reserves to the requisite bands.

Rationalization of reserves

If, in the opinion of a band which has within its control a number of reserves, it would be in its best interest to consolidate its reserve holdings, then the federal government should encourage and assist in that process. Some bands have many reserves not contiguous to each other and, in many cases unoccupied. The viability of existing reserve communities could be greatly enhanced if bands had the opportunity to exchange with government existing reserve lands for other lands of equal value. Lands received by bands in this way would be formally added to existing reserves or established as new reserves. Lands given back to government in exchange would cease to be reserve lands. In this way, the band leadership itself would have a direct hand in efforts to make their reserve communities more economically and socially viable.

It should be stressed that this is not a land give-away to natives or a land grab by government. Exchanges would be based on equal value as determined by independent and qualified appraisers. Whether such exchanges took place at all would be a matter wholly to be determined by the band leadership. It would only happen if a majority of the band agreed. Provincial government cooperation would be necessary because the land to be added to a reserve—if located within a province—falls under the jurisdiction and control of the province. In return, the province would have transferred to it the lands removed from existing reserves.

Transfer of ownership of reserves

It is both patronizing and demeaning to natives for the federal government to continue to hold title in its name to all the Indian reserves in Canada. Without delay, the beneficial ownership of reserves should be transferred outright to the band, as a collective interest of the band. A condition of the transfer should be that any time after five years from the date of such transfer, every band may have the right to divide and sell its interests in the reserve, or any part of it, provided that:

a) 75% of the band members agree in a democratically constituted election, and

b) if approved, that the proceeds of such a sale be distributed equally among the band membership at the time of sale.

In short, it is the bands that should have ownership and control of reserve lands thus allowing the bands themselves to ultimately decide whether their long term interests are to be achieved through the collectivity of land ownership or by the sale of reserve lands.

Self-government on reserves

Having achieved the rationalization of the reserve system and having conveyed the outright ownership of reserves to the bands themselves, the question then arises as to what degree of self-government should be extended to Indians living on reserves? That there should be some degree of self-government is supported by the application of legal principles. That is to say, if Indians are entitled to the collective ownership of their reserves, which they are, then they are entitled to manage their operation.

The debate that has raged throughout the country since the early 1980s around the issue of native self-government, is not whether a measure of self-government should be implemented but how and what kind. The constitutional conferences, described in Chapter 7, show a concerted effort by the native leadership to have recognized within the Constitution an undefined inherent right to native self-government. Fortunately, in my view, those efforts failed. Since then, the native leadership, aided and abetted by the views of the Royal Commission on Aboriginal Peoples, have argued that the right is somehow already implicit in the Constitution. Fortunately again, the Courts have rejected the idea. However, regretfully, DIAND and the federal government do not appear to have gotten the message.

The Sechelt experience

As this debate rages on at a somewhat esoteric level, practical examples of the establishment of self-government institutions on Indian reserves are taking place. The best example is the Sechelt band on the Sunshine Coast of British Columbia. On June 24, 1988, the Sechelt Indian Band celebrated the achievement of a long fight toward their model of native self-government. With the bringing into force of the

Sechelt Indian Band Self-Government Act (Canada), 1986, and companion provincial legislation, it was said:

> *"They celebrated freedom from the Indian Act, the establishment of their own band constitution, achievement of control of band lands and the establishment of relatively autonomous self-government with a wide range of powers."*[7]

It took the goodwill and best efforts of three parties—the Sechelts, the federal government, and, the provincial government to do it. The B.C. government of Bill Bennett was particularly keen on the Sechelt model going ahead to show that, while it opposed entrenching vague concepts of self-government into the Canadian Constitution, it was supportive of practical efforts to tailor particular solutions to particular cases—within the framework of the existing Constitution.

The Sechelt federal legislation provided that:

- the Sechelt Indian Band Council would exercise the powers and duties assigned to it under a band constitution, the contents of which would be approved, by the band in a referendum, and by the federal Cabinet;
- a further transfer of band powers to a quasi-local body known as the Sechelt Indian Government District would take place if the band, in a referendum, approved and if the Legislature of B.C. passed certain legislation in relation to the District. This has now been done;
- certain provisions of the *Indian Act* would no longer apply to the band but the tax exemption provisions would remain;
- all federal laws of general application would apply to the band and its members;
- all lands which were previously Indian reserves (32 of them covering 1,000 hectares or 2,532 acres) would be transferred outright to the band;
- the Minister of DIAND, with Cabinet approval, would negotiate block funding to the band with a maximum degree of flexibility to allocate the monies to match local needs.

The band constitution was adopted by band referendum on September 26, 1986, and approved by federal Cabinet. It establishes the composition of the band council, term of office, tenure of members, election procedures, and band council procedures. It provides for financial accountability of the council to band members, including audits and reports.

The powers which the Sechelt Indian Government District can exercise are municipal-like in nature. They include:

- general government;
- zoning and land-use planning;
- regulation of buildings;
- assessment and taxation of real property;
- regulation of noise, animals, waste disposal, and places of amusement;
- road construction, maintenance, and regulation;
- regulation of businesses, professions, and trades; and
- the imposition of fines or imprisonment for contravention of laws.

Assessing the Sechelt model

On paper, the Sechelt self-government regime would seem to represent a well integrated balance of interests. It has been described as "a judicious mixture of tribal and municipal institutions, in response to the fact that Natives and non-Natives live and work side by side on Band lands."[8]

And again:

"While the Sechelt have achieved self-government they have also realized their objective to remain an integral part of the larger local, regional and provincial community. At their wish, the Sechelt will participate politically in the regional district, hospital district and school board, receive relevant local services and pay all relevant regional property taxes. At the same time the Band is integrated with the provincial system, paying relevant provincial taxes, receiving the benefits of provincial programmes for local government and taking advantage of the provincial property assessment and land registration systems. The Sechelt have achieved all of this without prejudice to their aboriginal status, aboriginal land claims or whatever benefits are achieved through the constitutional entrenchment of aboriginal rights to self-governance."[9]

One serious flaw in the Sechelt scheme is the fact that non-band members living on Sechelt lands are not permitted to vote for, or participate on, the District Council. The only participation for non-Indians is through a non-voting Advisory Council. Democratic principles require more than this. Moreover, the tax exemption provisions of the

Indian Act should not apply to viable self-government communities such as this one.

It seems reasonably clear that the Sechelt Model could be used elsewhere in Canada. It is a model of self-government that warrants support where self-government on reserves is a viable option. It would be a mistake, however, to assume that it would be an appropriate model for all reserves. Self-government of this kind may not be appropriate, for example, to a band which occupies reserves having a weak economic base and which is more isolated and not part of an urban area.

The Sechelt Band is a highly urbanized, strategically located, relatively prosperous band, holding lands with immense development potential. In 1990, the population of the Band was about 700 or which 568 lived on Sechelt lands. These lands were also home to about 500 non-Indians for a total population of just over 1,000. It is expected that the non-Indian population in the future will grow significantly. The Sechelts appreciate the need to continue to integrate with the surrounding community and see benefits accruing individually and collectively from such integration.

The requisites for native self-government

Lessons learned from the Sechelt experience suggest that a new Canada-wide model for native self-government should have to meet these requirements:

1. Self-government would be limited to Indian reserves the full ownership of which has been transferred to the band.
2. The powers to be exercised by such band governments would be municipal in character, delegated to the band council and spelled out in the band's constitution.
3. The band's constitution would be required to be approved by a majority of band members in a referendum.
4. The band council which would exercise the limited law-making and administrative powers would be elected and function in accordance with democratic principles.
5. Laws passed by self-governments would comply with the Canadian Charter of Rights and Freedoms.
6. Federal laws of general application to Canadians would apply to band members as would similar provincial laws, except to the

extent that those matters fall within the powers given to the band council under 2.

7. Laws of band governments that adversely impact on surrounding non-reserve lands would be subject to provincial laws. Examples of this would be where reserve activities result in visual pollution (i.e. roadside third party billboards), or water or air pollution that extends beyond reserve boundaries.

8. Non-native occupiers of reserves would have specially elected representatives on band governments to prevent "taxation without representation."

9. Initially, a move toward self-government would have to be shown to have some reasonable prospect of economic and social viability measured by objective standards.

10. Self-governments of this kind would be expected to pay their own way within time-frames agreed to at the outset.

It is my view that it is this municipal kind of self-government on existing reserves that should be extended to native peoples. If properly done, it can be viable, practical, achievable, and affordable.

Is it one that is likely to be embraced by the present federal government? If the reported reaction of DIAND Minister Ron Irwin to a municipal-style self-government proposal put forward last year by the Sawridge Band of Alberta is any indication, prospects do not look good. When the proposal was put to him, he is reported to have rejected it out of hand and stormed out of the meeting because it did not go far enough toward the concept of the inherent right to self-government.[10]

The grand finale

When all elements of the new policy proposed in this chapter are put in place, two final steps must be taken:

1. Repeal the *Indian Act*, including the tax exemption provisions.
2. Ring down the curtain forever on ministries of Indian or Native Affairs both in Ottawa and in the provinces.

"Selling" a new native policy

Would this proposed new policy be enthusiastically embraced by the national native leadership? Not likely, because it does not fulfil the high hopes of sovereignty or self-determination to which they aspire. The national native leader will never enthusiastically agree to:

- land claim settlements that only recognize modest "traditional" aboriginal rights;
- abolishing special programs for natives and replacing them with all the programs—provincial and federal—available to other Canadians; and
- a delegated kind of municipal-like self-government.

But that lack of approval by the national native leadership to accept such changes should not deter government from making them nonetheless. Ordinary native people, many of whom live on reserves without even the basic municipal-like amenities, may well take a different view.

What it will take is governments with courage, committed to the view that a new policy must be totally in accordance with the rule of law and the Constitution and be governed by the principle of equality under the law. A policy that will work in the long-term interest of native and non-native Canadians alike and is conducive to continued Canadian nationhood.

Chapter 12 - Footnotes:

1. Cumming and Mickenberg, *Native Rights in Canada,* 2nd edition (Toronto: Indian-Eskimo Association of Canada and General Publishing), 193.
2. *Quebec Boundaries Extension Act, 1912,* S.C.1912 C.45, S2.
3. *The Aboriginal Peoples of British Columbia: A Profile* (Victoria: Ministry of Aboriginal Affairs, 1992), 1.
4. DIAND, Schedule of Indian Bands, Reserves and Settlements, December, 1990.
5. DIAND, *Basic Departmental Data,* 1992, 24.
6. *The Canadian Global Almanac, 1995 edition,* (Macmillan Canada), 48-49.
7. John P. Taylor and Gary Paget, *"Federal/Provincial Responsibility and the Sechelt,"* David C. Hawkes, ed., (Ottawa: Carlton University Press, 1989), 297-348.
8. Ibid., 341.
9. Ibid., 337.
10. "Don't confuse the minister with moderation," *Alberta Report,* March 7, 1994, 15.
11. As quoted in *The Canadian Almanac, 1995* (Canada: Macmillan), 113.

Defining the Terms

Who is an Indian?

The answer varies depending on the context in which the term appears and the purpose for which it is used. In generic terms, one Canadian dictionary defines "Indian" as "a member of any of the peoples who are the original inhabitants of the western hemisphere **south of the Arctic coast region**." By that definition the Inuit (or Eskimos) are not Indians and that certainly is the position of the Inuit themselves. However, the term "Indian" as used in section 91(24) of the Canadian Constitution has been found by the Supreme Court of Canada to include Eskimos (or Inuit). This means that the constitutional power which the federal government may exercise to legislate especially for "Indians" includes the same power with respect to Inuit. It does not mean that the **exercise** of the constitutional power, in the form of legislation and programs, must be the same as between "Indians" and Inuit. Indeed, it is not: the *Indian Act* does not apply to the Inuit.

Common sense suggests that the only true Indians are those of "pure" blood or close to it but that is not a popular concept because it immediately excludes those who have descended from intermarriage between Indians and non-Indians. To deal with this, undaunted by constitutional considerations, Parliament simply assumed the right to put into the *Indian Act* its own definition of "Indian" which is: "a person who pursuant to this Act is registered as an Indian or is entitled to be registered as an Indian."

The provisions of the *Indian Act* apply only to those persons who are registered or entitled to be registered. Sections 6 and 7 passed in 1985, set out the criteria for registration. These provisions are complex and are not of easy interpretation. Simply stated, registration is open to:

- *persons registered or entitled to be registered prior to April 17, 1985;*
- *a person who is a member of a body declared by the federal Cabinet to be a band since April 17, 1985;*
- *female persons previously deleted from the register by virtue of their marriage to a non-Indian and certain other persons previously deleted;*
- *children of parents, one of whom is registered or entitled to be registered;*
- *grandchildren, one of whose grandparents is registered or entitled to be registered but only if his or her parents are **both** registered.*

The term "status Indian" means those who have registered or are entitled to be registered under the *Indian Act* and also "treaty Indians"—those who are covered by past treaties. In both cases the benefits of the *Indian Act* apply.

Then there are Indians who have not maintained their rights as registered Indians and their right to live on reserves, but have accepted ordinary citizenship in the Canadian community. These are known as non-status Indians and receive no benefits under the *Indian Act* nor share in the federal special programs for Indians.

The final category of native people are Metis who live in Metis settlements or collectivities, mostly on the Prairies and who have their own cultural, social and linguistic characteristics based on their combined native and French or Scottish ancestries and heritage. Until 1982, no mention of Metis was made in the Canadian Constitution, or in the *Indian Act*, and the best opinion was that their legal rights, responsibilities and benefits were the same as all other citizens of the province in which they resided. Since 1992, by virtue of the definition of "aboriginal peoples" contained in section 35 of the *Constitution Act, 1982*, the "aboriginal rights" of the Metis, if any, are constitutionally "recognized and affirmed." Metis who have not chosen to be registered under the *Indian Act* receive no benefits under the *Indian Act* nor from the federal special programs for Indians.

Native populations

How many Indians are there in Canada? The 1995 *Canadian Global Almanac*, relying on the 1991 census, gives as the number of people who reported having their ethnic origins as North American

Indian, Metis and Inuit as their only ancestry or in combination with other origins at 1,002,675 people (or 3.7% of the Canadian population).

Of these I,002,675, Statistics Canada tells us that only 626,000 (2.3% of the Canadian population) identify with an aboriginal group and 553,316 of them (2% of the Canadian population) are status Indians. Status Indians in B.C. number 94,006 (3% of B.C.'s population). These are the people to whom the *Indian Act* applies and who benefit from an ever increasing array of special government programs. Of equal importance is the fact that, of these, only approximately 305,247 (1.1% to 1.2% of the Canadian population) actually live on reserves or native settlements. In B.C. the numbers living on reserves is 49,756 (1.6% of B.C.'s population).[1] The rest live in other rural or urban settings.

There has been a dramatic increase of 41% in the number of status Indians in the previous five years! What accounts for the increase? Statistics Canada says demographic factors such as changes in fertility and mortality cannot explain an increase of this size over a five year period. They account for it this way:

"Clearly, significant numbers of people who had not previously reported an Aboriginal origin did so in 1991, most likely due to heightened awareness of Aboriginal issues arising from the extensive public discussion of these matters in the period leading up to the 1991 census."[2]

"Heightened awareness" indeed, to say nothing of the attraction for the skyrocketing sums of money and other benefits which are expended by the federal government each year to those who claim they are entitled them. (More about this in Chapter 10).

Of the remainder, 212,650 identify themselves as Metis and 49,255 as Inuit.

Politicians supportive of the native cause tend to play fast and loose with the numbers. Recently, DIAND Minister Ron Irwin said there are 1.5 million aboriginal people in Canada. Ovide Mercredi talks in terms of 2 million. Both figures are sheer puffery.

---

[1]   *The Canadian Global Almanac, 1995 edition* (Macmillan Canada), 48-49.

[2]   Statistics Canada, *The Daily,* March 30, 1993, 2.

"AFS" means the Aboriginal Fisheries Strategy created by the federal Department of Fisheries and Oceans in 1992. It constitutes a separate commercial salmon fishery for certain native bands on the West Coast. It is the subject of Chapter 9.

"DFO" means the federal Department of Fisheries and Oceans.

"DIAND" means the federal Department of Indian and Northern Development. This is the department that administers the *Indian Act* and is the lead department in administering special federal programs for Indians.

"First Nations"

The term "First Nations" has come into common usage in recent years without so much as a public debate as to whether the tribes, bands and houses that make up the numerous native communities in Canada can properly be considered to be nations. Where possible in this book, I have refrained from using the term, not to cause offence but rather to underscore the fact that acquiesence in the terminology is to concede the debate. The fact is that there is little support in law for the view that the tribal societies that may have existed before the arrival of the white man constituted nationhood.[3]

Moreover, Indian treaties are not evidence of sovereignty. The word "treaty" in common parlance has several meanings. It can mean a compact between two or more independent nations or it can mean the negotiation of any agreement or contract.[4] The Courts have long since decided that Indian treaties are not international treaties in the sense of agreements between two or more independent nations.[5] Moreover, reputable historians state that not only did governments not consider the Indians to be independent nations at the time they entered

[3]   See Dickerson and Flanagan, *An Introduction to Government and Politics: A Conceptual Approach,* Third Edition, (Scarborough, Ontario: Nelson Canada, 1990), 39-40.

[4]   Cumming and Mickenberg, *Native Rights in Canada,* 2nd edition (Toronto: Indian-Eskimo Association of Canada and General Publishing), 54.

[5]   *Regina vs. White and Bob,* 52 WWR 193 (B.C.C.A.); affirmed by S.C.C., (1966) 52 DLR(2d), 481.

into the early treaties, but Indian negotiators themselves considered the Indian peoples to be subjects of the Crown.[6]

To be sure, Indian treaties created mutual obligations which the Courts have found to be legally binding.[7] By virtue of section 35 (1) of the *Constitution Act, 1982* these treaties are now "constitutionalized." But there is no support for the view that by entering into treaties there was a recognition of native sovereignty in a nationhood sense. In fact the opposite is the case.

"Native"

I have used this term to describe, in an all embracive way, the Indian, Inuit and Metis peoples that go to make up, what I could otherwise have described as the aboriginal peoples of Canada. Both the term "native peoples" and "aboriginal peoples" are in common usage and are generally accepted.

There are of course other meanings to the word "native." Persons born in Canada can properly consider themselves "native Canadians." It is in this sense that the words "native land" in our national anthem, "O Canada" is used. Moreover, the words "our home" in that anthem certainly embrace all those who have emigrated to this country and thereby made Canada their home.

---

[6]   A. Morris, *The Treaties of Canada with the Indians of Manitoba and the Northwest Territories,* (Belfords, Clarke & Co. Toronto: 1880).

[7]   *Regina vs. White and Bob,* Ibid.

Epilogue

In his address to commemorate the fiftieth anniversary of the D-Day invasion, delivered on Juno Beach, in Normandy, France, on June 6, 1994, Prime Minister Jean Chrétien said this:

> *"On the beach behind us,*
> *Canadians gave their lives*
> *so the world would be a better place.*
> *In death they were neither*
> *anglophones or francophones,*
> *not from the West or the East,*
> *not Christians or Jews,*
> *not aboriginal peoples or immigrants.*
> *They were Canadians."* [1]

If our bravest citizens can be just "Canadians" in death on a foreign battlefield, surely the rest of us can be just "Canadians" in life within our home **and** native land.